DEMOCRACY
AND ITS CRITICS

*Anglo-American democratic thought
in the nineteenth century*

JON ROPER
University of Wales, Swansea

London
UNWIN HYMAN
Boston Sydney Wellington

Published by the Academic Division of
Unwin Hyman Ltd,
15/17 Broadwick Street, London W1V 3FP, UK

Unwin Hyman, Inc.,
8 Winchester Place, Winchester, Mass. 01890, USA

Allen & Unwin (Australia) Ltd,
8 Napier Street, North Sydney, NSW 2060, Australia

Allen & Unwin (New Zealand) Ltd in association with the
Port Nicholson Press Ltd,
60 Cambridge Terrace, Wellington, New Zealand

First published in 1989

British Library Cataloguing in Publication Data
Roper, Jon
    Democracy and its critics : Anglo–American
    democratic thought in the nineteenth
    century
    1. Democracy. Theories 1750–1900
    I. Title
    321.8'01

    ISBN 0-04-445129-6
    ISBN 0-04-445130-X

Library of Congress Cataloging–in–Publication Data
Roper, Jon.
    Democracy and its critics: Anglo-American democratic thought in
    the nineteeth century/Jon Roper.
       p.   cm.
    Bibliography: p.
    Includes index.
    ISBN 0-04-445129-6.   ISBN 0-04-445130-X (pbk.)
    1. Democracy—History—19th century. 2. Politcal science—Great
Britain—History—19th century. 3. Political science—United
States—History—19th. I. Title
JC421.R627 1988
321.8'09—dc19

                                           88-17659
                                           CIP

Typeset in 10/11pt Imprint and printed in Great Britain by
Billing and Sons, London and Worcester.

Contents

ACKNOWLEDGEMENTS

I would like to thank Jack Greenleaf, Professor Emeritus of Political Theory and Government at the University of Wales, Swansea, for encouraging me to write this book, and for his subsequent faith in its progress. Professor Tom Ungs and colleagues in the department of Political Science at the University of Tennessee, Knoxville, invited me to join them for a term as visiting associate professor, and in that friendly and congenial environment I was able to complete the manuscript.

Gordon Smith, my editor at Unwin Hyman, has been a pleasure to work with, and I am grateful for the time and consideration he has put into the production of the text.

Sharon Hansard, in the American Studies Centre at Swansea, bore the brunt of the typing – at least until I came to terms with word-processing! My thanks also go to my elder brother, Tim, who has long understood the possibilities of new technology. His computing skills made the compilation of the index less haphazard than it otherwise might have been.

I owe a debt to all those who have helped along the way, and in particular to Nicola, who put up with both my absence – and my presence – while the book was written.

Jon Roper   American Studies

University of Wales, Swansea

Part one

Introduction

CHAPTER 1

Traditions of Democratic Thought

Consider democracy. In America it became part of that 'revolution in the principles and practice of governments' (Paine, 1969, pt. 2, p. 181), which accompanied and transcended the successful struggle for colonial independence. In Britain it implied a new set of political relationships within the old institutional order. Democracy in both countries, however, was not only a political concern. Nineteenth-century philosophical discourse also explored the moral, cultural and economic implications of this novel ideal. Sometimes democracy needed such theoretical justifications as the drunk needs the lamp-post, more for support than for illumination. However, the century recreated in itself a new 'spirit of the age'. A democratic tradition in America and in Britain was part of this invention.

The aim of this book is to investigate different aspects of this tradition in each country against the background of primarily nineteenth-century historical experience, and to do this through a consideration of the attitudes of contemporary commentators on and critics of democracy. It is a wide-ranging debate. The cast list of those who wrote and spoke is long: some famous, others less notorious. The views presented here are an eclectic rather than an idiosyncratic choice. Nor should they be overlooked in an age often concerned more with the empirical than the metaphysical. It has been tempting to distil the ingredients of the ideal as time has gone by, with the result that democracy is defined as a procedural mechanism, a process, a form of government, a way of doing things. There remains more to it than that.

This chapter lays the foundation of a broader view. It connects the idea of democracy in America and in Britain with values: the concept of individual liberty which anteceded it as a goal in Anglo-American philosophical discussion, and the notion of equality which is its foundation. More specifically, it discusses some of the political consequences of a democratic aim: the promotion of liberty as an equal right among all individuals. Here the problems begin. For equality as a value may imply more than an equal right to liberty. Indeed it may conflict with that right in the pursuit of other ends. The realization of the potential collision between liberty and equality in a democratic context provides much of the creative impulse for Anglo-American thinking on the subject.

To begin with, therefore, it is useful not so much to define democracy as to discuss the concepts of liberty and equality in the context of Anglo-American political thought. This in turn helps promote an understanding of the formation of different philosophical attitudes towards the democratic idea in America and in Britain. But it is only one path of analysis. Concern with other issues also structured opinions. In particular the notion of majority rule was, in the nineteenth century, a political and philosophical worry in each country. As part of the broader perspective, it is necessary also to look at the ways in which the ideal of democracy might impinge on matters of moral, cultural and economic concern. These too were affected by the democratic rhetoric of liberty and equality.

LIBERTY AND EQUALITY

The common heritage of Anglo-American liberal democratic constitutional thought is wrapped up in a commitment to the fundamental ideal of individual liberty. This liberty is a civil right protected by a political constitution. It is not the same as the liberty which exists in the philosophical state of nature that is prior to the creation of organized society. In Puritan America John Winthrop drew the important distinction between 'natural' and 'civil or federal' liberty. Natural liberty was 'incompatible and inconsistent with authority and cannot endure the least restraint of the most just authority'. Its essential consequence is the social and political anarchy of an unrestrained individualistic freedom.

In contrast, according to Winthrop:

> The other kind of liberty I call civil or federal; it may also be termed moral, in reference to the covenant between God and man, in the moral law, and the politic covenants and constitutions among men themselves. This liberty is the proper end and object of authority, and cannot subsist without it; and it is a liberty to that only which is good, just, and honest. (Quoted in de Tocqueville, 1945a, p. 44)

This is a liberty which connects individuals to society by ties of morality and authority. Religious conviction endorses rules of conduct, describing the sphere of morality within which liberty is constrained. To preserve such liberty, however, citizens must delegate power to governments to guard against anyone who transgresses the moral law. A contract is made by which natural individualistic liberty submits to lawful authority in order to preserve social harmony.

John Locke in Britain argued a similar case. Liberty in a social context was not absolute. It was restricted within the framework of a civil society of which government was a necessary part.

> Freedom of men under government is to have a standing rule to live by, common to everyone of that society, and made by the legislative power erected in it. A liberty to follow my own will in all things where that rule prescribes not, not to be subject to the inconstant, uncertain, unknown, arbitrary will of another man, as freedom of nature is to be under no other restraint but the law of Nature. (Locke, 1978, p. 127)

This regulated liberty is the liberty of non-interference: an idea of negative liberty extrinsic to individuals, prescribing an area free from the processes of government into which they can advance. It requires the building of a defensive stockade for liberty on the foundation of natural rights, utilitarian principles, or some such philosophical justification. Such theories became part of the baggage of Anglo-American liberal democratic thought.

If the liberty of the individual in the state of nature is absolute and unconstrained, within the structure of civil society it becomes a negotiable concept. The bargain must be struck which determines both an agreed sphere of individual liberty and the legitimate boundaries of public authority. Liberty and authority, indeed, are held in a state of creative tension, but the compromise can prove fragile. Problems emerge when individuals consider that government has overstepped the mark, or when it appears that the competing claims of individualistic liberty tear at the fabric of social harmony.

On the eve of the American War of Independence many in the colonies felt that the agreed balance between liberty and authority which was thought to exist within the British constitution had been tilted in favour of the Crown. This prompted a discussion of the meaning of liberty, in the context of a colonial past rather than a democratic future. In British constitutional thought in the late eighteenth century, the liberty of the individual was preserved within an institutional structure that few, if any, would have described as democratic. But it was this liberty which America too defended. In the act of declaring their independence from British rule, Americans argued their right to liberty not as something they had stumbled on in the colonies but as part of that which was their due under the terms of Britain's ancient constitution. So it was a conservative case.

5

Even Edmund Burke in Britain could not dispute it. Burke indeed saw the contradiction in British attitudes towards the colonies.

> In order to prove that the Americans have no right to their liberties we are every day endeavouring to subvert the maxims which preserve the whole spirit of our own. To prove that the Americans ought not to be free, we are obliged to depreciate the value of freedom itself; and we never seem to gain a paltry advantage over them in debate, without attacking some of those principles, or deriding some of those feelings, for which our ancestors have shed their blood. (Burke, 1912, p. 26)

There was a sense in which a battle to preserve an interpretation of British ideals was fought on American soil.

In political terms this version of the Anglo-American concept of liberty was expressed in the colonies in 1776 as the clarion demand for 'no taxation without representation'. It was hardly a revolutionary maxim. During the quarrel with Britain, however, 'the way opened' in America 'for reinterpreting John Locke in the spirit of Tom Paine' (Lynd, 1973, p. 37). Political theorists in the colonies picked up the idea of liberty and ran with it down novel and experimental constitutional paths. As the two countries parted company, in the newly independent states the notion of equality was associated with the ideal of liberty as the wellspring of another idea: an American republic. When Paine himself proclaimed in 1792, 'what Athens was in miniature, America will be in magnitude' (Paine, 1969, pt. 2, p. 202), he offered a new vision in the image of a nostalgic and romanticized conception of the republican past. For America was different. And that difference was marked by the commitment not only to liberty but also to the democratic value of equality.

If liberty was an aspiration, equality was a mood. Alexis de Tocqueville realized this. The existence of both values in the republic might be taken for granted, but on closer examination they could conflict. It depended on how equality was viewed. In the first volume of *Democracy in America*, de Tocqueville suggested two ways of regarding the idea. One involved 'a manly and lawful passion for equality that incites men to wish all to be powerful and honored'. On the other hand, 'there exists also in the human heart a depraved taste for equality, which impels the weak to attempt to lower the powerful to their own level, and reduces men to prefer equality in slavery to inequality with freedom' (de Tocqueville, 1945a, p. 56). If individuals *en masse* submit to this depraved taste for equality, individual liberty is jeopardized. To promote that idea of equality, governments are ceded the authority to limit successively individual freedoms in the name of conformity. This trend to enforced equality places barriers around the liberty to be different.

A democratic dilemma is simply put: 'the more equality, the less liberty' and vice versa. The promotion of the depraved form of equality may, moreover, be an inherent tendency in a democratic society that sees equality as a levelling rather than an elevating prospect. That at least was de Tocqueville's concern. It was shared by others. In Britain, where many were fighting the encroaching prospect of political democracy, the problem of reconciling the ancient ideal of liberty with the new prospect of equality was part of the direct confrontation over who should have the right to vote.

The development of democracy thus implied changes in the constitutional orthodoxies which had apparently safeguarded the value of liberty. Anglo-American political thought had to accommodate new ideas. A contrast is clear. In America the constitutional adaptations which accompanied the establishment of political democracy were revolutionary. In Britain they were evolutionary. If the War of Independence was fought to preserve British liberties, the creation of a republic was a unique American adventure. The British experience maintained a more direct continuity with the immediate past. This meant that democracy was not, as in America, woven into the fabric of political life. It was an overcoat imposed upon a constitutional and institutional structure that proved flexible enough to deflect the threat from the new republican persuasion. Britain could borrow the rhetoric of democracy without at core admitting its substance.

America's natural individualistic liberty – the pursuit of private interest at the expense of the community – was, on the other hand, civilized by a democratic faith. This faith was expressed in secular terms in the idea of republican virtue, and in the moral sphere by an appeal to religious belief. In Britain there was faith of another kind. Liberty might be defended against the euphoria of democratic equality if historical confidence were maintained in the influence of the social habit of deference. What emerged were two democratic traditions, facing connected problems and responding to them in separate ways.

AMERICA: REPUBLICAN VIRTUE AND THE ROLE OF RELIGION

The American democratic faith is documented. It is there in the Declaration of Independence. Jefferson's elegant prose announced that 'We hold these truths to be self-evident, that all men are created equal, that they are endowed by their Creator with certain unalienable Rights, that among these are Life, Liberty, and the pursuit of Happiness' (Commager, 1951, p. 125). That familiar litany presents the argument for America's democratic republican experiment: the ideas of equality and certain fundamental rights should be secured, Jefferson argued, through governments resting on consent. If they were not, then the people had the ultimate sanction to alter them, abolish them and find new forms. It seems to be an American version of the philosophy of John Locke.

Yet Jefferson's truths were not self-evident in the sense that Locke conceived them. Tom did not copy John. Jefferson's idea of a self-evident truth derived more from the influences of the Scottish Enlightenment – Frances Hutcheson and Thomas Reid – than from the seventeenth-century Englishman. In their view 'self-evident' embodied a communal sense of what was true. Such a truth was a shared wisdom, a consensus of that which to rational individuals was obvious. But for Locke a self-evident truth was an incontrovertible maxim which could admit of no nuances of interpretation. It was a truism and conceptually a different observation from the philosophically disputable assertion that 'all men are created equal'. The incontestable is confronted by the contestable.

If Jefferson had followed Locke's reasoning, he could not have phrased the Declaration in the way he did. He appreciated this. In 1814, repudiating the charge that he had plagiarized the author of the *Two Treatises of Government*, he wrote of the Declaration, 'all its authority rests then on the harmonizing sentiments of the day, whether expressed in conversation, in letters, printed essays, or in the elementary books of public right, as Aristotle, Cicero, Locke, Sidney, etc., &c.' (quoted in Wills, 1978, p. 172). Jefferson was ever eclectic. The greater significance of severing a traditional connection between Locke and the author of the Declaration, however, is that it draws attention to a myth. For the Declaration is less important for its intellectual debts than for what it says, what it is, or at least what it has become. It is quite simply a symbol. It represents the embodiment of the values which define the American democratic tradition. In many ways it created that tradition.

The fact that the Declaration embodied a prevailing sense of contemporary agreement on basic political ideas is one clue to the existence of the consensus necessary to the stability of America's experiment in republican democracy. It is not, however, the whole story. The War of Independence, of which the Declaration was a part, when won, left Americans with a post-revolutionary hangover.

What was to be done? In particular, how might the agreed values which Jefferson had proclaimed be translated into a constitutional and institutional system which would give them practical point. Ultimately it was the Federal Constitution which attempted to nail the vision down. According to its preamble it would 'establish Justice, insure domestic Tranquility, provide for the common defence, promote the general Welfare, and secure the Blessings of Liberty to ourselves and our Posterity' (Vile, 1976, p. 278). Together with the Declaration, the Constitution is a landmark in the creation of America's democracy. Between them these documents define the aspirations of American society. But neither is a passive charter. They demand a response from the citizens of the republic they create and preserve.

James Madison, a principal architect of the Constitution, saw that its permanence would rest on more than mere design. Although in 'Federalist 10' he argued that the purpose of the constitutional settlement was to accommodate minority and majority factions battling for political power, he realized that his republic was only as strong as people's commitment to it. Tyranny could be checked, republican liberty preserved. Yet this would occur only if there was a higher level of political and social consensus operating above the squabbles of America's pluralist society. The ground-rules had to be both agreed and respected. If the people were to be sovereign, if the republic was their creation and government their responsibility – and democracy was to work – then that democratic republican ethos imposed a reciprocal demand on its citizens. It required them to be virtuous.

The concept of republican virtue could be seen as a stabilizing force in American political society. It involved a sense of political and civic altruism: a commitment to the community and to the capacity to 'transcend private gain for public good' (Wills, 1981, p. 187). This quality was essential to the republic's existence and survival; indeed republican government might be impossible without it. Such virtue, moreover, was a characteristic of human nature which the republic itself could nurture. As people realized the benefits of the equal right to liberty they enjoyed as part of the republican lifestyle, they could be encouraged to support republican ideals.

For Madison, republican virtue persisted alongside those darker aspects of the human psyche which had so enraptured Thomas Hobbes. In 'Federalist 55' he observed: 'as there is a degree of depravity in mankind which requires a certain degree of circumspection and distrust, so there are other qualities in human nature which justify a certain portion of esteem and confidence. Republican

9

government presupposes the existence of these qualities in a higher degree than any other form' (*Federalist*, 1937, p. 286). So too did representative democracy.

In a further paper, 'Federalist 57', Madison describes the republican animus. It is 'the vigilant, and manly spirit which actuates the people of America – a spirit which nourishes freedom, and in return is nourished by it' (*Federalist*, 1937, p. 293). The republic is brittle. Without this idea of civic responsibility, of virtue, it is nothing. Structural designs to avoid the degeneration of the republican democratic experiment into a governmental tyranny implied by an excess of egalitarianism on the one hand, or an individualistic anarchy caused by a surfeit of unrestrained liberty on the other, could only go so far. Stability rested on the citizen's active association with the aims and aspirations of the ideal. Republicanism was not an easy option. In the end Madison had to rely on an optimistic faith in the virtuous capacity of his fellow Americans in a society defined by his Constitution and imbued with the rhetorical values of the Declaration of Independence.

The republican ethos, with its accompanying concept of virtue, became part of the secular faith which helped turn American democratic experiment into American democratic tradition. That faith had a religious dimension as well. Winthrop had observed that religion was a moral glue binding a code of social conduct to the institutional restraints of American constitutionalism, and this was as true in the federal republic as it had been in his Puritan colony. Americans could place their trust in God for reasons other than the purely spiritual.

As de Tocqueville recognized in the America of the 1830s, the indirect influence of religion was an important factor encouraging stability in the new republican democracy. Religious pluralism existed within an over-arching Christian commitment. 'All the sects of the United States are comprised within the great unity of Christianity, and Christian morality is everywhere the same' (de Tocqueville, 1945a, p. 314). This common moral ethic provided a pivotal point of reference. In America Christianity 'reigns without obstacle, by universal consent; the consequence is . . . that every principle of the moral world is fixed and determinate, although the political world is abandoned to the debates and the experiments of men' (ibid., p. 315).

Religion was a mould helping to shape liberty within the new republican ethos. It contributed to the underlying moral framework necessary to the experiment's success. In this way, 'while the law permits the Americans to do what they please, religion prevents them from conceiving, and forbids them to commit, what is rash or unjust' (de Tocqueville, 1945a, p. 316). Attitudes and outlook were influenced by republican culture and religious belief. Religion defined the limits of permissible freedom of action, reinforcing political institutions that were designed to check, balance and prevent the abuse of power.

From this observation that a shared Christian morality was a crucial factor in the survival of America's republican democratic creed, de Tocqueville could draw a more general conclusion. He argued that religious belief was 'more needed in democratic republics than in any others', precisely because there was no better anchor to keep liberty within bounds. Under other forms of government the tendency of unrestrained liberty towards anarchy was checked in other ways. Monarchies and aristocracies restricted the liberty of the individual through threat of coercion. Republics, where the people were sovereign, had no such countervailing power. De Tocqueville's rhetorical case was made. 'How is it possible that society should escape destruction if the moral tie is not strengthened in proportion as the political tie is relaxed? And what can be done with a people who are their own masters if they are not submissive to the Deity?' (de Tocqueville, 1945a, p. 318.) The role of republican religion is, as John Winthrop saw, to mould morality, encourage self-restraint and social responsibility, promote honesty and virtue, and supply a further dimension to the idea of an equal right to liberty within the democratic community.

The American democratic tradition can be characterized, then, in terms of a commitment to republicanism which is reinforced by the secular notion of virtue, and by what de Tocqueville referred to as the combination of 'the spirit of religion' and 'the spirit of freedom'. American democratic discourse involves, indeed, a 'mingling of political and religious thought' that is one aspect of the peculiar 'genius of American politics' (Boorstin, 1953, ch. 5). The ideas of republican virtue and the morality of religion have not always been articulated at a conscious level – although they often echo in American rhetoric as exhortations, appeals, or slogans. Defined in terms of its documents, the vision of democracy is nostalgic, glimpsed in the crucible of late-eighteenth-century political thought. In the annals of American oratory, however, it is an elevating, even utopian, prospect.

The idea of democracy in America could impinge on attitudes beyond the merely political, inspiring states of mind and influencing ways of looking at things. However, for some commentators the dimensions of American republican democracy were strictly political. For other critics democracy in practice failed to live up even to its political ideals. Its was a lapsed faith. The separation from Britain created new problems as it resolved old ones.

BRITAIN: HISTORY AND THE HABIT OF DEFERENCE

The Civil War came too soon. That republican interregnum in England which followed it from 1649 to 1660 did not have the philosophical insights of later Enlightenment rationalism to use as a guide. The constitution did not adapt well to revolutionary ideas of self-government. There remained a strong attachment to the general principle of monarchy, even after the head of a specific king – Charles I – had been detached. It has been suggested, indeed, that 'the lofty ideals of the Commonwealth thinkers missed realisation because they took inadequate account of the vigour of those ancient institutions, those venerable traditions, those firmly-established conventions, those ineradicable prejudices, which they aimed at sweeping aside' (Hearnshaw, 1918, p. 118).

After the Restoration, the English constitutional settlement was established in the realm of tradition. Locke's *Second Treatise of Government*, which was taken to inspire America's later republican idealism, was written after all to justify the Revolution of 1688, when Parliament substituted William III for James II as English monarch. So to speak of a British democratic tradition is in a way to talk of a tradition within a tradition. It is a strand to be teased from the apparent continuity of historical habit, custom and practice. In Britain even political democracy had a tough nut to crack.

It was not that constitutional change was impossible. Rather the range of possibilities – leaving aside full-blooded social revolution – was thought to be limited by the inherited weight of historical experience. The strength of Britain's unwritten constitution has been taken to lie in its adaptive capacity: its ability to meet and assimilate new circumstances without altering its outward forms. The evolution of political democracy in Britain took place within the framework of a system defined by its constitutional monarchy, and became a matter of almost purely pragmatic concern.

In Britain the issue of what constituted political liberty had been largely settled in terms of the prevailing relationship between Crown and Parliament. During the nineteenth century, however, a realization of the consequences of the demand for political equality forced the concept of democracy into the arena of public debate. The liberal intellectual view may have been philosophically dominant, but it was weaker in the sphere of practical political influence than it was in arguing the finer points of theory. Among British conservatives the view gained currency that democratic stability was to be built upon the encouragement of apathy and ignorance.

Since it was a political concern, moreover, democracy arrived in Britain with minor impact upon entrenched social attitudes. In turn those attitudes effectively determined the nature of the British democratic tradition. For nineteenth-century Britain was a class-conscious society. Everyone had, and it was important that everyone should accept, their social place. Naturally the upper classes governed the lower classes and the relationship was decently paternalistic. Sir Robert Peel was not alone in considering that 'the existence of the territorial aristocracy as the governing class of England was essential for the welfare of the nation' (Blake, 1970, pp. 25–6). The idea that the right to vote should be extended beyond those who assented to and were sustained by this natural right to govern, provoked the customary fears of an outraged self-interest. Yet in this class-based society lay the key to the assimilation of the impetus towards political democracy. The acceptance of paternalism implies deference.

Britain's democratic faith is not expressed in terms of a nostalgic commitment to documented ideals. Its confidence is in its institutions, and is informed by a sense of the inherited wisdoms contained in its social hierarchy, of which they are a reflection. The constitutional division between monarchy, aristocracy and democracy was given institutional force in the notional separation of powers of the king, the House of Lords and the House of Commons. This system was glued together by a social consensus which believed that the arrangement was peculiarly appropriate to British needs. It was the 'genius' of British politics. Membership of particular institutions was the prerogative of social class. Whatever resentment such a social and political structure engendered was more than balanced by a sense of deference among the many who regarded it as the natural order of things.

Democracy in nineteenth-century Britain could be seen in a limited institutional context. It involved an appreciation that there should be a widespread right to vote for the only representative national institution, the House of Commons. That right could be defended on abstract grounds of social justice. More often, however, it was viewed as a concession to be granted: a safety-valve which would avoid the creation of potentially more disruptive political pressures. As a result of its wider representative base, the House of Commons could assume more power in the constitutional triumvirate, but the social hierarchy was shaken rather than stirred. As long, that is, as deference was maintained.

Disraeli's Tory administration which passed the second Reform Act in 1867 thus extended the suffrage to a wider cross-section of the community. But at least some contemporary politicians – and philosophers – who made this 'leap in the dark' had a shrewd idea of where they would land. Frederic Harrison, the philosopher of positivism, predicted:

> All will remain very much as before. Power and wealth will control elections; the rich governing class will furnish nineteen-twentieths of the members. The corrupt boroughs, the bribery system, the nominee system, the jobbing system will perish hard and slowly. Rank will exert its time-honoured spell, petty interests will divide constituencies as of old, and Beer will be king time and again. The Millennium that the Radical hails, the Chaos that the Tory dreads, are alike the creation of delusion or of panic. The whole thing is in embryo as yet. (Harrison, 1975, p. 177)

It was hardly the stuff of democratic dreams.

If deference ensured that the battle for political democracy in Britain did not cause many casualties in the social hierarchy, it was the monarchy which emerged as the pivot on which the concept turned. Walter Bagehot, describing the deferential society which existed in mid-century, realized that the symbolic role of the monarchy transcended its curtailed political influence. Again, Frederic Harrison was another who made the point. He described the function of the monarchy in British society with brutal candour:

> It is the embodiment of the *status quo*. It is the keystone of our social system. Thus, though of very small account in itself, it is a most potent symbol. To the governing classes it is the sign of their right to govern . . . In fact, the governing orders in England could no more manage the plebeians without the mystical rites of monarchy than the Roman aristocracy could have ruled without augurs and sacred chickens. (Harrison, 1975, pp. 332–3)

Confined within the strait-jacket of a constitutional monarchy, held enthralled by deference, the democratic tradition in Britain appeared capable of only limited aspirations.

Underlying the faith in deference and social consensus, however, was an equally widespread concern that these traditional forces might not withstand the political and social changes which accompanied the transition to a new industrialized society. The consciousness of class was apparent in both policy and debate. While conservatives acted surreptitiously, liberals agonized openly. The political literature of the nineteenth century was full of references to class, and in particular nervously raised the possibility of unchecked working-class political power. The rhetoric of class structured the sphere of political analysis and discussion. In a society which recognized the antagonisms of class, therefore, there were those who argued that democracy – as it implied an equal right to liberty – would disrupt the habits of social deference. They searched for alternative ways of checking the new ideal.

Other critics in Britain became concerned with democracy not as a means to an end, nor even as an end in itself. They were outsiders looking on: predicting the consequences of economic and social changes and offering a range of suggestions intended to help guide or preserve the ethos of British political life in the new industrial age. Not all their solutions involved the notion of democracy, but their views structured a philosophical environment in which some dimensions of that ideal, could be explored. If the constitutional issues were decided, the intellectual battles were not. Argument continued. Perspectives varied. It became a matter of connecting ideas and ideology.

The democratic tradition in Britain can hence not be viewed entirely within the realm of constitutional developments. The ideological dimension should not be overlooked. Ideology in Britain incorporated attitudes towards a political world in which, during the nineteenth century, democracy became an important part. Interpretations of democracy as an ideal reflected different ideological persuasions in the same way as contemporary views on social and economic issues were the outcome of ideological belief. In brief, then, democracy did come to mean different things to conservatives, liberals and socialists. Conservatives resisted the change, or at least tried to control the practical consequences of the new ideal. Liberals worried about the demand for equality and its likely impact upon an overriding ambition: the preservation of liberty. Socialists broadened the argument, realizing democracy's claims to be multi-dimensional, involving political, religious, social and economic considerations. That clash of ideas, ideals, ideologies, effectively determined the nature, character and scope of British democracy in the nineteenth century.

In America, then, the political outcome of an acceptance of the idea of an equal right to liberty was a Constitution which attempted to create, in Abraham Lincoln's words, 'government of the people, by the people, for the people' (Commager, 1951, p. 153). Contrast this with Lord Bryce's definition of democracy in Britain as 'government in which the will of the majority of qualified

15

citizens rules' (Bryce, 1921, vol. 1, p. 26). The distance between those perspectives, though small, is significant. In America all had been created equal; in Britain each had to qualify for the privilege of being so regarded. In both countries, however, the implications of basing democratic decisions on the will of a majority raised issues of basic concern.

MAJORITY RULE

The concept of majority rule represents an attempt to legitimize the decision-making process in society. In Anglo-American thought it is an idea again associated with the philosophy of John Locke. For Locke, majority rule was a necessary consequence of the transition from the state of nature to political or civil society. It involved a recognition of the need to compromise natural liberty, and thus the absolute power individuals had over their own lives in the state of nature, in order to achieve a social organization. In the *Two Treatises of Government*, Locke concluded that 'wherever . . . any number of men so unite into one society as to quit every one his executive power of the law of Nature, and to resign it to the public, there and there only is a political or civil society' (Locke, 1978, p. 160). As the sovereignty of the individual is transmuted into the sovereignty of the people, however, the question remains as to how this society reaches communal decisions.

Locke suggested that the only way it could reach such decisions legitimately was by following the will of the majority. In any political society, he claimed, 'the majority have a right to act and conclude the rest' (Locke, 1978, p. 165). It is a purely pragmatic suggestion, but it became central to American and British ideas of democracy. The majority is in a position to claim legitimacy for its viewpoint simply because that outlook is agreed by more people. Individuals must accept the determination of the majority because otherwise the majority will secede from the body politic and society disintegrates back into the state of nature. The majority can thus pick up the contractual football and leave the field of play. Locke, however, avoids by this argument the resolution of another problem. What happens when the minority no longer feel constrained to obey this social contract? It was a dilemma which occurred in America immediately after the election of Abraham Lincoln. The result was civil war.

There may be limits, therefore, to both the legitimacy and the efficacy of majority rule, but it became one of the principles associated with the democratic tradition as it emerged in America and in Britain. The concept had two practical outcomes in both countries. First, the idea of majoritarianism was applied to the popular vote by which the legislature was to be constituted – the electoral system came to be based on the rule that the candidate with the greater number of votes won. Secondly, the internal regulation of the legislature was to be based upon the decision of the majority – a majority was needed to pass legislation. The search for an organized and reliable majority within the legislature was aided by the development of political parties.

The drawback to the principle of majority rule, however, is that it places a premium on the weight of sheer numbers: a fault that John C. Calhoun, James Fenimore Cooper, de Tocqueville and John Stuart Mill among others were, for different reasons, concerned to point out. In a society which has a mixed and balanced constitution with a restricted franchise this need not be a major problem. But democracy could bring majority rule a bad name. In America, during the founding period, suspicion developed that a majority might dominate government and rule in its own interest rather than in the interests of the people of the republic. In Britain the association of the idea of a numerical majority with the working class appeared a threat to constitutional complacency. The 'tyranny of the majority' was one end of a spectrum of political ills bounded at the other extreme by 'arbitrary government'.

Majority rule remained a problem for nineteenth-century critics of democracy in both America and Britain. The concept was revisited from time to time in the hope of fresh insights. In the end there appeared to be no obvious alternative procedure. The problem with majority rule, moreover, grew with the sophistication of the analysis. It became a social as well as a political issue: a qualitative as well as a quantitative concern. The majority not only won votes and determined policies, it also influenced attitudes. That view, again popularized by de Tocqueville, was one which defenders of the democratic ideal had to debate. Discussion of democracy could not avoid the critique of the implied consequences of rule by the majority.

DIMENSIONS OF DEMOCRACY

In the nineteenth century the association of the ideal of democracy with the idea of an equal right to liberty, created a climate of aspirations and expectations. Democracy could be regarded as a method of running a society which was qualitatively better than other arrangements. The invitation was there to judge by results. The democratic ideal was coloured by experience. In both America and Britain, moreover, discussion of democracy involved more than purely political polemic. Some fundamental questions might be asked. What, indeed, was the point of a democratic polity if its ideals were abused elsewhere? What might be the moral, cultural and economic dimensions of democracy? Together they too formed part of its broader ideology.

America remained captivated by the democratic vista. But what of slavery? As an institution it was at odds with the republican democratic ethos: self-evidently inimical to liberty, equally anti-egalitarian. If America's democratic experiment was to appear as an example and an inspiration, and if it was to be tied to the rhetoric of the Declaration of Independence, the continued existence of negro slavery within the republic was difficult to explain, let alone defend. Abraham Lincoln realized, as did others, that the morality of democracy could not condone it.

On the other hand, the defence of slavery involved a critique of the assumed connection between the idea of democracy and the value of liberty. In 1856 George Fitzhugh, the southern apologist, maintained:

> democracy and liberty are antagonistic; for liberty permits and encourages the weak to oppress the strong, whilst democracy proposes, so far as possible, to equalize advantages, by fairly dividing the burdens of life and rigidly enforcing the performance of every social duty by every member of society, according to his capacity and ability. (Fitzhugh, 1960, p. 82)

The southern sociology questioned the fundamental values of the American republic in an attempt to condone an institution which remained the antithesis of the republican ethos.

For much of the nineteenth century, then, the nature of American democracy was debated against the background of the continued existence of slavery. On a political level defenders of the institution prolonged a discussion which involved interpretations of the Constitution: the boundaries that had been drawn between the liberty of the states and the authority of the union. But in human terms the fact of slavery demanded a decision on a straightforward, yet ultimately progressively contentious issue: which individuals among America's inhabitants should be granted the equal right to liberty promised in its founding documents? If the democratic republic was established on the presumption of the existence of God-given rights, then could those rights be exclusive to members of a particular race? To answer such questions was to determine the extent to which democracy's claims to be a morally superior form of social organization could be realized.

America's democratic faith might rest initially on concepts like republican virtue and the morality of religion. Yet as the argument over slavery developed and the nation tumbled into a civil war it became apparent to some that the prospect of harmony in a free and equal society might require a new affirmation. As Lincoln confirmed the nation's political aspirations in the Gettysburg address – another of the documents of America's democratic faith – so the outlines of a broader vision could be sketched. The idea of a democratic culture was to create the sense of America's difference as an example to itself and to the world.

In this way, it was argued that the evolution of a democratic culture would stamp a unique hallmark upon America's experiment in democracy. The outward signs of a functioning democratic polity – elections, political parties, political debate and freedom of discussion, among them – were a veneer. Democracy should be identified with an American way of life. It should be an all-encompassing vision, a socializing faith, which was informed by and drew its inspiration from its own 'native expression-spirit' (Whitman, 1982, p. 365). In these terms, America's nationalism would be defined by its democratic commitment, reflected in art, music and literature. A culture that was both American and democratic would, in the era after the Civil War, be confirmed as a crucial piece in the Founders' jigsaw. It provided America with a national identity, explaining its purpose and maintaining its sense of a democratic destiny.

During the nineteenth century another problem impinged upon the nature of American democracy. It was realized that democratic values might clash with economic priorities: indeed, the very attempt to promote such values could have unintentional repercussions. In 1848, as Marx and Engels were concerned with the first publication of the *Communist Manifesto* in Europe, Frederick Grimké noted the irony in the United States: 'it is the principle of equality there which introduces all the inequality which is established in that country' (Grimké, 1848, p. 54). It was not the equal right to liberty which was the problem. Rather, it had to be conceded that equality of opportunity did not necessarily lead to equality of lifestyle once the opportunity had been taken. On the contrary, as population increased, 'on the one hand capital accumulates to such a degree as to create a large class of rich . . . on the other hand labour becomes superabundant, which gives rise to a still larger class of poor' (ibid., p. 46).

In the economic sphere, the liberty of *laissez-faire* combined with the progressively uneven distribution of wealth to create a society where some appeared more free and equal than others. The values which seemed to underlie the ethos of capitalism were remote from the ideals of political democracy. The economic system could compromise both liberty and equality. In America, in the *ante-bellum* period, this did not escape the apologists of the south. Fitzhugh argued that the wage-slaves of the north were just as much victims as were the negro slaves of his region. Indeed, the slaves were better served by the paternalism of the 'peculiar institution' than they would have been by the factories of the north. Was free labour a contradiction in terms?

Fitzhugh suggested it was, and claimed that 'our southern slavery has become a benign and protective institution, and our negroes are confessedly better off than any free laboring population in the world' (Fitzhugh, 1960, p. 201). This was because 'capital supports and protects the domestic slave; taxes, oppresses and persecutes the free laborer' (ibid., p. 203). The abolitionist argument was undermined, the north's hypocrisy exposed. 'Set your miscalled free laborers actually free, by giving them enough property or capital to live on, and then call on us at the South to free our negroes' (ibid., pp. 223–4). The Civil War forced that issue: the negro slaves were granted – notionally – an equal right to liberty. The conflict was not, however, a dispute over the consequences of economic theory. Capitalism emerged unscathed.

In the period after the Civil War the focus of social criticism in America shifted from a moral condemnation of negro slavery to a similar concern with the consequences of industrial capitalism. The so-called 'Gospel of Wealth' which was the triumphant outcome of allying the idea of equality of opportunity with *laissez-faire* economics was challenged by the advocates of a 'Social Gospel' which tried to reassert the original values of the American republic in the context of the emerging industrial society. The conclusion that a Jeffersonian interpretation of liberty and equality might conflict with the ideals of capitalism led to a search for economic theories which admitted this democratic dimension.

Industrialization could be accompanied by the realities of poverty, unemployment and social deprivation. In this atmosphere, one new industry flourished. In the last quarter of the nineteenth century in America a large number of utopian novels were published, offering speculative escapes from contemporary misery through the construction of economic systems based upon democratic values. They were popular. Underlying this connection between democracy, economics and utopia, moreover, was the ideology that in many ways accompanied the transition to the new industrial order. That ideology was socialism.

In Britain concepts of morality, culture and economics meshed with the ideal of democracy in other ways than in America, but common themes emerge. The consequences of industrialization and urbanization were felt there, too, in the nineteenth century, producing a strand of social criticism which questioned the morality of the underlying economic ethos of *laissez-faire* capitalism. Such criticism, however, was not from those who necessarily subscribed to a democratic faith. The cure for the ills of society was not seen in terms of the promotion of values like liberty or equality. Those remedies, indeed, were sometimes thought likely to cause greater social injuries than they might relieve. In Britain democracy was always a concern, never a panacea.

It was in such a context, too, that the concept of culture emerged in the mid-nineteenth century not as an essential requirement in a broad view of the democratic ideal but as yet another barrier to be placed in its way. Given the suspicion that a democratic society would tend to level rather than elevate general standards of taste and aesthetic appreciation, it was argued that the descent into collective mediocrity could be ameliorated if due account was taken of culture as an educational force. In this sense, culture is a term which incorporates an aspiration towards the creation of a civilized society: a mannered society, a society with standards. Culture could supply Britain with the code of conduct which in America was the natural outcrop of republican virtue and religious sentiment. It constrained the prospect of unbridled democratic liberty in much the same fashion. As such it was an antidote to anarchy.

The development of political democracy within the framework of Britain's constitutional monarchy made reliance on devices such as culture to counter the potential excesses of the new ideal largely superfluous. This and other suggestions of ways of confronting the demand for democratic equality were symptomatic, however, of a perennial concern with the quality of life which could be enjoyed as the force of change was felt in nineteenth-century Britain. The philosophical criteria which different critics brought to such a question were structured by views filtered through ideology. And in looking for the democratic values of liberty and equality to be emphasized in reply, it is again commonly in the literature of socialism that we find most favourable references. Indeed, as in

America, British socialists used utopian fiction as a vehicle for an explanation of their version of the democratic ideal. At the end of the century, the strand of Anglo-American analysis which best articulated the philosophy of democracy connected with values can be found in both countries as a theme in socialist thinking.

CONCLUSION

De Tocqueville's insight was profound. 'I accord institutions only a secondary influence over the destiny of men', he wrote. 'I am thoroughly convinced that political societies are not what their laws make them but what they are prepared in advance to be by the feelings, the beliefs, the ideas, the habits of heart and mind of the men who compose them' (quoted in Herr, 1962, p. 35). Here the case for a broad conception of the democratic ideal is made. It is necessary to look behind the definitions at the ideas and ultimately at the ideologies that inspire them. America and Britain may nowadays be regarded as liberal democracies, but it is evident that the convictions each brings to the characterization are different. In the nineteenth century, then, it is not enough to see democracy as matter of politics. The democratic ethos – differing in the nature of its impact in America and in Britain – influenced attitudes towards other issues as well. The advent of democracy may have 'shattered the old framework of political society' (Ostrogorski, 1902, vol. 1, p. 3). It did much else besides.

This book suggests some of the themes which combined to characterize the democratic tradition as it emerged in America and in Britain during the nineteenth century. It structures the material in the following manner. Part Two describes the context of American democracy in the founding period, and traces the political evolution of the institutions of the republic from the Constitution to the presidency of Andrew Jackson. It then considers the views of some representative critics of the central concept of majority rule: John C. Calhoun, James Fenimore Cooper and de Tocqueville, who more than any individual brought America's democratic experiment to the attention of Europe. Finally, it surveys the way in which the values which determined the nature of American democracy impinged on attitudes towards issues of moral, cultural and economic concern. This involves a discussion of the debate over slavery between Abraham Lincoln and Stephen Douglas, the views of Walt Whitman, notably in his book *Democratic Vistas* (1871), and the economic analysis of American democracy offered by Henry George, Edward Bellamy and Henry Demarest Lloyd.

Part Three turns attention to Britain, and pursues a similar path. A general discussion of different interpretations of the nature of the British constitution in the late eighteenth and early nineteenth century provides the context for a description of the evolution of political democracy in this country. This development is analysed with reference to the concern at the likely consequences of extending the right to vote: some antidotes to working-class majority rule are presented in the contrasting views of John Stuart Mill, Walter Bagehot and Matthew Arnold. Finally, there is a survey of a representative sample of the Victorian critics of democracy, who based their ideas on a concern about its impact upon the nation's moral conduct, aesthetic sensibilities and economic well-being. In this context, the views of Thomas Carlyle, John Ruskin and William Morris are discussed. Part Four, the concluding section, ties together some common themes connecting democracy, values and ideology as elements within the overall framework of the democratic tradition in each country.

The book focuses attention, then, on a wide-ranging democratic debate concerned with 'what ought to be' rather than 'what is', and discusses this against the background of the changes during the nineteenth century which were the product of new ideas and circumstances. Distinct traditions of democratic thought emerged on both sides of the Atlantic, although there were some common themes. As the narrative follows a broadly chronological path, it begins in America on the eve of the democratic millennium. So consider democracy in 1776.

Part two

The democratic debate in America

CHAPTER 2

The Founding of the American Republic

As Francis Lightfoot Lee observed in 1776, '*Constitutions* employ every pen' (quoted in Wood, 1969, p. 128). And behind such frantic scribbling there was a common desire in the newly independent states not only to implement some of the aspirations set out in the Declaration of Independence but also to construct institutions that might avoid the corruption and abuses which had inspired Jefferson to write it. Some put their faith in the people or at least their representatives. In many of the former colonies there was a systematic down-grading of executive power in favour of the legislature, where the representatives of the people might deliberate and determine the future of the community. That experiment began to break down once it was realized that legislative tyranny, arbitrary power in the hands of a majority, could be as real a possibility as had been the abuse of executive authority.

Meanwhile the first tentative steps were taken towards transforming the union of the states into the United States. But the Articles of Confederation, agreed in 1781, proved to be unequal to the task. These two developments – the instability of the state constitutions and the ineffectual nature of confederation – came together to provoke a pragmatic response. In 1787 the Philadelphia Convention was a chance for those who appreciated such problems to experiment with new ideas: a form of democracy resting on values and constructed on a national scale, a constitution that, as Madison suggested, would 'decide forever the fate of republican government' (quoted in Wood, 1969, p. 467).

It did. Federalism was united with the separation of powers. Republican principles were established. The Constitution worked. Justified and rationalized by Hamilton, Madison and Jay in *The Federalist*, the Constitution was ratified and became another part of the myth, another symbol of American democratic achievement. The problem of a republican constitution may have been solved, but the

'American dilemma' was not. Slavery existed within and alongside the democratic experiment. The issue was never dormant. It awaited the catalysts which nudged it towards a reaction, the process of fission which would lead to the catharsis of the Civil War.

The immediate problems were more prosaic. The institutions set up under the Constitution also had to work. The twin democratic outcrops, an electoral system and a party system, ultimately gave American democracy its characteristic flavour. In 1800, indeed, the electoral system, admittedly not with total facility, brought about a peaceful change of office between two parties: the first time such an event had happened in the United States, and possibly the first time it had happened on such a scale anywhere. Although President Jefferson ushered in a period of one-party dominance which would in the course of time culminate in the 'Era of Good Feelings', republican harmony was transitory. Tensions re-emerged. Jacksonian democracy represented a new phase. It was Jeffersonianism metamorphosed into a novel, dynamic, aggressive, populist, democratic partisanship.

These initial themes are representative of a chapter in American democracy. It was a formative period in which, if the colonial mould was broken, the democratic one was set as these elements were poured in. Before they are lost in the melting-pot it is worth examining some in slightly more detail, as the attempt was made to put the idealism of the Declaration to a practical test.

A REPUBLICAN CONSTITUTION

As Thomas Paine wrote in the year that America declared its independence, 'these are the times that try men's souls' (Paine, 1953a, p. 55). The war was still to be won, and the post-independence period was inevitably one of uncertainty and flux. It was also a time to test the intellect. No democratic master-plan existed for the victorious colonists to follow. They were not rejecting British rule in favour of a clear-cut alternative. Republicanism would be an experiment: so too democracy. New constitutional theories had to be devised, but they were not created in the abstract. Britain was at once the bogey-man and the guide. On the one hand America reacted against what was seen to be the corruption of the British system of mixed government and a balanced constitution. On the other it was still to British theories of constitutionalism that Americans turned when building their own systems of government.

At the same time, Americans had new and different priorities. However vague and inchoate the feeling, there was as part of the post-independence outlook a revolutionary stirring towards what would in time be recognized as a commitment to democracy. And democracy was a long way off in Britain. So there had been 'a democratic revolution in American *thought*' in the 1770s, and 'although the aspirations of the "democrat" rarely extended as far as simple majority rule, or universal manhood suffrage, there was a rejection of monarchical and aristocratic principles that had earlier been accepted' (Vile, 1967, p. 120). Insistence upon an equal right to liberty resulted in a conscious denial of ideas of government which enshrined principles of social hierarchy.

Such a 'democratization of mind' led to a situation in which 'somehow for a brief moment ideas and power, intellectualism and politics, came together – indeed were one with each other – in a way never again duplicated in American history' (Wood, 1978, pp. 102–3). It was almost as if, at the start of its democratic republican experiment, America found not one but several philosopher kings. Even if it was not his explicit motive, Jefferson, in writing the Declaration of Independence, had given America its charter. And the Founding Fathers were moved in part by similar idealism: the Constitution endured because there was an intellectual coherence underlying it and because it came to embody the secular and spiritual faith in republicanism which inspired it.

The irony of what became the American Revolution, rather than a mere struggle for colonial self-determination, was that these intellectuals, the political philosophers and the pamphleteers who set the ball rolling – Benjamin Franklin, Jefferson, Madison, even Paine – were, to mix the metaphor, flattened by the democratic juggernaut. 'In the end nothing illustrates better the transforming democratic radicalism of the American Revolution than the way its intellectual leaders, that remarkable group of men, contributed to their own demise' (Wood, 1978, p. 128). As de Tocqueville and John Stuart Mill among others were to point out, democracy elevated the common man, and politics and ideas became a common preserve. The uncommon individual was displaced not only from a position of power but also from a position of influence. Intellectuals no longer mattered. The Founders, then, inspired the ethos; it was up to the people to preserve it and the memory of those who were responsible for its creation. In America democracy endured largely because of such deference to the past – the critical era of the founding period.

Not only did Americans criticize Britain, but also, inspired by this democratic sentiment, they realized that new constitutional arrangements in the former colonies had to avoid the pitfalls of the British system and had to be suited to the unique circumstances of their own experience. Yet Britain still had something to give, for 'constitutional thought in America in the period leading up to the creation of the Federal Constitution reflects a number of interwoven influences at work. English thought, and the pattern of English institutions, inevitably provided the starting point for American development' (Vile, 1967, p. 121). That said, it was also true that Americans had little or no constitutional or even democratic heritage of their own to graft on to this British foundation. They had to make one.

It was a matter of *Common Sense*. Paine's pamphlet was among the better-known attempts to provide a critique of the imperial power and to offer an alternative. Part of this involved a commitment to republicanism and the rejection of the idea of monarchy. This was far more than a symbolic gesture – a ritual thumbing of the nose – to give substance to the separation from George III and Britain. For it allowed Americans to think about new forms of government, unhampered by the constitutional shackles which confined attitudes elsewhere. Although there was a lot of anti-monarchical literature published during the struggle for independence, *Common Sense* stood out because it destroyed the mystique of monarchy.

Paine 'said things about monarchical government that had not been said before', and the pamphlet 'broke through the pre-suppositions of politics and offered new ways of conceiving of government' (Wood, 1978, p. 110). Given that government was made necessary, as Paine observed, 'by the inability of moral virtue to govern the world' (Paine, 1953a, p. 6), it could be shown that there was little that was moral or virtuous about monarchs. Consider Paine's description of William the Conqueror: 'a French bastard landing with an armed banditti and establishing himself king of England against the consent of the natives' (ibid., p. 15). It leaves little scope for argument. An edifice of British constitutional tradition, amalgamating monarchy, aristocracy and democracy, blending them in supposed mixture and balance, had emerged none the less to legitimize the position of such kings.

To Paine, monarchy and aristocracy were merely examples of a corrupt hereditary tyranny: self-seeking autocrats had no need of public virtue. Between them they propagated a constitutional myth. 'To say that the constitution of England is a *union* of three powers, reciprocally *checking* each other, is farcical; either the words have no meaning, or they are flat contradictions' (Paine, 1953a, p. 7). America, however, need not adopt a constitutional system suited only to the demands of historical accident. It might plan something better. As Paine observed: 'a government of our own is our natural right;

and when a man seriously reflects on the precariousness of human affairs, he will become convinced that it is infinitely wiser and safer to form a Constitution of our own . . . than to trust such an interesting event to time and chance' (ibid., pp. 32–3). Britain, nevertheless, was still an example of sorts. In that three-fold division between the monarchy, the aristocracy and the democracy within the constitution lay the principle – that of a separation of powers – which, together with federalism, was to become the basis of a constitution for the United States.

THE SEPARATION OF POWERS AND FEDERALISM

The theory of a separation of powers had a long European tradition. In Britain the concept had been explored by Locke. On the Continent it had been publicized by Montesquieu. And indeed the idea appeared to correspond to the natural British order of things. The monarchy, the aristocracy and the democracy – the king, the House of Lords and the House of Commons. Each institution had distinct powers – a separation based upon that most characteristic of British traits, class. So the king could be the executive, the House of Lords might have part of the legislative function and be the ultimate arbiter in judicial matters, and the House of Commons could share in the powers of legislation. Mixed, balanced and fairly neat, it was a constitutional arrangement which, if it worked, gave Britain an enviable stable, if not qualitatively superior, political system.

It was this theory of the separation of powers which American thinkers extracted from the wreckage left by their criticism of the practical consequences of British constitutional arrangements, in which, they argued, the executive king had arrogated power, and in collusion with the aristocracy had reduced the legislative House of Commons to the status of a cipher. But there was a crucial distinction in the way in which the concept made the crossing. Separation of class was far less an issue than separation of function. Executive, legislature and judiciary became elements of republican government, and there was neither the need nor the desire to allocate responsibility according to a perceived hierarchy of political privilege. The executive and the judiciary were part of the people's government and might be accountable to them in the last resort.

In Britain, moreover, mixture had not implied control, and balance had not meant accountability. In America no function of government was to be independent of the people merely because it owed its status to the accident of birth and the contrivance of hereditary

31

succession. After the War of Independence few would contemplate the wholesale importation of the British system, which as it stood could not be grafted on to republican principles. But even during the conflict some had realized that the separation of powers according to function might have a part to play. As John Adams wrote in 1775: 'a legislative, an executive and a judicial power comprehend the whole of what is meant and understood by government. It is by balancing each of these powers against the other two, that the efforts in human nature towards tyranny can alone be checked and restrained' (quoted in Vile, 1967, p. 133). Balance indeed was crucial. It had to be right. The problem of the early state constitutions in America was that what was considered right in the 1770s and 1780s reflected the disillusionment with arbitrary executive power which had sparked the conflict with Britain in the first place. This resulted in an over-ambitious faith in the possibilities of representative authority invested in state legislatures.

The theory of a separation of powers having been accepted, therefore, the central problem was to decide upon the different powers to be distributed among these separate institutions. In this, there was a general conscious down-grading of executive authority. Popular election was thought to be no guarantee against the possibility of arbitrary executive rule once the election was over, and there was a concern not to replace the hereditary monarch with an elected substitute. Suspicion was acute. 'The executive power is ever restless, ambitious, and ever grasping at encrease [sic] of power', wrote William Hooper in 1776 (quoted in Wood, 1969, p. 135).

It was not enough to insulate the legislature from executive interference, although some states, such as Pennsylvania and Vermont, adopted an almost 'pure doctrine' of the separation of powers. Rather, it was the legislature which often pre-empted the political powers and responsibilities which had previously been the prerogative of the executive. On this see-saw of constitutional responsibility the weight was on the side of the legislature, and there was the danger, soon realized, that the executive might be catapulted off altogether. As the South Carolinan, Thomas Tucker, put it in 1784, after ridding themselves of an arbitrary monarch, Americans had 'vainly imagined that we had arrived at perfection, and that freedom was established on the broadest and most solid basis that could possibly consist with any social institution. That we have in some points been mistaken is too evident to be denied' (quoted in Wood, 1969, p. 430). A strong, but not over-mighty, executive might after all be a constitutional asset.

By the 1780s, then, the idealism which had emerged out of the War of Independence, and which had inspired revolutionary constitutional experimentation in the former colonies, appeared to be corrupted in practice. The value of liberty implied at least freedom from arbitrary authority and control. The value of equality presupposed republican government, which in turn placed its trust in the civic virtue and responsibility of the people. But the state constitutions had not realized such aspirations. The people proved fickle. Majorities and minorities brought with them factions. Legislative power unchecked could oppress freedom by law. It was seen that 'power abused ceases to be lawful authority and degenerates into tyranny. Liberty abused or carried to excess is licentiousness' (Henry Cumings, quoted in Wood, 1969, p. 403). Independence brought instability.

Republican virtue was stifled. The state legislatures, controlled by factions and unchecked by executive power, might impose what John Adams had appreciated in 1776 was a theoretical contradiction but a real possibility, a 'democratic despotism'. The radical demand for frequent elections, sometimes annual, contributed to the atmosphere of confusion. Legislative assemblies rested on the uncertainty of shifting factional control. Laws passed in one legislative session might be repealed in the next. Madison was moved to comment in the year before the meeting in Philadelphia that the absence of *wisdom* and *steadiness*' in legislation was the 'grievance complained of in all our republics' (quoted in Wood, 1969, p. 405). The republican idea, with its democratic underpinning contained in the values expressed in the Declaration of Independence, seemed to have gone awry.

Nor could America take comfort from attitudes elsewhere. In Britain there were some sympathizers with the revolutionary ideas which had emerged from the struggle for independence. Others, however, saw the instability in the states as confirmation of the impression that in throwing off their colonial status they were trying to run politically before acquiring the ability to walk constitutionally. In January 1787 the London-based *Gentleman's Magazine and Historical Chronicle* reported a letter from Dr Richard Price, a revolutionary fellow-traveller, to a friend in New York which recounted the prevailing sentiment in Britain.

The conclusion is that you are falling to pieces, and will soon repent your Independence. But the hope of the friends of Virtue and Liberty is . . . that whereas the kingdoms of Europe have travelled to tranquillity through seas of blood, the United States are travelling to a degree of

33

tranquillity and liberty that will make them an example to the world, only through seas of blunders. (*Gentleman's Magazine*, 1787, vol. 57, p. 631)

The idea of a separation of powers appeared too weak a constitutional theory to stand on its own.

The British magazine did not share its correspondent's hopes for America. The prospect of the Philadelphia Convention only appeared to confirm such pessimism. America was

on the verge of being thrown into popular ferment; delegates are being sent from every State to Philadelphia, to form a convention for the purpose of reviving, altering, or perhaps totally annihilating, the different constitutions of the country. This will, no doubt, produce a scene of confusion and anarchy. (*Gentleman's Magazine*, 1787, vol. 57, p. 632)

From the stability of the balanced constitution some British onlookers saw the chaos of the degenerating republican experiments. The future seemed somewhat bleak.

The states could not look to the nation. There was no such thing: no embodiment of the one republic, the United States. The idea had been mooted, and the Articles of Confederation, drawn up in 1781, provided a fleshless skeleton. They committed the states only to 'a firm league of friendship with each other for their common defense, the security of their liberties, and their mutual and general welfare . . .' (reproduced in Cooper, 1885, bk. 4, p. 6). Representation in Congress varied between two and seven members according to the size of the state, but each state had only one vote in this national assembly. This form of confederation did not seize the popular imagination. In 1783 Paine seemed almost to have forgotten its existence when pointing to the need for a strong national government. 'That which must more forcibly strike a thoughtful, penetrating mind, and which includes and renders easy all inferior concerns, is the *union of the states*. On this our great national character depends. It is this which must give us importance abroad and security at home' (Paine, 1953b, p. 67). For those who came to the Philadelphia Convention four years later with the intention of saving the republican experiment, the Articles of Confederation offered little foundation. They rejected them.

A viable national government appeared the only way to provide a republican focus which might overcome the difficulties encountered in the atomistic autonomous states. Yet, having abandoned the Articles, the delegates had little to fall back upon except more constitutional theorizing and a desire to avoid previous mistakes. In this sense the Constitution was a retreat from the democratic efforts of the states insofar as they had entrenched the legislature as the dominant element in their designs. That form of democracy had a tarnished reputation. The new government worked out new accommodations, checking and balancing separate powers in different ways.

At the Convention some would have preferred to abandon the democratic republican prospect. Edmund Randolph observed that: 'our chief danger arises from the democratic parts of our constitutions. It is a maxim which I hold incontrovertible, that the powers of government exercised by the people swallows [sic] up the other branches. None of the constitutions have provided sufficient checks against the democracy' (McHenry, 1927, p. 925). Maybe Britain was best. There was a feeling that the state governments had not achieved an appropriate blend of the separate functions, and that at least under a system of mixed government the liberty of the people could be counterbalanced by the monarchy and the aristocracy, so constraining the slide towards 'licentiousness'. This view short-circuited once more to the idea that separation of powers should necessarily be based on hierarchy and class.

Alexander Hamilton argued such a case in a five-hour speech to the Convention on 18 June. The proceedings were *in camera*, fortunately, as to committed American republicans his views would have appeared nothing short of subversive. Hamilton may have been playing devil's advocate, but Madison took him seriously enough to record that 'in his private opinion, he [Hamilton] had no scruple in declaring, supported as he was by the opinions of so many of the wise & good, that the British government was the best in the world: and that he doubted much whether anything short of it would do in America' (Madison, 1927, p. 220). Hamilton encapsulated the democratic republican conundrum: 'Give all power to the many, they will oppress the few. Give all power to the few, they will oppress the many.' The answer was old and familiar: 'Both therefore ought to have power, that each may defend itself against the other' (ibid., p. 221). As the delegates cast around for a constitutional framework which achieved such a compromise, the British model once more came into its own. Not republican, not democratic, it nevertheless achieved Hamilton's balance.

It was necessary, then, to build defences against arbitrary executive authority on the one side and unbridled popular power on the other. Hamilton, perhaps punning, called the British House of Lords a 'noble institution', which did this by forming 'a permanent barrier against every pernicious innovation, whether attempted on the part of the Crown or of the Commons' (Madison, 1927, p. 221). Such a fulcrum of constitutional responsibility was what America then lacked. Hamilton thus advocated one branch of the legislature holding 'their places for life or at least during good behaviour' (ibid., p. 222). In similar fashion he also argued that the executive should have tenure 'for life'. Indeed no good executive 'could be established on Republican principles', and 'the English model was the only good one on this subject' (ibid., p. 221).

The other major account of the Convention proceedings confirms Hamilton as potentially an apostate republican and certainly no democrat. 'Can a democratic assembly, who annually revolve in the mass of the people be supposed steadily to pursue the public good? Nothing but a permanent body can check the imprudence of democracy. Their turbulent and uncontrolling disposition requires checks' (Yates, 1927, p. 781). Hamilton's prospect, then, was a constitution under which the executive was elected or appointed for life. One branch of the legislature was to be similarly constituted to balance the other representative part. It would have been the king, the Lords and the Commons: monarchy, aristocracy and democracy. Britain recreated in America.

Others argued that the British example was quite simply no longer relevant. The very expression of the Declaration of Independence ensured that. And as Charles Pinckney pointed out at another session of the Convention:

> the United States contain but one order that can be assimilated to the British Nation – this is the order of Commons. They will not surely then attempt to form a Government consisting of three branches, two of which shall have nothing to represent. They will not have an Executive and Senate (hereditary) because the King and Lords of England are so. (Madison, 1927, p. 273)

Separation of powers was not to be based on class. America was different, and in that difference lay a possible answer. A bi-cameral system, with an unelected second chamber balancing the disturbingly democratic tendencies of one elected by the people, seemed an appropriate model to follow. But, whereas in Britain the qualification for membership to the House of Lords lay in an accident of birth or the gift of the monarch, America's Senate could still be a representative institution, not of the people but of the states.

In this way the federal House of Representatives 'was to be the grand depository of the democratic principle of the Government. It was, so to speak, to be our House of Commons' (Madison,

1927, p. 125). The Senate, however, could check this democracy by counterbalancing the people with the states. Federalism was the happy result of circumstance: there had been the 'accidental lucky division of this Country into distinct States' (ibid., p. 143). It was this principle which brought some stability to American government, and allowed the concept of separation of powers according to function to operate as part of the national democratic republican experiment. So federalism, the incorporation of the states as distinct units within the national government, seen most obviously in the Senate – but present also as a principle in the Electoral College system for deciding the executive – was the missing link in maintaining the republican ideal.

Federalism, then, implied something more than merely the states' presence in national government. It also meant the division of political power between the centre and the periphery, between the national and the state governments. In deciding the relative division of powers between them, the Founders were concerned to bring the state experiments in republican democracy under control. And the decision also reflected a theory of balance re-entering American constitutional thought: balance not between classes but between units of government.

The success of the new Federal Constitution thus rested on this balance. The division of powers was between the national government and the state governments, and within the national government between the separate functions of executive, legislature and judiciary. A stage further and the balance within the legislature between the House of Representatives and the Senate, the people and the states, was also significant. In this sense the Constitution was a complex series of compromises, designed to bring about the institutional sleight of hand: national government without eradicating state sovereignty, republican government without endangering political stability, and democratic government without a degeneration into popular tyranny.

The Articles of Confederation had not attempted such a subtle engineering of constitutional confidence. It had proved difficult to intrude in areas where the states regarded themselves as sovereign and independent units, yet such intrusion was necessary to impart a feeling of stability to American government. As Madison pointed out at the Convention, 'all the examples of other confederacies prove the greater tendency in such systems to anarchy than to tyranny, to a disobedience of the members than to usurpations of the federal head' (Madison, 1927, pp. 250–1). Confederation confounded the democratic republican experiment. Federalism became its foundation.

There were, then, two sorts of balanced inter-locking relationships within the American Constitution. The one, a separation of powers according to function, enabled the creation of a powerful, but not too powerful, government at a national level. The other, federalism, divided power between the central government and the states. At least that was the theory. Between them these principles supplanted the ideas of mixed government and a balanced constitution in such a way that republicanism could persist and there could be no return to monarchy, aristocracy and a class-based division of political power. The Federal Constitution provided the secure foundation for the American version of republican democracy to proceed.

Its success, however, might be measured not only in the extent to which it preserved the republican ideal: the Constitution had to provide a framework within which the greatest threat to the survival of that ideal could be met. Factionalism had been seen to be a potentially evil and divisive product of state constitutions built upon ideas of popular sovereignty and majority rule. Epidemic in the states, it might be endemic in the nation. 'Faction, dissension and the consequent subjection of the minority to the caprice and arbitrary decisions of the majority' (Frances Corbin, quoted in Wood, 1969, p. 502) was a complaint associated with the republican institutions of the states. How might the national government avoid a similar disease? The Constitution itself did not pronounce on the theory – it was only concerned with the mechanics. But then the operating manual of the document, *The Federalist*, was always available for consultation.

THE FEDERALIST AND FACTIONS

Madison Avenue is aptly named. Hamilton contributed much to *The Federalist*, John Jay also wrote a few. But it was James Madison who really advertised the Constitution, not only to New York but also to posterity. He was its greatest publicist. His first contribution to the series was possibly his finest. 'Federalist 10' opens with the famous assertion: 'Among the numerous advantages promised by a well-constructed Union, none deserves to be more accurately developed than its tendency to break and control the violence of faction' (*Federalist*, 1937, p. 41). Madison goes on to argue, with elegant logic, how this would occur, establishing an idea of political pluralism as the dynamic force contained within the constitutional framework.

The criticisms levelled against republican government are confronted head on. 'The instability, injustice and confusion introduced into the public councils, have in truth, been the mortal diseases under which popular governments have everywhere perished.' How was America to avoid this? Already it might be too late.

> Complaints are everywhere heard . . . that our governments are too unstable, that the public good is disregarded in the conflicts of rival parties, and that measures are too often decided, not according to the rules of justice and the rights of the minor party, but by the superior force of an interested and overbearing majority. (*Federalist*, 1937, p. 41)

Thus, 'a factious spirit has tainted our public administrations', (ibid., p. 42), a spirit which sat uneasily with the ethos of republican harmony.

Madison's ideas as to how to control such factions have been well rehearsed. Briefly, having concluded that removing the causes of faction would be worse than the malady itself, he argues that there are indeed ways of moderating the effects. A minority faction can be dealt with by the procedural mechanism of majority rule. It can be out-voted. Problems re-emerge when the faction becomes a majority. The Federal Constitution, claims Madison, avoids this happening. In a representative system operating in a large country – and size is crucial – potential majority factions will be broken up.

> Extend the sphere, and you take in a greater variety of parties and interests; you make it less probable that a majority of the whole will have a common motive to invade the rights of other citizens; or if such a common motive exists, it will be more difficult for all who feel it to discover their own strength, and to act in unison with each other. (*Federalist*, 1937, p. 47)

Pluralism within a large republic – *ex una plures* – was the safeguard.

Republican democracy of the kind envisaged by Madison was thus different from other forms of democracy, not necessarily in values but rather in structure. As he wrote to Jefferson in October 1787, the month before 'Federalist 10' was published, a simple democracy – which Madison called a 'pure republic', and which could be seen as similar in type to the constitutional experiments in the states – would be inherently unstable as long as there were different selfish interests in society. Republican virtue implied unanimity on one point: the republican interest transcended all others, and without that over-arching commitment its future was threatened. Given the existence of opposing interests, however, there was another republican model which could subordinate factions such that virtue might triumph.

If then there must be different interests and parties in society, and a majority when united by a common interest or passion cannot be restrained from oppressing the minority, what remedy can be found in republican Government, where the majority must ultimately decide; but that of giving such an extent to its sphere, that no common interest or passion will be likely to unite a majority of the whole number in an unjust pursuit. (Quoted in Padover, 1960, p. 361)

In Madison's terms, the subsequent pursuit of America's manifest destiny was in part the fulfilment of this republican mission.

Pluralism could work in a republican democracy, as previously and perversely it had in corrupt autocracies. 'Divide et impera, the reprobated axiom of tyranny, is under certain qualifications the only policy by which a republic can be administered on just principles' (Madison, quoted in Padover, 1960, p. 361). This was the point that Madison developed in 'Federalist 10'. 'The influence of factious leaders may kindle a flame within their particular States, but will be unable to spread a general conflagration through the other States' (*Federalist*, 1937, p. 47). Federalism and the separation of powers thus helped to set republican virtue back on the pedestal from which self-seeking majorities had threatened to swipe it, and 'in the extent and proper structure of the Union, therefore, we behold a republican remedy for the diseases most incident to republican government' (ibid., p. 48).

The theme is a consistent one. In 'Federalist 51', it was reiterated in a discussion of the merits of a separation of powers incorporating checks and balances. 'Ambition must be made to counter-act ambition' (*Federalist*, 1937, p. 264). To this end, American 'society itself will be broken into so many parts, interests, and classes of citizens, that the rights of individuals, or of the minority, will be in little danger from interested combinations of the majority' (ibid., p. 266). So republican democracy of this type need not, as anti-federalists feared, inevitably degenerate into tyranny. Locked in cleverly arranged conflict within the 'extended sphere', the factions had their impact deflected and dissipated.

The Federalist provides a guide to the constitutional thought of those whose arguments prevailed in Philadelphia, and a justification for the institutional arrangements that were to be adopted. The papers show a healthy regard for the possibilities of corruption, whether at a state or at a federal level, or within the executive, legislative or judicial functions of government. That can be avoided by constitutional contrivance. At times the admiration for such institutional engineering borders on the self-congratulatory. Despite the artful designs to outwit tyranny, the driving force behind the republican ideal, however, was still a confidence in its capacity to nurture virtue: a belief in the ability of the people to exercise the right of self-government, and to submit to the greater good of the republic rather than merely exploit the community for their own short-term gain. Inherent in such a concept are the values of democracy – equality and liberty – which Jefferson had designated part of the American faith. But whatever the democratic belief, the republican ethos, and however good the institutional framework designed to encapsulate it, one fundamental blot remained: slavery.

SLAVERY AND DEMOCRACY

The contradiction between the proclaimed principles of equality and liberty and the fact of slavery in America was so obvious that for some future observers it could have been resolved by the Founders only through a subtle process of constitutional doublethink. Otherwise it might prove impossible to square the appeal to freedom and the rejection of arbitrary power, power to compel by threat or force, with the existence of domestic slavery in several states. Americans loved liberty and hated slavery. For themselves that is. A slave was not an American. Indeed a slave was not a man.

Some, in the era of the fight for independence, could happily blame the 'peculiar institution' on Britain. Jefferson originally drafted a paragraph in the Declaration cataloguing slavery as yet another evil perpetrated by George III. 'He has waged cruel war against human nature itself, violating its most sacred rights of life and liberty in the persons of a distant people who never offended him, captivating and carrying them into slavery in another hemisphere, or to incur miserable death in their transportation thither.' Not content with inflicting slaves on America, the king was now inciting them to insurrection, causing the colonists additional concern.

> He is now exciting those very people to rise in arms among us, and to purchase that liberty of which *he* has deprived them by murdering the people upon whom *he* also obtruded them: thus paying off former crimes committed against the *liberties* of one people, with crimes which he urges them to commit against the *lives* of another. (Billington, 1950, vol. 1., p. 85)

Jefferson, a reluctant slave-owner, was outraged enough to look for scape-goats.

The problem of slavery transcended both the War of Independence and George III. It would not go away with the British. It may have been, therefore, that to salve their democratic consciences some Americans adopted a simple but compelling outlook. Liberty and equality, they may have held, rested upon a belief in the inalienable rights of man. Slaves were not human, so they had no such rights. Yet this was a static and unsustainable view when confronted with a rising tide of rationalist idealism. The argument changed. Negroes, it was suggested, indeed had the same rights as all humans. But at that time they could not actually exercise them, and they could not be provided with the necessary safeguards or power to test such potential. That would come. Slavery was a moral travesty of the democratic sentiment but it was unavoidable. It entered the democratic structure because it was part of the establishment. Slavery came in by the back door, 'grudgingly, unacknowledged, on the presumption that the house would be truly fit to live in only when it was gone, and that it would ultimately be gone' (Storing, 1978, p. 225). The Constitution and *The Federalist* show the transition from one view to the other.

The Constitution does not mention the word. 'Slavery' does not appear in the document. Two references in particular, however, imply a recognition of the issue which bugged the debates of the Convention. The first concerns the apportionment of representatives and direct taxes among the states. This is to be done: 'according to their respective Numbers, which shall be determined by adding to the whole Number of free Persons, including those bound to Service for a Term of Years, and excluding Indians not taxed, three-fifths of all other persons' (Art. 1. s. 2). Slaves were 'all other Persons' (Vile, 1976, p. 278). They were to count for 60 per cent of a free individual. Tax-evading Indians counted for nothing.

The second reference comes later, and is potentially more significant still in showing the awareness of the fluid nature of the issue. 'The Migration or Importation of such Persons as any of the States now existing shall think proper to admit, shall not be prohibited by the Congress prior to the Year one thousand eight hundred and eight, but a Tax or duty may be imposed on such Importation, not exceeding ten dollars for each person' (Art. 1. s. 9) (Vile, 1976, p. 283). Migration was not such an issue in these terms as was importation. Congress was given power to act in the future to curb the slave trade: in the meanwhile it could at least tax it.

Taken together these constitutional formulations are more than stylistic niceties. They demonstrate some humanitarian idealism in the Founders' view of their future republic. The circumlocution of the first reference avoided cursing the Constitution with a word that the second reference aimed to start making redundant. When the republic came of age, Congress could ban the slave trade: democracy in the shape of an equal right to liberty might slowly be extended to all individuals, although it would take some time for this to happen. The Founders welded idealism to realism. But the prospect was there, and it was the prospect which was important.

The Federalist gives the pragmatic arguments behind the constitutional phrases. Again, there is an evident antipathy towards the institution of slavery. 'Federalist 54' argues that slaves have been included for apportionment purposes as taxable assets and fractions of a representative unit since they are both property and people. They are property because they are owned by and work for a master, and because the master can sell them to another. A slave is also property since he is 'subject at all times to be restrained in his liberty and chastised in his body by the capricious will of another' (*Federalist*, 1937, p. 278). Equally, however, the slave counts as a person: an important concession in the face of contrary claims. The slave has some legal protection against abuse, and may also be held responsible for actions towards others. In this way, a slave is 'no less evidently regarded by the law as a member of the society, not as a part of the irrational creation; as a moral person, not as a mere article of property' (*ibid*, p. 278). *The Federalist* suggested that although the masters defined the rules, they could not have the argument all ways. A slave was property for taxation purposes but almost a person for the calculation of representation, and legally a person in matters of transgression. The Constitution and the law said so.

As a further argument in favour of anti-slavers supporting the Constitution, 'Federalist 54' used the point that the Constitution disagreed with the southern ploy that slaves were not human.

> Might not some surprise also be expressed, that those who reproach the Southern States with the barbarous policy of considering as property a part of their human brethren, should themselves contend that the government to which all the States are to be parties, ought to consider this unfortunate race more completely in the unnatural light of property than the very laws of which they complain? (*Federalist*, 1937, p. 279)

In the end it had to be admitted, however, that this was a unique issue. 'Let the case of the slaves be considered, as it is in truth, a peculiar one.' Then 'let the compromising expedient of the Constitution be mutually adopted, which regards them as inhabitants, but as debased by servitude below the equal level of free inhabitants; which regards the *slave* as divested of two-fifths of the *man*' (ibid., p. 280).

43

Here again it is the fact of slavery that creates the problem, rather than any intrinsic assessment of the worth of the slave as human. The institution was at fault, not those who suffered under it.

Further evidence that some of the Founders looked on slavery with abhorrence is shown in 'Federalist 42', where Madison comments on the clause that might be used eventually to ban the slave trade. It might be argued that Congress should have been given immediate power to prohibit the importation of slaves. But the climate of opinion was not suitable: law was no substitute for voluntary change of attitude.

> It ought to be considered as a great point gained in favour of humanity, that a period of twenty years may terminate for ever, within these States, a traffic which has so long and so loudly upbraided the barbarism of modern policy; that within that period it will receive a considerable discouragement from the federal government, and may be totally abolished by the concurrence of the few States which continue the unnatural traffic in the prohibitory example which has been given by so great a majority of the Union. (*Federalist*, 1937, pp. 213–14)

Abolition of the slave trade was hence seen as a step in the direction of a more general emancipation. The Founders, or at least some of them, realized that the ideals of republican democracy would be dogged by the existence of slavery until time resolved the issue.

The 'peculiar institution' was thus profoundly reassessed in the light of the sentiments of the War of Independence and the American Revolution, and it bore the marks ever after. Freedom versus slavery: the conflict remained at the core of the American republic and the emerging character of its democratic tradition. It took a civil war to clarify the issue and an insistence on civil rights to bring some substance to constitutional amendments. Slavery was and remained a problem of morals and ethics as much as a problem of politics. It is the perennial dilemma – the American dilemma – still.

There were also other difficulties. 'The new Constitution possessed neither tradition nor the backing of organized public opinion' (Morison and Commager, 1930, vol. 1, p. 323). The republican commitment had to exist beyond the confines of the convention hall, and the means to preserve the experiment had to be endorsed by a population who not only took a lead from the Founders but also, in the main, agreed with them. Unanimity on the chimerical Constitution proved as impossible as it had been unlikely. Ratification was not achieved without a tussle, and the institutions of the United States only gradually acquired the aura of legitimacy that comes with age and successful operation.

The constitutional principles thus found expression in the functional elements of the executive, legislature and judiciary, but two further institutions were necessary to impart a dynamic to the system and to complete the process of organization. A federal electoral system and a national political party system were these missing links. Both came to characterize in different ways the nature of American democracy. If representative government presupposed elections, however, it did not inevitably imply parties. Many were not too sure about them. Some would not come to their aid; even good men eschewed them.

The development of the federal electoral system and the evolution of political parties followed separate but interrelated paths in the early years of the republic: overlapping and inter-twining, but ultimately the result of different purposes and ideas. For both institutions 1800 was a memorable year, although it was only in the Jacksonian period that each took on its modern guise.

THE ELECTORAL SYSTEM

The states had the power to legislate the rules under which the first federal elections would take place. The Senate was not elected by the people, but the House of Representatives was, and indirectly, through the Electoral College, so too was the president. Senators caused little controversy. They were chosen by the individual state legislatures, and 'within the respective assemblies, the action taken was usually a perfunctory registration of votes for men more or less important in the local political life' (Stephens, 1909, p. 10).

The electoral system for the House and for the Electors attracted more of a debate. The choice might appear technical, but it was realized that the method of election had severe consequences for the character of representation. It did not take long to weigh up the possibilities: by 1812 the governor of Massachusetts had devised that political reptile the gerrymander. In the first federal elections, then, two methods of election were canvassed: by district, within the state, with each such constituency electing one or several representatives; or by 'general ticket', whereby the whole state acted as one electoral unit. Since it was an electoral horse-race, decided by the 'first-past-the-post' method, where there were different districts a variety of representatives supporting various points of view could be elected. But where the 'general ticket' was used, a 'slate' of candidates committed to one outlook could effectively monopolize representation. Districting diffused influence; the general ticket consolidated it.

The two sides of this debate were widely discussed in contemporary newspapers. In July 1788 the *Pennsylvania Gazette* printed the eye-catching headline: '*Numa to the Inhabitants of the States that have adopted the New Constitution*'. 'Numa' proposed a compromise between districting and the general ticket.

Divide the state into as many districts as there are members to be chosen, and direct the electors to fix upon a member from *each* district, and then let the whole state vote for the whole number of members. By these means a knowledge of the local interest of every part of the state will be carried to Congress, but in such a manner as not to interfere with the interest of the whole state. (*Pennsylvania Gazette*, 16 July 1788)

Support for this idea came from the equally epigrammatic 'Pompilius' in the same paper a week later.

The reply to both came from 'a friend to Agriculture, Trade and Good Laws' who argued that any form of districting would destroy the representative base of those elected to the federal lower house. It would: 'narrow them down from representatives of Pennsylvania to representatives of districts, and would reduce me from an elector from a confederated state to an elector for part of a state. I think this is contrary to the spirit of the new confederation, and to the nature of confederacies in general' (*Pennsylvania Gazette*, 23 July 1788). Later still it was argued that there could be no doubt that districting '*will tend to destroy and undermine the state governments*' (*Pennsylvania Gazette*, 30 July 1788). These articles contributed to a persistent debate which newspapers kept to the attention of their leaders: the *Pennsylvania Mercury* reprinted the views of 'a friend to Agriculture' some two months after they had first appeared elsewhere.

The newspaper debate, which went on in most states – Massachusetts offers another example – throughout the summer and autumn of 1788, provided the background for the subsequent discussions in the state legislatures towards the end of the year. The choice between the electoral systems was by no means clear-cut. The argument continued between those who thought that local interests within the states should be represented, and that this was the intention of the Founders and others who considered that the state should act as an indivisible unit for electoral purposes.

Eventually this controversy was resolved through practical experience. By 1832 most states had moved to presidential balloting under the rules of the general ticket. This method of election was felt to preserve the influence of the state as an autonomous unit within the Electoral College, and has determined the strategy of presidential elections ever since. On the other hand, congressional legislation in 1842 demanded districting for elections to the House of Representatives. The legislature was hence seen as a place where variety of representation should not only be encouraged but also endorsed. At the outset there was no such bifurcation of electoral systems, but by the mid-nineteenth century the mechanics for executive and legislative elections had assumed their modern form.

The first federal elections, however, demonstrated a plethora of systems for choosing both representatives and presidential electors. Whatever the theoretical rationalizations, at a practical level the struggles in the state legislatures persisted between factions who supported and those who opposed the new Constitution; they were in a position now to influence its electoral system and thus the expected outcomes of those contests. Their perception dictated their preferences. Their political clout determined the exact arrangements.

The Founders remained largely aloof from the mechanics and the infighting except to pass comment, as Madison did to Jefferson in a letter written in October 1788. Observing that the general ticket had been adopted in Pennsylvania, Madison wrote:

> the act proposes that every citizen throughout the State shall vote for the whole number of members allotted to the State. This method of election will confine the choice to characters of a general notoriety, and so far be favourable to merit. It is, however, liable to some popular objections urged against the tendency of the new system. In Virginia, I am inclined to think, the State will be divided into as many districts as there are to be members. In other States, as in Connecticut, the Pennsylvania example will probably be followed. And in others, again, a middle course be taken. It is, perhaps, to be desired that various modes be tried, as by that means only the best mode can be ascertained. (Madison, 1884, vol. 1, pp. 420–1)

Madison's remarks reveal the prospect as much as the retrospect. The debate over the electoral system reflected the image of a Constitution which provided a framework within which the institutions of a representative government had to be developed. Again it was custom and practice, expedience and accident, that characterized the procedures and processes, as the attempt was made to translate the ethos of republican democracy into practice.

THE PARTY SYSTEM

Competitive elections eventually came to involve the idea of a party system. Indeed, political parties alternating in elected office is often seen as a functional characteristic of a liberal democracy. It was not always the case. To many Americans the concept of a political party was, during the founding period, not only novel but hardly compelling. Much of the theorizing behind the Constitution involved an effort to dissipate the effects of factionalism – the achievement which Madison lauded in 'Federalist 10'. Factions squabbled over the political prospects of the state republics. Parties might equally battle for federal control. The early history of political parties in the United States can appear as a well-intentioned desire to throttle them at birth.

Attitudes change. From the notion of 'party as evil' in the immediate post-independence period, a predominant shift of outlook occurred to 'party as good' in the Jacksonian era. Again, this was the product of experience. The apparent harmony of sentiment which found its ultimate expression in the 'Era of Good Feelings' persisted in the end only through clenched political teeth and politicians' stiff upper lips. Jacksonian democracy released a pent-up partisanship which established parties as inevitable outcrops of the American democratic tradition. But they still had their critics.

Suspicion of political parties had a long and distinguished history as a strand in American political thought. The Founders were products of an era in which a general consensus existed that parties should be avoided as they could embody only a partial vision of the public good. Harmony of sentiment and unanimity of outlook would reinforce the belief that the republican interest should somehow transcend all others. Evidently that ideal was unlikely; but the idea persisted that if divisions did arise the dominant viewpoint would eventually absorb the rest.

Controversy was thus to be transient, and was not to be reflected in permanent forces ranged against one another. Republican commitment filled a party divide which difference in ideology would find difficult to widen. Enlightenment rationalism sought consensus. Solutions were neat, right and unique. George Washington in his farewell address as president summarized the sentiment, warning 'in the most solemn manner, against the baneful effects of the spirit of party generally'. In a monarchical system, parties might act as rallying points for the expression of the sentiment of liberty. But in a republican government liberty was a foundation rather than a cause, and the spirit of party was not to be encouraged. Washington explained why:

The alternate domination of one faction over another, sharpened by the spirit of revenge, natural to party dissensions, which, in different ages and countries has perpetrated the most horrid enormities, is itself a frightful despotism . . . The disorders and miseries which result, gradually incline the minds of men to seek security and repose in the absolute power of an individual; and sooner or later, the chief of some prevailing faction more able or more fortunate than his competitors, turns this disposition to the purposes of his own elevation on the ruins of public liberty. (Reproduced in Cooper, 1885, bk 2, pp. 14–21)

The spirit of party was thus 'a fire not be quenched, it demands a uniform vigilance to prevent its bursting into a flame, lest, instead of warming, it should consume' (ibid.).

With a quieter rhetorical flourish, Washington's successor, John Adams, agreed that 'a division of the republic into two great parties . . . is to be dreaded as the greatest political evil under our Constitution' (quoted in Hofstadter, 1969, p. 38). He was shutting the theoretical door after the party horse had bolted. For although the prevailing sentiment against political parties could almost be accorded the status of a self-evident truth that they were bad, nevertheless the early years of the republic were marked by a rudimentary party system emerging at a national level.

The uneasy way in which this occurred is epitomized by the changing attitudes of the party founders, Hamilton and the ubiquitous Madison. Hamilton had apparently thrown his hand in with the winners when at the New York ratifying convention he declared that 'we are attempting by this Constitution to abolish factions, and to unite all parties for the general welfare' (quoted in Hofstadter, 1969, p. 17). Who, however, decided what was the general welfare? Hamilton had an answer. Taking advantage of the initial difficulties of organizing the federal Congress, 'a leaderless herd' which set 'no direction of its own for the new government' (Chambers, 1963, p. 38), Hamilton set about forming a group of like-minded representatives who could give some support to the legislative initiatives he orchestrated from within the executive branch at the Treasury department. By the 1790s he had achieved this modest ambition.

It was counteracted by Madison. For the good of the republic and to establish 'political equality among all' he aimed to deflect threats to the republican ideal of liberty which might result from Hamilton's centralization of power. The evils of Hamiltonianism could be combated 'by making one party a check on the other, so far as the existence of parties cannot be prevented, nor their views accommodated' (quoted in Hofstadter, 1969, p. 81). By the 1790s Madison too had recognized that the party writing on the wall might be more than political graffiti. Or to put it more elegantly, 'the pragmatic pressure of political conflict has already begun to modify

49

his theoretical system' (Hofstadter, 1969, p. 84). The Hamiltonian Federalists were opposed by Madison's Republicans, with Madison persuading his old collaborator, Jefferson, to act as leader. Two parties had emerged, and in the presidential election of 1800 an interesting result shattered the predominance of the Federalists. The Republicans won.

It was a significant event. The contest was as much about person-alities as it was about politics, as much about electoral mechanics as it was about party competition. The electoral system was an electoral football: in Virginia, the district system was changed to general ticket to ensure a home-state whitewash for Jefferson. But the Federalists – the incumbents – did their best elsewhere to manipulate events. Indeed, 'on the surface it appears as if the Federalists were almost as strong as ever. In reality they were saved from a much more crushing defeat than they experienced by measures which the political morality of our time would condemn' (Stanwood, 1903, p. 61).

So the Republicans did not win without opposition: in fact they appeared to deliver only a technical knockout. Their candidates, Jefferson and Aaron Burr, tied the Electoral College in knots with 75 votes each, beating the Federalists but not each other. John Adams and Charles Pinckney for the Federalists were better prepared: 65 electors voted for the former, one less for the latter. This was to surmount the problem that the two executive positions – president and vice-president – were not then elected independently (although a subsequent and rapid constitutional amendment would ensure that this was changed) and to avoid the republican mess. The dead-heat meant that the presidential election reverted to the House of Representatives, where each state could cast its vote and a simple majority was needed to win. Here there was a further difficulty over the necessary numbers. After 36 ballots, Jefferson emerged the winner. It was by no means a case of attrition ensuring success. A contemporary account relates that 'the means existed of electing Burr, but this required his co-operation. By deceiving one man (a great blockhead) and tempting two (not incorruptible) he might have secured a majority of the States' (James Bayard quoted in Stanwood, 1903, p. 73). Jeffersonian democracy wheezed its way to centre stage.

The inaugural address could not have been more conciliatory.

Let us, then, fellow citizens, unite with one heart and one mind. Let us restore to social intercourse that harmony and affection without which liberty and even life itself are but dreary things. And let us reflect that having banished from our land that religious intolerance under which mankind so long bled and suffered, we have yet gained little if we countenance a political intolerance as despotic, as wicked, and capable of as bitter and bloody persecutions. (Jefferson, 1943a, pp. 384–5)

The attitudes of the previous administration, in particular as they had informed the Alien and Sedition Acts, could have little place in a republic built on 'harmony and affection', but Jefferson was content to remonstrate rather than condemn. To the new president a unanimous commitment to the republic should be the underlying ethos of American society, and the Constitution accordingly should be above politics.

The famous argument was presented in support. 'Every difference of opinion is not a difference of principle. We are all republicans – we are all federalists.' The era which would lead to 'good feelings' could begin. The republican ideal was encapsulated in that idea: 'would the honest patriot, in the full tide of successful experiment, abandon a government which has so far kept us free and firm . . .?' As Jefferson observed, 'sometimes it is said that man cannot be trusted with the government of himself. Can he, then, be trusted with the government of others? Or have we found angels in the forms of kings to govern him?' (Jefferson, 1943a, p. 385.) History would decide that question.

Jefferson's inaugural address is a remarkable speech in the same way that Lincoln's later Gettysburg address is notable, or as the Declaration and the Constitution are such significant documents. All contribute to the invention of the American democratic tradition. Jefferson sought to unite partisan spirit and divided opinions, through an appeal to patriotism, in support of his version of an American republic resting on democratic values. He looked for and found a coalition of sentiment which backed his effort to rescue the republic from what he saw as the centralizing 'monarchical' tendencies of federalist philosophy, and to recreate it anew. Jefferson's 'great society' would thus be based on decentralization of power, mistrust of nascent industrialism, a belief in the virtues of individualism, and faith in the capacities of a bucolic citizenry. It was intriguing enough to be tried, and sensible enough, in the context of its time, to work.

Part of the strategy was to abolish parties. Jefferson's conviction was based on consensus. Agreement could be achieved through absorption. An attempt was made to win over a majority of the Federalist party, leaving a residual rump rather than a fully fledged opposition: a party to end parties was the goal. Democracy could operate without the challenges of party competition. Three weeks after the inaugural, Jefferson wrote: 'nothing shall be spared on my part to obliterate the traces of party and consolidate the nation, if it can be done without abandonment of principle' (quoted in Hofstadter, 1969, p. 151). Later still he expressed the hope 'to be able to obliterate or rather to unite the names of federalists and republicans' (quoted ibid., p. 155). He did. Opposition more or less crumbled away. Jefferson retained the presidency in 1904, winning 162 Electoral College votes to Pinckney's 14, and Republicans outnumbered Federalists by four to one in the Senate and five to one in the House of Representatives. In his second inaugural address the president was able to congratulate the country on 'the union of sentiment now manifested so generally', and he anticipated that an 'entire union of opinion' might not be long in forming among his fellow countrymen (Jefferson, 1943b, p. 414).

This vision of harmony that is sometimes taken to characterize the period between Jefferson's presidency and the emergence of Jackson is, at core, another myth. An example of wish-fulfilment, Jefferson may have believed it, and John Quincy Adams, elected president in 1824 as a result of the 'corrupt bargain', may have rejoiced over 'the decline of internal dissensions in the country', repudiating 'the spirit of party' (Hofstadter, 1969, p. 233). But it was not true. Divisions were evident within the all-conquering Republican party, and whatever the outer veneer of unity and harmony the internal cracks went deep. It became increasingly evident that the practice of federal politics had to be freed from the intellectual constraints of eighteenth-century anti-party doctrines which tried to confine the democratic republic in a strait-jacket of spurious contentment.

The Federalists and the Republicans of the late eighteenth century were beguiled by visions of republican harmony, and to that end schemed to absorb, annihilate, or avoid party sentiment. The result was romance. The 'Era of Good Feelings' was in the end a period not of stabilization but of transition. Many American politicians began to appreciate that party organization might have its advantages, that it could be a positive principle, and that two-party competition was an asset to the public interest.

It was not a lightning revelation. Pro-party attitudes were present in the Enlightenment. As early as the 1730s it had been suggested that opposition 'is not only necessary in free governments but of great service to the public', and that parties 'are a check upon one another, and by keeping the ambition of one another within bounds, serve to maintain public liberty' (quoted in Hofstadter, 1969, p. 35). Parties could be seen as part of a system of checks and balances. In the 1750s another writer argued that 'parties in a free state ought rather to be considered as an advantage to the public than an evil', because of their possible contribution to a 'balanced' society. Some went further, claiming that a one-party society effectively stifled republican principles such as liberty or representation. 'Whenever men are unanimous on great public questions, whenever there is but one party, freedom ceases and despotism commences' (quoted ibid., p. 36).

Opposition might be important. First, because it provided a focus for criticism of the party which was controlling the government. Secondly, because it provided the possibility, through the mechanism of the electoral system, for government to be replaced. The advantages of party competition had thus been realized in theory before its application in practice brought about the alternation of 1800 and then finally put an end to the 'Era of Good Feelings'.

That happened in 1824. Good feelings turned sour. The presidential electoral contest showed that. Factionalism had become endemic in the one unanimous and united party, and four candidates emerged – Jackson, Adams, Crawford and Clay. Jackson won the popular vote but did not have a majority in the Electoral College. As in 1800 the election reverted to the legislature, where Clay's influence delivered the presidency to Adams by the margin of one vote. Andrew Jackson was understandably piqued. Democratic practice such as this left little room for values: a 'corrupt bargain' had been struck, and Henry Clay became Adams's Secretary of State. Whichever way it was judged the whole process seemed a long way from the ethos of republican virtue in which the Founders had placed their trust. As one nineteenth-century commentary puts it, 'the election of Mr. Adams was perfectly constitutional, and as such fully submitted to by the people; but it was a violation of the *demos krateo* principle' (Cooper, 1885, bk 1, p. 26). The representatives of the people had been putty to Clay.

The outcome of 1824 boosted the development of a new model party system, designed by Martin Van Buren and rapidly bought by Jackson. Van Buren subscribed to the more favourable opinion of parties which grew up in the 1820s. His attitude to parties was thus 'to recognize their necessity, to give them the credit they deserve' (quoted in Hofstadter, 1969, p. 225), and to work to create rather than destroy party competition. This was an important new departure. Van Buren was among those who had come to appreciate the importance of the concept of a party system: the existence of more than one party, and indeed the idea of a legitimate opposition to a party in government. Political parties could become institutions which might provide the electorate with democratic choice.

Rejecting the nostrums of good feelings, together with Monroe's 'fusion policy' of the 1820s, which was an attempt to sponsor them anew, Van Buren thus entered federal politics with the express intention 'to revive the old contest between federals and anti-federals and build up a party for himself on that' (quoted in Hofstadter, 1969, p. 227). For Jackson 1824 was a democratic betrayal. For Van Buren it was a vindication. He became a leading opponent of Adams, and from his political base in the Senate he started looking round for a presidential candidate to support in 1828. He settled on Jackson.

The candidate needed a party. Jackson became the nucleus around which the atavistic Democrats were formed. Organization was the key, with committees established in Jackson's home state of Tennessee and in the federal capital, Washington, to proselytize, create and foster interest in the states. In turn state organizations established 'Jackson clubs' or committees in each county and most localities. So once it was completed the Democratic structure consisted of a network of small groups of supporters, built as a pyramid from the localities to the counties to the states and to the central national committees.

Swerving around the congressional caucus which had largely determined presidential nominations, this new party, founded on democratic populism, entered the 1828 contest. Jackson beat the incumbent Adams by 178 Electoral College votes to 83. Opposition existed, but was slow to react to this new phenomenon: a party which wanted to polarize rather than conciliate, to contest rather than absorb, and to provoke rather than to agree. It was not until 1832 that a 'Young Men's National Republican Convention' met in Washington and agreed upon a number of resolutions inspired by a common dislike of Jacksonian democracy. The stirrings of such opposition became during that decade the Whig party.

CONCLUSION

The consolidation of the federal electoral system and the development of a political party system occurred within half a century from the moment Jefferson declared the values of an independent democratic republic. The experiment had yielded some results: a constitutional theory appropriate to prevailing sentiment, and an institutional system that sought, however imperfectly, to give it practical effect. Within this time, though, a fundamental transition took place: from Jeffersonian to Jacksonian democracy.

It is a measure of the initially fluid nature of the details of American democracy that these epithets are used. Once the institutions of the Jacksonian period gained a firm tradition of custom and practice and a legitimacy borne of repeated and successful operation, the American style was no longer borrowed from its chief executive. There is no Lincolnian democracy or Rooseveltian democracy not merely because of euphonics but also because after Jackson the basic character was formed. From the early years of the republic, through Jefferson's own presidency and on to the election of Jackson, the underlying ethos may have been republicanism but the outward images of American democracy could be traced through different scenes.

This was in part a function of industrialization, in part a product of settlement and expansion and the widening gulf between the agrarian south and the progressive north and west. But it was also the result of an emerging institutional maturity. A realization that democracy – as it involved politics – could work most effectively through political parties was coupled with an appreciation that contested elections had a symbolic significance: that alternation in office was dynamic evidence of a viable system of government that transcended a pious and spurious hope for republican unanimity. Substantive changes were important. Jackson's democracy was populist where Jefferson's had been patrician. It was experimental and optimistic, where too often Jeffersonians tended to lament a mythical past. And as such it was less inclined to talk of values than it was concerned with practical success. Not everybody liked it. Jackson may have formed the character of modern American democracy, but there was still concern about some of its traits.

In this sense Jacksonian democracy was still a partial vision. The nascent industrialism began to appreciate the bouquet of capitalist organization, and the values prevalent in that economic world became difficult to square with those of democracy. Slavery remained an issue unresolved. Jacksonian democracy was not the complete embodiment of the aspirations of 1776. Its critics pointed this out, and it is in the writings of a representative sample, Calhoun, Cooper and de Tocqueville that the defects, drawbacks and detractions of Jacksonian democracy, or at least democracy as it had emerged by the time of Jackson, are catalogued. Calhoun and Cooper provide some native reflections, but it was de Tocqueville's work which had a major impact, not only within America but overseas as well. Ultimately then these critics are significant and democracy in America cannot be appreciated without understanding *Democracy in America*.

CHAPTER 3

Democracy's Critics: Why Should Numbers Count for More?

John C. Calhoun, James Fenimore Cooper and Alexis de Tocqueville in their separate but related ways each criticized the majoritarian mystique of American democracy. The American system was built upon the honourable Lockean principle that the will of the majority should prevail. But the idea gave rise to certain problems. For if the numerical majority was unchanging and immovable, what chance had the minority in electoral terms? And if parties existed to organize the spoils of power gained through the majoritarian electoral system, did this not call into question the role of the responsible democratic citizen? And, further, what prospects were there for the individual in a society suffused by the cult of the majority, where attitudes, tastes and prejudices were formed by the weight of numerical opinion? The nature of Jacksonian democracy – populist, pragmatic and based on the creation of party – prompted these questions. Calhoun, Cooper and de Tocqueville attempted an analysis of American democracy that took account of the majority principle while denying it central importance as an operative mechanism. They indicted what they saw as its sinister effects. Why should numbers count for more?

JOHN C. CALHOUN (1782–1850)

Calhoun was the product of a particular and peculiar intellectual and social environment. His roots were in the *ante-bellum* south: the plantation-owning, slave-holding, cotton-picking south. As a politician he served in the South Carolina state legislature and the federal House of Representatives, before becoming secretary of war, vice-president and, apart from another brief spell in the executive branch, a member of the federal Senate. As a political theorist he was equally distinguished, although the argument remains as to whether he was a mere apologist for a sectional interest or whether

56

he transcends such surroundings to address some of the ubiquitous issues of American democracy.

On the one hand, Calhoun has been called 'the one major speculative political philosopher' of his times, yet 'also the one whose speculations were the most irrelevant to American experience' (Commager, 1950, p. 311). On the other, he has been described without qualification as 'the one outstanding political thinker in a period singularly barren and uncreative' (Parrington, 1930, vol. 2, p. 69). The puzzle of Calhoun is the puzzle of the south, and, to the extent that it is difficult indeed to prise him out of his southern context, before discussing the philosophy it is first necessary to look to the region that informed the ideas.

Part of the United States, the south in the nineteenth century nevertheless became uneasily self-conscious about its 'differences' within the union. The reasons for this are easily rehearsed. There was cotton. This economic mainstay of southern wealth was profitable for some, but at the same time it was inevitably interwoven with another differentiating factor. Slavery threaded its way as an issue, a concern, and eventually a threatening problem for the fabric of American democracy. The debate was constant as expansion continued. 'Extend the sphere', Madison had advised, in order to create the pluralist republic; but the acquisition of territories and the transition to statehood – Louisiana and Texas were instances – opened the prospect of a further spreading of the cotton economy. With that could come more exploitation, more slavery. Free labour states and slave states co-existed in the democracy and confronted each other, nowhere more directly than in the federal Senate. There for years a balance was maintained with all the aplomb and all the risks of running along a tight-rope with eyes firmly shut.

Again, the south's aggressive agrarianism clashed with the north's equally energetic industrialization. When it was thought that domestic industry might best expand under the protection of tariffs, the south, surviving on the export of its primary product, feared retaliation from abroad. Economic sectionalism fuelled regional conflict: Calhoun took time to offer an exposition of and protest against the north's sharp practice. Then the north expanded faster than the south, at least in terms of numbers. In 1790, when Calhoun was eight and the first decennial census was taken, the population of the two regions was about equal. By 1850, the year of his death, the population of the north had reached about 13 1/2 million, that of the south was roughly 6 1/2 million.

Numbers influenced representation. The voting strength of a state was determined by its population, with the south's compromised additional counting of its slaves as three-fifths of a free individual an advantage progressively eroded as the north's population increased. In the federal House of Representatives southerners became an increasingly entrenched, embattled and embittered minority. By 1836 Calhoun was pointing out that in the Congress the representatives from his region were out-numbered by the solidarity of a growing northern majority. And what was true of the legislature could also be true of the executive, since population was also the basis of allocating a state's votes in the Electoral College. Without numbers, influence was lost. The rules of the electoral game were stacked against the south.

The problem for American democracy, then, was that the majority and the minority became increasingly fixed. The majority became always the north: the minority ever the south, with each region held together by the glue of distinct and different outlooks and priorities. This was the cataract on Madison's pluralist vision. His solution to the problems of faction – 'Federalist 10' – assumed that a kaleidoscope of different alliances, groupings and interests across the diverse union would constantly form and reform. Minority groups could gain allies to transform themselves into temporary majorities. Majorities would lose friends, and be relegated to a subordinate influence. Such a democracy was energetic, shifting, changing, such that the prospects of a permanent majority, uniting for unworthy or even benign reasons, or of a regional hegemony were unlikely. But this free-wheeling interplay of pluralist politics solidified into the monoliths of the compass point: the north versus the south.

The south became, in Calhoun's words, 'a fixed and hopeless minority' (quoted in Hofstadter, 1948, p. 77). The idea that their position was permanent fuelled the pessimism of southerners, who saw that majority rule would not just counteract but effectively perpetually frustrate their ambition. It was the perennial problem for the democratic republic: reconciling majority rule and minority rights in a situation where the minority felt resentful of their inferior status. Jefferson had faced up to it in his first inaugural address. 'Though the will of the majority is in all cases to prevail, that will, to be rightful, must be reasonable . . . the minority possess their equal rights, which equal laws must protect, and to violate which would be oppression' (Jefferson, 1943a, p. 384).

No doubt the north thought it acted 'reasonably', but the south still felt 'oppressed'. It was a matter of perception. If majority rule denied the south effective political power, however, it was not deprived of all political response. An insistence upon States' rights, proposals to overturn federal law through nullification and the ultimate threat of secession were ever more bludgeoning shots in the armoury. The south's case was made to its supporters: it still had to be argued to its opponents.

Enter Calhoun. He provided an intellectual respectability for sectional priorities by casting them in general terms. He took issue with the Founders, and those who had tried translating their ideas into practice. He rejected the philosophical and political analysis of his peers. In this way 'Calhoun's critique was an extensive commentary upon, and correction of, *The Federalist*'s remedy for "the diseases most incident to republican government" ' (Lerner, 1963, p. 924). He broke from prevailing orthodoxies and asked the awkward questions. His case against the numerical majority was not merely destructive, however. His strength was that he offered an alternative which to some was a beguiling prospect. The idea and the ideal was the 'concurrent majority'. In two books, the *Disquisition on Government* and the *Discourse on the Constitution and Government of the United States*, Calhoun worked out a new political philosophy.

His advantage over the Founders was history. Whereas Madison's ideas were a future prospect, Calhoun could look at the republic's past, and to him it didn't work. The first book, then, was a general treatise exploring the nature of civil government and arguing the case for a rejection of numbers in favour of the 'concurrent majority'. The second work was culturally specific, referring the theory more closely to the experience of the United States. In 1853 both works were published posthumously.

The *Disquisition* raises some familiar issues. Why is government necessary? Is abuse of governmental power inevitable? How might such abuse be controlled or prevented? Calhoun argued that government was needed to avoid the universal state of conflict which without it would result from the fact that individuals live together in a social context but are basically self-interested. Government is essential to the existence of society. Yet the inescapable trait of self-interest implies that governmental power, the power that should be used for the promotion of the good of all, or at least to prevent a war of all against all, might be abused by individuals who were less than altruistic. A constitution, then, was the potential controlling influence, since a properly designed constitution could create a framework aimed at preventing corruption.

This was exactly the same concern as had motivated the Founders. The operative word, however, is 'design', since a constitution 'stands to *government*, as *government* stands to *society*', but the difference is that 'constitution is the contrivance of man, while government is of Divine ordination' (Calhoun, 1968a, pp. 7–8). In other words, God,

59

creating individuals, anticipated society as an essential adjunct. It has been left to humanity to devise a constitution appropriate to the control of government. That was the task which Calhoun undertook on behalf of his fellow Americans.

The essential problem was again familiar. Calhoun confronted it. 'How can those who are invested with the powers of government be prevented from employing them, as the means of aggrandizing themselves, instead of using them to protect and preserve society?' (Calhoun, 1968a, p. 8). Evidently the right to vote is useful: in a sense government does become responsible to 'the people'. But once the mechanism of majority rule has been established, and 'the people' have agreed that representatives of that majority can command the heights of governmental power, then the argument becomes circular – how can such representatives be made to use that power responsibly? 'Nothing is more difficult than to equalize the action of the government, in reference to the various and diversified interests of the community; and nothing more easy than to pervert its powers into instruments to aggrandize and enrich one or more interests by oppressing and impoverishing the others' (ibid., p. 15).

Once this is realized, the object of political life immediately becomes to gain power, and as a result different interests in society battle to form themselves into a majority and so dominate government. At this point, Calhoun, a product of the generation that had seen 'good feelings' crumble into Jacksonian partisanship, appreciated the inevitability of party as the instrument of majority rule. During his career, philosophical vestiges of the Founder's anti-party sentiment remained in American political thought, even though in practical terms politicians accepted their existence. For Calhoun, the fact of party confirmed his suspicion of majority rule.

Parties thus aggregated a set of interests which, if combined as a majority, would rather hang together for the advantages that conferred than squabble separately in self-indulgent impotence. Calhoun concluded that 'the community will be divided into two great parties, – a major and minor, – between which there will be incessant struggles on the one side to retain, and on the other to obtain the majority, – and, thereby, the control of the government and the advantages it confers' (Calhoun, 1968a, p. 16). The concurrent majority was an antidote to this. It was an anti-party device, or at least a way of avoiding interest groups losing an identity in the quest to aggregate a numerical majority. It also gave a chance to those groups which would never compromise their interest to the larger concern of mere numbers.

Where parties are coalitions, the concurrent majority affirms a principle of 'separate but equal'. There is a need to take account of diversity rather than to use the excuse of numbers to ride roughshod over differences, a need to recognize 'the sense of each interest or portion of the community . . . separately through its own majority, . . . and to require the consent of each interest, either to put or to keep the government in action'. Here is the principle of the concurrent majority. Calhoun suggested its formula: 'by dividing and distributing the powers of government, give to each division or interest, through its appropriate organ, either a concurrent voice in making and executing the laws, or a veto on their execution' (Calhoun, 1968a, p. 25). It is all right for interests to exist, but not for them to combine.

The concurrent majority is a kind of institutionalized pluralism, effectively stymying governmental power and preventing it being used – abused – through the antics of a numerical majority of interests: a party. It is the veto power which is important, far more than the hope that all interests could be a part of the legislative and even executive process. Calhoun admitted that 'it is this negative power, – the power of preventing or arresting the action of the government, – be it called by what term it may, – veto, interposition, nullification, check or balance of power, – which in fact forms the constitution' (Calhoun, 1968a, p. 35). Such a power had to counterbalance the coalitions of convenience, and indeed would render them unnecessary, since they existed only to promote an artificial majority: a majority which rested not on sentiment but merely on the numerical superiority necessary to gain power.

To accept the idea of a concurrent majority is to open up a vista of utopian perfection, built upon the 'disposition to harmonize'. Giving each interest its independent power-base of the veto would create a society in which 'instead of faction, strife, and struggle for party ascendancy, there would be patriotism, nationality, harmony, and a struggle only for supremacy in promoting the common good of the whole' (Calhoun, 1968a, p. 49). The individual's self-interest and the party's manipulation of power wilt before Calhoun's self-indulgence: the concurrent majority presented as the salvation of democracy's deficiency.

The aspiration may be noble, even inspiring, and attractive to some, but at root the concurrent majority substitutes problems for problems. What constitutes a legitimate interest group in society? Who is to be allowed the veto? Is the criterion the number belonging to a group, the loudness of its collective voice? Is size indeed important? Can groups have overlapping memberships? What is the internal democracy of the group? Would this system not encourage splintering, factionalism, and the *reductio ad absurdum* of an individual with power to veto a decision that appeared to be inimical to a perceived interest? Calhoun did not rescue himself from many of these charges – that was left to critics and commentators. Rather he evaded them through an unstated or at least understated assumption. This was that the legitimate basis of the concurrent majority was to be found in America in the institutional device of federalism.

Again, the sectional perspective holds sway. The concurrent majority allows the south a voice; it prevents the north controlling federal politics for its own ends. Once that is appreciated it can be argued that 'Calhoun rejected an infinite regress by which the sense of every portion would be determined by the concurrent majority of *its* parts. Within each portion the numerical majority would rule. This is not to assume internally homogeneous portions, but rather the presence of an interest that overrides many lesser interests' (Lerner, 1963, p. 926). That overriding interest was the south. The interest groups were the states themselves.

This much is emphasized when Calhoun brings the discussion down to specifics in the *Discourse*. The United States, he claims, 'is a democratic, federal republic' (Calhoun, 1968b, p. 112), and the states agreed the Constitution as 'a compact *between* them' rather than 'as a constitution *over* them' (ibid., p. 131). And there is no equivocation when he discusses the nature of American political society: it is the states which emerge as the significant elements of the system.

> There is, indeed, no such community, *politically* speaking, as the people of the United States, regarded in the light of, and as constituting one people or nation . . . The whole, taken together, form a federal community: – a community composed of States united by a political compact; and not a nation composed of individuals united by what is called a social compact. (Calhoun, 1968b, p. 162)

The states, then, were part of the community. As such they could be counted as having distinct and different interests that should legitimately find representation within the union. The concurrent majority was designed for them.

It is in the juxtaposition of state and federal power that Calhoun finds an ignored justification of his theory. Such division of authority embodied the essence of the idea of the concurrent majority. Unfortunately, most Americans did not appreciate the subtlety of this constitutional design. 'It is not an uncommon impression that the government of the United States is a government based simply on population, that numbers are its only element, and a numerical majority its only controlling power . . . No opinion can be more erroneous' (Calhoun, 1968b, pp. 168–9). Instead the principle of federalism meant that the United States was naturally and appropriately designed for the implementation of Calhoun's idea. Calhoun insisted that:

> It was the object of the framers of the constitution, in organizing the government, to give to the two elements of which it is composed, separate but concurrent action; and consequently a veto on each other, whenever the organisation of the department or the nature of the power would admit: and when this could not be done, so to blend the two as to make as near an approach to it in effect as possible. (Calhoun, 1968b, p. 181)

He was right. The whole design of the Constitution was to prevent tyranny through the consolidation of power in the hands of anybody, either an individual or a minority or a majority. The Constitution was to promote republican democracy – equality, liberty and the values of the Declaration, and not the cause of party or mere numbers. Calhoun had the temerity, and the conviction fuelled by sectional pride, to suggest that things had not worked out.

In the *Discourse* this theme is re-emphasized, with geographical division and numbers the chief culprits: the northern states predominated in the federal government, and a centralized authority had been created against which the minority southern states had no chance. The federal government had come to dominate the states which had brought it into being, and the section which controlled that government thus had great influence in determining matters of public policy. Numerical supremacy had given the north the advantage in the House of Representatives and in the Electoral College. Northerners could use the federal government for their own ends. The south was powerless, helpless. The options were clear:

> With us the choice lies between a national, consolidated and irresponsible government of a dominant portion or section of the country, – and a federal, constitutional and responsible government, with all the divisions of powers indispensable to form and preserve such a government in a country of such vast extent, and so great a diversity of interests and institutions as ours. (Calhoun, 1968b, p. 268)

Democracy was not majority rule: democracy was diffusion of power, representation of interests, recognition of minorities. 'The will of a

63

majority is the will of a rabble. Progressive democracy is incompatible with liberty' (quoted in Schlesinger, 1946, p. 405). Calhoun's perspective appears to be that of a committed nineteenth-century British liberal.

Except, however, that the plea for a recognition of diversity, and the concern to protect minorities – indeed the entire pluralist persuasion – obscures the dull beat of dualism that is at the heart of Calhoun's ideal. This much has been recognized: Calhoun, it has been suggested, 'seems to have taken a dualist, not a pluralist view of politics' (Current, 1963, p. 147). His democracy was bi-focal. For it was not groups that Calhoun sought to protect through federalism and the concurrent majority but a group – the southern states – and it was not minorities that must be insulated against majority rule but a minority – the south. In the end the sectional roots were strongest. The general principle that Calhoun sought to establish was built on a dominant concern for one cause. 'The South asks for justice, simple justice, and less she ought not to take' (Johnson and Woodburn, 1927, vol. 2, p. 157). Calhoun was adamant. And he was happy to argue the case.

For those who saw that Jacksonian democracy might yet elevate numbers to a position of democratic pre-eminence, Calhoun did offer an alternative. The concurrent majority could still be cast as a pluralist antidote to majority rule if seen in a slightly wider context than as a mechanism of positive discrimination to advance the cause of sectionalism. Calhoun then becomes 'the chief American representative of that world-wide school of thought which challenged the ideas of natural rights and popular sovereignty' (Heckscher, 1939, p. 586). His insight was to recognize that since the state 'is composed of individuals – not in isolation, but organised as "great interests". The assent of all the great and distinct interests must be given to the measures of the government' (Heinberg, 1932, p. 467). There is no doubt that he isolated a problem in democratic theory and in American democratic practice. The worth of his solution depends on whether it is seen merely as special pleading for an illiberal minority view, or whether the concurrent majority can have a relevance which transcends its sectional origins. That is an issue which Calhoun himself had no reason to confront.

His critique was trenchant. 'The ideal of democracy he conceived to be the noblest in the whole field of political thought, but misunderstood and misapplied as it had been in America, it had become the mother of every mischief' (Parrington, 1930, vol. 2, p. 77). His criticism was consistent. Calhoun's speeches echoed the analysis presented in his books. In the Senate, in the year he died, he was still arguing that 'what was once a constitutional federal republic is now converted, in reality, into one as absolute as that of the Autocrat of Russia, and as despotic in its tendency as any government that ever existed' (Johnson and Woodburn, 1927, vol. 2, p. 139). His pessimism was profound. In the same speech he predicted that 'the South will be forced to choose between abolition and secession' (ibid., p. 147). Calhoun could see where the collision between a fixed majority and a determined minority would end. Democracy as it had evolved in America could not accommodate such tensions, and could not resolve such conflict. In the end, Calhoun's faith in the concept was eroded.

He has been described as 'a minority spokesman in a democracy, a particularist in an age of nationalism, a slaveholder in an age of advancing liberties, and an agrarian in a furiously capitalistic country' (Hofstadter, 1948, p. 90). He was an outsider in terms of the temper of his times: but his criticism of contemporary democracy remains perceptive. And he stuck to the south, even though in many ways his outlook, sentiments and persuasions – elitist, liberal, idiosyncratically democratic – might have found him a home in nineteenth-century Britain. But his slaves would have had to stay behind. Or at least he would have had to pay them.

JAMES FENIMORE COOPER (1789–1851)

James Fenimore Cooper was a Yankee. His concern to warn of the dangers of majority rule was not motivated by sectional chauvinism. Rather he was an American de Tocqueville. He dissected the democratic experiment and pointed out the deficiencies that he saw were the result of its fundamental reliance on the principle of obedience to the aggregated will of the majority. His conclusions were remarkably similar to some of those de Tocqueville reached in *Democracy in America*. As H. L. Mencken pointed out, Cooper saw 'how the rule of the majority must tend toward a witless and malignant tyranny, anti-social in its motives and evil almost beyond endurance in its effects' (introduction to Cooper, 1931, p. xii).

In such works as *Home as Found* and most significantly *The American Democrat*, both published in 1838, Cooper observed this tyranny of the majority – a tyranny both quantitative and qualitative in its impact – even as de Tocqueville was coining the phrase. And whereas de Tocqueville came to America to study the democratic experiment, Cooper's understanding of his native land was deepened by going abroad. His *Gleanings in Europe* (1837) enabled him to see the United States in a wider comparative cultural context. When he returned to America in the Jacksonian period, his suspicions as to the nature of its democracy were confirmed. He became a jaundiced critic. His angst was expurgated in his books: notably *The American Democrat*, a shorter, less well-known domestic counterpart to de Tocqueville's more widely read analysis.

Cooper was born in 1789, coincidentally with the institutions of the United States. In 1790 the family moved to Cooperstown, New York. James Fenimore Cooper was brought up in the town of which his father William had been a pioneer founder. The son went to university – Yale – but was expelled for misconduct. He had a brief career in the navy, before becoming a 'gentleman farmer' in New York state. In 1822 he moved to New York city and set himself up as a professional writer – publishing among other works a perennial favourite *The Last of the Mohicans* (1826). He then took off for Europe for seven years and after his return in 1833 he eventually resettled at Cooperstown.

After 1837 his work became more polemical and political than literary as he became enmeshed in the Three Mile Point controversy – a squabble over land supposed to be for common use through custom and picnicking practice, but reclaimed by Cooper as part of the family estate. This dispute inspired a series of books intended to explore the implications of the row. Cooper was widely criticized for his actions and these attempts at self-justification. In the 1840s he retreated to the realm of historical romance, remaining a prolific writer until his death on 14 September 1851, the day before his sixty-second birthday.

Cooper's milieu, then, was not the same as Calhoun's. He belonged to a world concerned more with culture, and the relationship between democracy, majority rule and the artistic or literary minority, than with the balancing of sectional interest groups arguing over institutional protection to pursue their different moral and economic philosophies. His personal experience of the impact of democracy on the individual – in his case as a literary figure and a property owner – conditioned his outlook. If America's democratic experiment was to work, it should be judged not according to whether it resolved political problems and the structural difficulties associated with majority rule but in terms of its capacity to bring about an acceptable quality of everyday life for the citizen living in such a society. Cooper's conclusion that the democratic life could not necessarily claim this qualitative superiority promoted his final disillusionment. Democracy might work. American democracy did not.

Public opinion was to blame, or rather the fear of crossing prevailing attitudes which meant that the individual in a democracy deferred to public sentiment. One of Cooper's *Gleanings in Europe*, was the observation that 'the besetting, the degrading vice of America is the moral cowardice by which men are led to truckle to what is called public opinion' (Cooper, 1982, p. 304). This opinion was fickle, and subject to constant change, and was often influenced by sections of the community bent on the pursuit of dubious policies. American life was enervated. The result was that American society was characterized by mediocrity. Democracy had created a monster: the myth of the omnipotent people led to the apotheosis of public opinion. The republic was not about liberty or even equality; it was about not alienating the dread uniformity of mediocre public sentiments and attitudes.

The United States had lost its way. In *Home as Found*, two of Cooper's characters, Aristabulus Bragg and Steadfast Dodge, are observed to have been seduced by the myth into a belief that public opinion was all-powerful. The exotically named duo

> made a mistake which is getting to be too common in America, that of supposing the institutions of the country were all means and no end. Under this erroneous impression they saw only the machinery of the government, becoming entirely forgetful that the power which was given to the people collectively, was only so given to secure to them as perfect a liberty as possible in their characters of individuals. (Cooper, 1961, p. 223)

Home as Found was a dismal place. These themes recur in Cooper's criticism. He concluded that 'the grossest enormities are constantly committed in this good republic of ours, under the pretence of being done by the public and for the public . . . Men will have idols, and the Americans have merely set themselves up' (ibid., p. 240).

In sum, therefore, 'in America the gross mistake has been made of supposing that, because the mass rules in a political sense it has a right to be listened to and obeyed in all other matters – a practical deduction that can only lead, under the most favorable exercise of power, to a very humble mediocrity' (Cooper, 1961, p. 317). Democracy might elevate the common man to a position of political superiority, but where the mass also took it upon itself to set the social and cultural standards of the republic the unusual was sacrificed to the average. This was due also to other flaws in American society which Cooper characterized as 'provincialisms', small-minded prejudices that inspired general satisfaction with standards of mediocrity.

In Cooper's democracy the citizen's tastes and attitudes are moulded by the pressure to conform with prevailing popular opinions. The individual genuflects like Calhoun's south: a victim, powerless.

There is a sense that this analysis is edged with personal feeling – Cooper finding himself in the Three Mile Point dispute – and that it is tinged too with the fear of unpopularity that would be enough to destroy the literary reputation of someone whose commercial success lay at the mercy of popular taste. The best advertisement for an author was a claim to a wide readership. Cooper was aware of the thin line between obscurity and high repute. His critique of majority rule is a cry of insecurity, a complaint against an unenlightened and uninspired public.

In *The American Democrat* the arguments are presented in their most mature and decisive way. Cooper claims he is a democrat, indeed 'as good a democrat as there is in America' (Cooper, 1931, p. xxiv), but he is a democrat of a distinct hue. He is no egalitarian. Ignoring the Declaration of Independence, he suggests that 'equality is nowhere laid down as a governing principle of the institutions of the United States, neither the word, nor any inference that can be fairly deduced from its meaning, occurring in the constitution' (ibid., p. 54). He is a libertarian. In theory, he argues, there is the possibility of constructing a democratic polity which preserves the value of liberty – a negative liberty defined 'to be a controlling authority that resides in the body of a nation, but so restrained as only to be exercised on certain general principles that shall do as little violence to natural justice, as is compatible with the peace and security of society' (ibid., pp. 65–6).

There is a problem. For if the people are in essence the 'controlling authority', that authority has to be exercised through an established procedure, and majority rule is of itself but a trite answer to the organizational difficulties of democracy. 'The common axiom of democracies . . . which says that "the majority must rule", is to be received with many limitations. Were the majority of a country to rule without restraint, it is probable as much injustice and oppression would follow, as are found under the dominion of one' (Cooper, 1931, pp. 57–8). Politically something might be done. A constitution might limit the areas in which majority rule could legitimately claim to hold sway. But majority rule can extend beyond the political sphere to influence opinions and social and cultural mores. 'Since the tastes, knowledge and principles of the majority form the tribunal of appeal' (ibid., p. 83), the argument then short-circuits back to the issue of democratic mediocrity.

Popular taste is vulgar. High standards of intellectual or aesthetic appreciation are absent. 'Thus do we find in literature, the arts, architecture and in all acquired knowledge, a tendency in America to gravitate towards the common center in this, as in other things;

lending a value and estimation to mediocrity that are not elsewhere given' (Cooper, 1931, p. 83). This is the non-institutionalized tyranny of the majority. A constitution can only do so much. It is a political device, as Calhoun also pointed out, but the influence of the majority can extend beyond politics. 'It is a besetting vice of democracies to substitute public opinion for law. This is the usual form in which masses of men exhibit their tyranny' (ibid., p. 84). Such is *The American Democrat*'s raw nerve.

It is an argument which is worried at, chewed over and reiterated, as if repetition enhances its force and reinforces its *gravitas*. 'Whoever opposes the interests, or wishes of the public, however right in principle, or justifiable by circumstances, finds little sympathy; for, in a democracy, resisting the wishes of the many is resisting the sovereign in his caprices' (Cooper, 1931, p. 103). Again:

> In this country, . . . there is a strong and dangerous disposition to defer to the public, in opposition to truth and justice. This is a penalty that is paid for liberty, and it depends on the very natural principle of flattering power. In a monarchy, adulation is paid to the prince; in a democracy to the people, or the public. (ibid., p. 184)

And again:

> Men have been so long accustomed to see oppression exercised in the name of one, or in the name of a few, that they have got to consider the sway of numbers as the only criterion of freedom. Numbers, however, may oppress as well as one or a few and when such oppression occurs, it is usually of the worst character. (ibid., p. 231)

The point had to be emphasized, since it had only been addressed as a suspicion before, and the constitutional design was expected – despite the criticisms of Calhoun – to circumvent it. The influence of de Tocqueville had yet to make the 'tyranny of the majority' a stock phrase in the liberal democratic vocabulary. The democratic belief that 'the majority was not only just rightly absolute but absolutely right' (Railton, 1978, p. 167), had led Americans to consider that the majority could not only decide on legislative questions but could also act as final arbiter on all moral, cultural and aesthetic issues, irrespective of its capacity to do so, and often in conflict with the standards of truth, justice and liberty.

The omnipotence of the majority, uneducated and ignorant, put democracy at the mercy of one type of individual. 'The peculiar danger of a democracy arises from the arts of demagogues' (Cooper, 1931, p. 101). Those who can seize the imagination of the masses can control and direct the inchoate opinions of an amorphous public. The demagogue can tell the people what their opinions are. Attitudes have to be formed, outlooks moulded, prejudices confirmed. The demagogue is the most direct practitioner of such political propaganda, usually for the sake of a vested self-interest. If public opinion cows the individual, it in turn is conned by the demagogue. Democracy is reduced to a spurious populism – Jacksonianism was an obvious example of such political faddism. As Cooper put it, 'the true theatre of a demagogue is a democracy' (ibid., p. 121). The stage was set. Jackson acted. He was the democratic demagogue incarnate: the people were swayed, beguiled and misled. Cooper knew it. They did not.

If the democratic demagogue was an individual to be mistrusted, so too was a collection of individuals bent on some purpose on which they all agreed. Political parties had corrupted the body politic. In *Home as Found* Cooper observed that 'party is never an honest or a disinterested expounder' (Cooper, 1961, p. 313). In *The American Democrat* he drew the vital distinction between being 'a democrat' and belonging to 'what is called a democratic party'. To be a democrat implied 'independence and an entire freedom of opinion'. Parties, on the other hand, were 'incompatible with either' (Cooper, 1931, pp. 229–30). The concept of 'party as evil' loomed large in Cooper's democratic demonology, and his catalogue of the deficiencies of political parties amounts to little more than diatribe.

Parties encourage prejudice, partisan policies, corrupt legislation; they destroy local representation and patriotic feelings; they result in power-broking, incompetence and manipulation; they overshadow truth, justice (and every other public virtue). The case is damning. Cooper concludes that 'no freeman, who really loves liberty, and who has a just perception of its dignity, character, action and objects will ever become a mere party man' (Cooper, 1931, p. 230). Parties are a nineteenth-century canker on the republic. Cooper agreed with the prevailing ethos of the Founders: democracy should not be about partisanship and faction.

So the dominance of public opinion resulted in tyranny and mediocrity, and threats also existed from demagogues and political parties. What chance had democracy? The implication of Cooper's work is that a recognition of these problems is a major part of overcoming them. In particular,

It ought to be impressed on every man's mind, in letters of brass, *That in a democracy, the public has no power that is not expressly conceded by the institutions, and that this power, moreover is only to*

*be used under the forms prescribed by the constitution. All beyond this
is oppression, when it takes the character of acts, and not unfrequently
when it is confined to opinion.* (Cooper, 1931, p. 185)

Once it is appreciated that the public is potentially so tyrannical, the
only remedy, however, is to keep an eye on it 'as in other countries
kings and aristocrats are to be watched' (ibid., p. 187). Cooper can
offer no institutional solution to something that is not at root an
institutional problem. The 'concurrent majority' could not safeguard
the liberty of individual opinion; the force of public sentiment is not
a procedure to be reformed. Vigilance is the only hope, and a pious
one at that; the idea that mere observation, publicity and concern
can produce a refuge for individualism until a proper conception of
democracy holds popular sway.

Cooper's concern then is the fundamental shared belief of the
liberal ethic: the protection of the liberty of the individual. Political
liberty meant life under the forms of the Constitution; moral autonomy was the liberty to follow an individual rather than a collective
conscience. It is a transcendental persuasion. Eccentricity should be
encouraged as each pursued happiness according to a unique set of
aspirations. Society was thereby enriched.

> All greatness of character is dependant on individuality. The man who
> has no other existence than that which he partakes in common with all
> around him, will never have any other than an existence of mediocrity.
> In time, such a state of things would annihilate invention and paralyse
> genius. A nation would become a nation of common place labourers.
> (Cooper, 1931, p. 232)

It is a bleak prospect, to re-echo in Thoreau's assertion that 'the
mass of men lead lives of quiet desperation' (Thoreau, 1981, p.
263). An accent on individualism was the force that could break
this mould.

In this way, 'the pursuit of happiness is inseparable from the
claims of individuality. To compel all to follow this object in the
same manner is to oppress all above average tastes and information.
It can only be done at the expense of that which is the aim of
liberty' (Cooper, 1931, p. 232). Cooper welded one aspiration of the
Declaration of Independence firmly to his liberal democratic creed.
He was in this sense a Jeffersonian democrat. Like Jefferson his faith
was in the land – the basis of social solidarity and the guarantee
of social and cultural continuity. The feeling of the Jeffersonian
patrician pervades his outlook at a time when Jacksonian populism
was assuming centre stage.

71

Cooper, then, could consider himself an aristocrat among democrats, since aristocracy was not about social status but rather the counter-point to that dread mediocrity: the best was preferred to the lowest common denominator. As an aristocrat in the flood-tide of egalitarianism he was forced to romanticize the past as he became increasingly disillusioned with his present. In 1846 in *The Redskins* he wrote of 'the innate dislike which is growing up in the country to see any man distinguished from the mass around him in anything, even though it should be in merit' (quoted in Bewley, 1970, p. 242). Although he professed himself a democrat the tensions remained.

It was there in his writings. The blending of moralist and novelist, it has been suggested, was such that 'what Cooper brings to the study of politics . . . is a moralist's commitment to truth and a novelist's preoccupation with the discrepancy between appearance and reality, profession and practice, names and things' (Dekker and Johnson, 1969, p. 9). If America's democracy had become a masque, then Cooper was right to dismiss its prevailing myths. Democracy had room for aristocrats, for, as he reportedly claimed the year before he died, 'it takes a first-class aristocrat to make a first-class Democrat' (quoted in Bewley, 1970, p. 233). Aristocracy of the right kind – of Cooper's kind – was what Jacksonian America was lacking. Like Calhoun, therefore, for different reasons, Cooper ended his life disillusioned with his country's experiment in republican democracy.

ALEXIS DE TOCQUEVILLE (1805–1859)

And so to de Tocqueville. His work *Democracy in America*, published in two parts in 1835 and 1840, presented America to itself as it represented the United States to the outside world. He absorbed and reflected the concerns of those like Calhoun and Cooper who saw the dyspeptic as well as the euphoric side of democracy in action. America became democracy's petrel. Calhoun's dread, the danger of an overbearing centralized authority, and Cooper's criticism, the omnipotence of majority opinion, were also de Tocqueville's warnings. *Democracy in America* was among the first comprehensive studies of the political and social institutions of the United States. And it was written by a foreigner. Whereas Calhoun's political theories were rooted in the peculiar problems of the south, and Cooper's analysis was based on his experience as an American literary luminary, de Tocqueville's work was coloured by his European background. Moreover, he brought American democracy to Europe. His volumes on America had as profound an impact not only in France but also in Britain as the writings of Montesquieu and Locke had had on Americans a generation earlier.

For many Europeans, and in particular for France, Jackson's America was still the democratic laboratory: experimental, unpredictable, volatile. To some it offered a prospect, to others it was an endorsement of inherited prejudice. As de Tocqueville was later to point out in *The Ancien Regime and the French Revolution*:

> To the rest of Europe the American Revolution seemed merely a novel and remarkable historical event; whereas the French saw in it a brilliant confirmation of theories already familiar to them . . . Indeed, the Americans seemed only to be putting into practice ideas which had been sponsored by our writers, and to be making our dreams their realities. (De Tocqueville, 1971, p. 168)

For de Tocqueville the American experiment was worth studying. By the 1830s the United States had come to embody 'a new science of politics for a world itself quite new' (Krause, 1983, p. 67). He came to see America 'as Marx saw France: the land of political culture' (ibid., p. 70). At the same time, the United States could prove to be Europe's democratic mentor.

The old world was tagging behind the new. De Tocqueville's purpose was therefore not so much to understand America on its own terms as to filter the democratic experience and possibly to refine it for European consumption. As a contemporary reviewer observed, 'the problem that disturbed M. de Tocqueville and that brought him to the United States is the problem of European democracy' (quoted in Horwitz, 1966, p. 295). He was looking for lessons. Whereas a later generation of Americans would be inspired by the idea of making the world safe for democracy, de Tocqueville travelled to America in 1831 with the intention of seeing if democracy could be made safe for the world.

So he did not come with an uncluttered mind. For de Tocqueville the advance of democracy was inevitable. The egalitarian ethic was a tidal wave cresting irrepressibly through history. He viewed it with alarm. Such philosophical baggage was included along with the luggage he took to the United States and remained with him during his 7,000-mile, nine-month tour of North America. Gustave de Beaumont, his travelling companion, recorded that prior to the journey de Tocqueville was considering four major problems which he thought confronted a democratic society. Could equality and liberty be reconciled rather than sacrificed one to the other? Did the exercise of power inevitably become, if such power existed, absolutist and tyrannical? Was there some countervailing force to be found in a society in which all were equal, but at the same time equally weak in their capacity to resist it? And if these questions could not be resolved, was modern society doomed to a democratic despotism? (Zetterbaum, 1967, p. 43). The Frenchman visited the Americans to see if they had turned the democratic trick.

The problems were interrelated. Like the Founders, de Tocqueville saw that the democratic values of equality and liberty could clash, and that it was possible that the desire to promote the one might involve degrading the other. The quest for equality in the name of democracy could involve indulging government with power to infringe individual liberties in the name of the people. That was the key. In a democracy the people were sovereign and their government became the organized expression of that sovereignty. They might invest more and more power in such a symbol of their authority, to reinforce its substance. As Harold Laski pointed out:

> The tendency, therefore, of every democracy is a concentration of authority in the central government . . . Liberty . . . is sacrificed to the demand for equality; and it is the tragedy of a democratic society that the masses are persuaded to accept the erosion of individuality by the administration as a benefit for which they should be grateful. (Laski, 1931, pp. 106–7)

What Laski described in the twentieth century was a problem that had confronted Madison in the eighteenth and worried de Tocqueville in the nineteenth.

So society might be misled. If the absence of liberty meant the exercise of tyranny, then a democratic society was capable of tyrannizing itself. It was a well-beaten path of political philosophy, and it was precisely this problem which the Founders had tried to resolve when they designed the Constitution. Hence the deliberate attempt to avoid consolidation of power. The countervailing principles were established; federalism, separation of powers, administrative and institutional decentralization, were thought to be barriers against a concentration of democratic sovereignty. De Tocqueville acknowledged that America's political and institutional system appeared to have overcome some of the theoretical problems associated with democratic society.

This was not the end of the story. Another problem appeared which in many ways transcended the rest. The 'tyranny of the majority' was again not a new idea; and Cooper as a contemporary was among those who would advance the notion that the sovereignty of mediocre public opinion might drag democracy down. Indeed, the whole earlier constitutional wrangling had been in essence an effort to avoid it. The middle course was felt to be between the Scylla of such democratic tyranny and the Charybdis of arbitrary rule, although, as Calhoun observed, an uneasy tension might exist also between majority rule and a pluralist republic. But de Tocqueville's insight, like Cooper's, was to recognize and publicize the criticism that a qualitative tyranny, which was the result of public opinion presuming to influence standards of aesthetic and cultural taste, went hand in hand with the quantitative drawback of majority rule, which meant that popular sovereignty, expressed through an arithmetical counting of heads, could determine public policy against the wishes of the minority. De Tocqueville's advantage in advancing this point was that among Europeans it might be amplified to a wider and more receptive audience.

Like Cooper, then, de Tocqueville suggested that the tendency to adhere slavishly to the will of a majority stifled minority opinion and promoted a collective mediocrity. He argued that:

> it is evident that the opinions, the prejudices, the interests and even the passions of the people are hindered by no permanent obstacles from exercising a perpetual influence on the daily conduct of affairs. In the United States the majority governs in the name of the people, as is the case in all countries in which the people are supreme. (De Tocqueville, 1945a, p. 180)

More significantly he noted that although 'the majority may be mistaken on some points . . . it is always right and *there is no moral power above it*' (quoted in Schleifer, 1980, p. 192). Not even religion provided a check; indeed in some ways its orthodoxies substantiated the point. The 'tyranny of the majority' became a social as well as a political disease.

This insidious tyranny prevented freedom of individual opinion, and promoted a kind of political and intellectual oppression worse than that which characterized the undemocratic states of Europe. De Tocqueville claimed that:

> at the present time the most absolute monarchs in Europe cannot prevent certain opinions hostile to their authority from circulating in secret through their dominions and even in their courts. It is not so in America; as long as the majority is still undecided, discussion is carried on; but as soon as its decision is irrevocably pronounced, everyone is silent, and the friends as well as the opponents of the measure unite in assenting to its propriety. (De Tocqueville, 1945a, p. 273)

Why? Simply because the will of the majority was backed by moral authority as well as by political power and it could claim both in implementing its decisions via the legislative and executive processes.

The majority in a democracy had this overwhelming advantage. No monarch, however absolute, could succeed in coercing all opposition in the same way. But the moral force of majority will reinforced by the political weight of majority rule was unstoppable. The result was that 'the majority possesses a power that is physical and moral at the same time, which acts upon the will as much as upon the actions and represses not only all contest, but all controversy' (de Tocqueville, 1945a, p. 273). De Tocqueville's 'tyranny of the majority' was thus a subtle, pervasive and ultimately numbing force.

It was a social and intellectual problem rather than a purely political one: a fact the Founders had missed when they carefully balanced institution against institution and checked power with power. Now, to de Tocqueville, there was 'no other country in which there is so little independence of mind and real freedom of discussion as in America'. The outcome was that 'in America the majority raises formidable barriers around the liberty of opinion' (de Tocqueville, 1945a, p. 274). The impact of this stultifying majoritarianism was the creation of a society that frowned on the liberty to be different. Idiosyncrasy and eccentricity, sometimes the creative motors of a free society, were viewed with suspicion. In this way, it has been suggested that:

> the majority problem in America was not a symptom of society in conflict but of its antithesis: a society with a frightening degree of moral agreement . . . In fact 'tyranny of the majority' was a particularly misleading phrase, suggesting a community divided into permanent and rigid majorities and minorities. Rather, as Tocqueville implied, 'tyranny of unanimity' would be a more appropriate concept for the American scene. (Horwitz, 1966, p. 305)

The pluralist republic was not one in which a panoply of different opinions, lifestyles, outlooks and ideas co-existed. On any major issue, all groups had to bend to the will of the majority. The decisions of that arbiter were arbitrary, but they were obeyed, and the ripples of uniformity spread through the 'extended sphere'.

Beaumont, de Tocqueville's companion in America, made the point with equal force. 'In the United States the masses rule everything and forever – and they are constantly jealous of any superiority that indicates itself, and prompt to break down any that has succeeded in making itself to be recognized. Middling understandings reject great minds, just as weak eyes abhor the broad light of day.'

The result was that 'the uniformity which reigns in their political world is equally apparent in their civil society', and although 'the American nation recruits itself from all the nations of the earth, yet no one, take it all in all, presents such an uniformity of character' (quoted in Lockhart, 1835, p. 300). The Europeans, observing the Americans, independently reached a similar conclusion.

In his travel journal de Tocqueville wrote in the same vein of the monotone society he found in America.

> It may be either rich or poor, humble or brilliant, trading or agricultural; but it is composed everywhere of the same elements. The plane of uniform civilization has passed over it. The man you left in New York you find again in almost impenetrable solitudes: same clothes, same attitude, same language, same habits, same pleasures. (Quoted in Horwitz, 1966, p. 301)

So just as 'majority' might really imply 'unanimity' so 'tyranny' could be too strong a term for this cultural enervation. The majority were not malicious, merely boring. The 'torpor of unanimity' describes the malaise of this democratic society more accurately than the 'tyranny of the majority', although with less of a rhetorical flourish. De Tocqueville's tyranny is a matter of opinion.

De Tocqueville could not avoid commenting on slavery. Here, apparently, was a concern that contradicted his belief that American democratic society preserved a monolithic inscrutable uniformity in its approach to issues of fundamental importance. Slavery was the divisive problem, the intractable dilemma which aroused passions strong enough to disrupt the passivity of American democracy. For de Tocqueville, however, the intolerance of slavery among some in the north showed that mobilization of public opinion was in action: that ultimately once the majority agreed that slavery was a moral outrage then that view would have to prevail. Conflict was inevitable.

> Whatever may be the efforts of the Americans of the South to maintain slavery they will not always succeed. Slavery, now confined to a single tract of the civilised earth, attacked by Christianity as unjust and by political economy as prejudicial, and now contrasted with democratic liberty and the intelligence of our age, cannot survive. (De Tocqueville, 1945a, p. 397)

The south thus had no adequate rationalization of their 'peculiar institution' in the face of demands for an equal right to liberty. On the other hand, although the social consensus may have abhorred slavery, it might still condone racism.

77

This observation was made by Beaumont in his novel *Marie ou L'Esclavage aux États-Unis*. He reported 'a melancholy truth. Public Opinion so beneficent when it protects is, when it persecutes, the most cruel of all tyrants.' In America he saw the unchecked hatred that was reserved for the negro. There was no method of influencing attitudes through legislation. 'In general it belongs to the wisdom of legislators to correct manners by laws, which laws are again corrected by manners. This moderating power has no existence in the United States.' The sovereign people were generally racists. The consequence was that 'the coloured race in America undergoes the government of hatred and contempt: everywhere I was forced to recognize the tyrannies of the popular will' (quoted in Lockhart, 1835, p. 295). The attitude towards negroes could be taken as another facet of the tyranny of the majority, bending attitudes towards a prevailing ethos of racism, even though the issue of slavery involved questions of such basic moral concern that private opinion could still be open to persuasion.

In *Democracy in America*, however, de Tocqueville retreats from the assessment of his travel journal that his trip through America presented him with images of a society painted only in grey. For there were differences between north and south. Such variation was due to the institution of slavery. On the one hand, 'the American of the North has not only experience but knowledge: yet he values science not as an enjoyment, but as a means and is only anxious to seize its useful applications'. On the other hand, 'the American of the South is more given to act on impulse; he is more clever, more frank, more generous, more intellectual and more brilliant' (de Tocqueville, 1945a, pp. 411–12). There was a clear contrast to be drawn between northerner and southerner in terms of their comparative European social ranks. 'The former, with a greater degree of activity, common sense, information and general aptitude, has the characteristic good and evil qualities of the middle classes. The latter has the tastes, the prejudices, the weaknesses, and the magnanimity of all aristocracies.' This was the function of owning slaves. De Tocqueville concluded that 'slavery, then, does not attack the American Union directly in its interests, but indirectly in its manners' (de Tocqueville, 1945a, p. 412). The south confronted him with a problem. It was the home of illiberal aristocrats.

He admired aristocracy. And indeed, the preservation of aristocratic values might be the antidote to some of the drawbacks of democracy and majority rule. The masses could be 'led astray by ignorance and passion', but 'an aristocratic body is too numerous to be led astray by intrigue, and yet not numerous enough to yield readily to the intoxication of unreflecting passion. An aristocracy is a firm and enlightened body that never dies' (de Tocqueville, 1945a, p. 245). De Tocqueville had a blind spot with regard to rule by the few. He was convinced that an aristocracy kept absolutism at bay. It acted as society's lynch-pin. It 'made a chain of all members of the community, from the peasant to the king; democracy breaks that chain and severs every link of it' (quoted in Zetterbaum, 1967, p. 59). The description of the society of southern aristocrats in *Democrácy in America* is thus almost wistful.

As a committed liberal, de Tocqueville could not tolerate the south's attachment to its 'peculiar institution'. An American aristocracy might have stood against the democratic egalitarian tide and the encroaching 'tyranny of the majority'. In a way the south did just that – but while some southerners owned slaves they sacrificed the right to be considered true aristocrats who were committed to freedom rather than democratic equality. As long as it condoned slavery, the south believed in neither.

Fortunately the south was not the only preserve of an American aristocracy. De Tocqueville also found the values he thought so important in the legal profession. The judiciary, he argued, represented the one enlightened force that might counter the democratic despotism imposed by majority rule and majority opinion.

> In America there are no nobles or literary men, and the people are apt to mistrust the wealthy; lawyers consequently form the highest political class and the most cultivated portion of society. They have therefore nothing to gain by innovation, which adds a conservative interest to their natural taste for public order. If I were asked where I place the American aristocracy, I should reply without hesitation that it is not among the rich who are united by no common tie, but that it occupies the judicial bench and the bar. (De Tocqueville, 1945a, p. 288)

The legal profession becomes the watchdog in the democratic society. Not only can it assume a role in political life, it can also influence the attitudes of ordinary citizens, by enlisting their help as jurors and educating them in the law.

In this way, 'armed with the power of declaring laws to be unconstitutional the American magistrate perpetually interferes in political affairs', and 'it is especially by means of the jury in civil causes that the American magistrates imbue even the lower classes of society with the spirit of their profession. Thus the jury, which is the most energetic means of making the people rule, is also the most efficacious means of teaching it how to rule well' (de Tocqueville,

1945a, pp. 289 and 297). The aristocrats might educate the democrats.

There is far more to the rich discussion of *Democracy in America* than the complaint about majority rule. As one contemporary review of the work put it:

> M. de Tocqueville has, then, written the book he wished to write, and we are grateful to him for having written a work on higher political philosophy of the first order, a profound and conscientious analysis of a most complex social condition, but therefore all the more worthy of study in that it harbors within its depths the future of the world. (De Tocqueville, 1945b, app. 2, p. 407)

That future was perhaps not quite as rosy as some of the Founders might have believed. The character of America's democratic tradition was not to be found in the operation of political institutions alone. De Tocqueville's skill was to raise the curtains of democratic rhetoric to let some light in upon its reality.

CONCLUSION

The debate over the consequences of majority rule revolved around the claims of the many and the interests of the few. Obedience to the decisions of the majority was a principle that was a controversial part of the democratic experiment – or at least of the Jacksonian version of it. Calhoun, Cooper and de Tocqueville were among those who argued that the idea that numbers should determine the nature of decisions taken in the republic, and even the character of its life, was mistaken. Quantitatively and qualitatively majority rule could be accepted only with severe reservations, and if there were plausible alternatives maybe the notion could be dispensed with altogether. Such was the drift of the critics' contribution.

However, the discussion had another side, and supporters of Jacksonian democracy presented it. The initial editorial of the *United States Magazine and Democratic Review*, first published in 1837, summarized the issues involved. The relative status of majorities and minorities in a democracy had not changed since Jefferson had tried to define it in his first inaugural address, for the *Democratic Review* presents the case in much the same way.

> Though we go for the republican principle of the supremacy of the will of the majority, we acknowledge in general a strong sympathy with minorities, and consider that their rights have a high moral claim on the respect and justice of majorities; a claim not always fairly recognized

in practice by the latter, in the full sway of power, when flushed with triumph and impelled by strong interests. (Rozwenc, 1963, p. 20)

This had always been the criticism to which democracy had been most vulnerable: that majorities would ride roughshod over minority rights.

The case against majority rule is argued in a standard, if not classic, form. It is impossible to justify the claims of the majority on strict utilitarian grounds by appealing to the 'greatest good of the greatest number' since 'it by no means follows that the greatest number understands its own greatest good'. Majority rule can be faulted also on two further grounds: if the majority is slim, then its moral margin of victory may be difficult to sustain; and majorities can be wrong or open to abuse their power just as often as minorities. The 'anti-democratic' side of the argument endorses a campaign of 'conservative checks' on the majority by the minority (similar to Calhoun's protectionism) or recourse to greater guidance from the 'more enlightened wisdom' of the 'better classes' (as Cooper and de Tocqueville would have agreed).

The *Democratic Review* then does justice to the case in favour of majority rule. First, it is argued, the majority is 'more likely' to know and to follow its own 'greatest good' than is the minority. Secondly, minority rule is far more open to selfish abuse of power than is rule by the majority. Thirdly, 'there does not naturally exist any such original superiority of a minority class above the great mass of a community, in intelligence and competence for the duties of government.' In addition, widespread education and access to information, and freedom of the press, 'make the pretensions of those self-styled "better classes" to the sole possession of the requisite intelligence for the management of public affairs, too absurd to be entitled to any other treatment than an honest, manly contempt' (Rozwenc, 1963, p. 21).

The two sides of the majority-rule debate thus came to rest upon the prejudice of a persuasion. Those who feared the mob – in European, if not American terms, the aristocrats – pressed their criticism almost as an assertion of fact. Those who had faith in the people *en masse* – the democrats – did not fear majority rule, even though they appreciated its potential drawbacks. So 'have we but a choice of evils'? The *Democratic Review* argued: only if belief in majority rule shades into a conviction that government by the majority must be active, interventionist, centralized and strong. The tyranny of the majority is expressed through its actions. The use of governmental power encourages its abuse, and the over-mighty government is more to be feared than the overbearing majority. If republican government is actively oppressive, all the defects of democracy are present.

> Hence the demagogue – hence the faction – hence the mob – hence the violence, licentiousness, and instability – hence the ambitious struggles of parties and their leaders for power – hence the abuses of that power by majorities and their leaders – hence the indirect oppressions of the general by partial interests – hence (fearful symptom) the demoralization of the great men of the nation, and of the nation itself, proceeding . . . gradually to that point of maturity at which relief from the tumult of moral and physical confusion is to be found only under the shelter of an energetic armed despotism. (Rozwenc, 1963, p. 22)

On the other hand, if government withdraws from all but the minimum of legislative activity, then the individual is left free from the niggling laws its majority dictates, and the rights of minorities are left untrampled. The problem is thus not with democratic government but rather with democratic government that tries to do too much.

The *Democratic Review* makes a determined statement in favour of negative liberty. 'Legislation has been the fruitful parent of nine-tenths of all the evil, moral and physical, by which mankind has been afflicted since the creation of the world, and by which human nature has been self-degraded, fettered and oppressed. Government should have as little as possible to do with the general business and interests of the people' (Rozwenc, 1963, p. 23). In essence the question is begged. It was precisely the criticism of Calhoun among others that the federal government had become too centralized and too interventionist. Whatever the theory, the practice might be at odds with it, and it was America's democratic practice which attracted the brickbats.

In shifting the ground of the debate from majority rule as a principle to government as the real issue, the Jacksonians' *Democratic Review* could be accused of missing the point. In the end, if the critique was really only concerned with the role of government and the impact of majority rule on legislation, then it was merely the machinery of democracy that was under discussion. As Cooper and de Tocqueville suggested, however, democracy could not be taken as an end in itself. The quality of democratic life was also important. So although the mechanism might be adjusted – on the ground that 'the government is best which governs least' – or even radically changed to admit the claims of a concurrent majority, that could not be the end of the affair.

Values remained significant. It was not enough for democracy to be seen as a political method: the perennial concern of some was that the democratic way of life should express the fundamental values – equality and liberty – of the Declaration. The vision was still nostalgic. America's democratic experiment, as it continued in the nineteenth century, can be seen as an attempt to resolve the conflict over those values. Freedom versus slavery and equality against privilege were contests joined not only in the political but also in the moral, cultural and economic arenas.

The criticism of American democracy endured although the focus of it changed. The critics of the democratic practice of the Jacksonian period, represented by Calhoun, Cooper and de Tocqueville, were generally presenting arguments that most contemporary liberals could accept, even if they might not condone the motives which could be imputed to Calhoun. It was, indeed, the issue of slavery that provoked another discussion about the moral implications of accepting such an institution in a self-proclaimed democratic republic. Later in the nineteenth century further dimensions of democracy would be explored: the nature of a democratic culture and the ideal of a democratic political economy. Some felt that the American republic might yet become a democratic commonwealth. If the earlier critics thus filtered their views through the ideology of liberalism, these later commentators were more likely to be the product of a socialist persuasion. And separating the two generations, of course, was the Civil War.

CHAPTER 4

Interpretations of the Democratic Ideal

'This slavery question has been the only one that has ever endangered our republican institutions – the only one that has ever threatened or menaced a dissolution of the Union – that has ever disturbed us in such a way as to make us fear for the perpetuity of our liberty' (Angle, 1958, pp. 313–14). Abraham Lincoln was right. Slavery was the choke-chain of American democracy. A republic which was based on a self-proclaimed belief in equality and liberty had necessarily to come to terms with its innermost contradiction. The issue of slavery was undeniably complex. It involved questions not only as to the nature of the 'peculiar institution' but also as to the character of democracy itself. Was slavery to be construed purely as meaning the subjugation of the negro? Or could it also mean wage-slavery in the emerging industrial leviathan? Was republican government about self-government, sovereignty and federalism? Or should it incorporate a sense of moral purpose: a claim to differentiate between good and evil, right and wrong?

The Civil War was a hiatus in the argument. It resolved one contradiction only to focus attention upon others. American democracy in the nineteenth century was a perennial battleground of ideas. Was democracy a process of government or an ethical concern? If it appeared that the latter persuasion – involving a commitment to abolish slavery as an outrage to the moral democratic conscience – was a cause precipitating Civil War, then the latter part of the century seems to have been a period when the moral mission was sublimated to the demands of economic expansionism.

It is too harsh a judgement to claim, however, that in the reconstruction period all those who had seen democracy as a moral crusade were seduced by the rewards of capitalist enterprise. It was not the case that 'the idealism of the transcendentalists had perished in the smoke of the Civil War. For a generation after 1865, America worshipped material gods and the intellectual protest was insignificant' (Feuer, 1959, p. 546). For there were critics. In the latter part of the century, the so-called 'Gospel of Wealth', supported by appeals to the 'self-made man' and social Darwinian theories, was challenged by those who believed in a 'Social Gospel'. These advocates looked back nostalgically to Jeffersonian values, as they constructed a future commonwealth by adding the concept of a democratic political economy to the framework of the republican past.

Although the focus of the debate changed, the themes are consistent. The clash between those who saw democracy as a political method and those who invested it with a moral commitment can be seen on both sides of the Civil War divide. It is simple yet convenient to associate these different attitudes about democracy in the *ante-bellum* period with the regions, north and south. Behind the northern notion that part of the democratic faith should be invested in a moral crusade against negro slavery was a religious belief, and indeed the abolitionists of the north were in many cases products of the old Quaker communities. The historian George Bancroft noted that in the 1830s and 1840s 'there is fast rising in New England a moral Democracy, in harmony with Christianity . . . in harmony with the progress of Civilization. Democracy is practical Christianity' (quoted in Craven, 1959, p. 22).

On the other hand the southerners maintained a different outlook. Democracy and their 'peculiar institution' need not be at odds. Black slavery could be presented as the foundation upon which white democracy was built. In the south democracy reached its full political expression where slaves were occupied with the menial drudgery, so permitting the white population to pursue honest efficient public service in their supposedly egalitarian community. The argument could only be sustained if it was accepted, as it was in the south, that different moral criteria applied to black people and white people. Racism gave the slavery problem another dimension. Even after slavery was abolished, racism remained. What would have happened after the Civil War had the slaves been white?

The idea that democracy could be harnessed to Christianity and progress towards a better civilization nevertheless fuelled a religious conviction that slavery in any form was an intolerable affront to American values. God was a powerful ally. Even if capitalism and democracy were linked after the Civil War by the seductive myth that each individual had an equal opportunity to achieve material prosperity, doubts remained about the morality of the relationship. The theme of democracy as the secular equivalent of a Christian faith re-emerged in the late nineteenth century as the basis for a critique of an industrial and economic system which seemed to deny the prospect of such an elevating moral vision.

In between the moral and economic explorations of the democratic ideal there was also an attempt to understand the nature of a democratic culture. Walt Whitman, the 'poet of American democracy', promoted the idea of such a culture as a unifying force in a nation recovering from the divisions that had resulted in the Civil War. The United States could continue its democratic republican experiment as an example to itself and to the rest of the world. And it could do this through becoming aware that its difference was expressed not merely in terms of its institutions but also in terms of its art, literature, poetry and music. The achievement of preserving the United States as one nation was not to be squandered.

Whereas the social critics of the late nineteenth century often looked back to Jefferson as the inspiration of the republican ideal, Whitman appreciated the importance of a hero less remote. It was no accident that his candidate was Lincoln, the alchemist of the democratic experiment in its most crucial period. There could in the end be no finer tribute:

This dust was once the man,
Gentle, plain, just and resolute, under whose cautious hand,
Against the foulest crime in history known in any land or age,
Was saved the Union of these States.

(Whitman, 1965, p. 339)

ABRAHAM LINCOLN AND THE MORAL IMPLICATIONS OF DEMOCRACY

Political parties in the north discovered the moral aspect of democracy in arguing for abolition. Slavery gave birth to the Republican party, growing out of abolitionist sentiment to a point where, in 1856, it was able to put up a respectable showing in the presidential electoral contest. The party openly claimed to defend the values of Christianity and democracy and to promote the more earthly concern of progress. This moral crusade was based on an interpretation of the established American political tradition. The Republicans found their inspiration in Jefferson's Declaration and attempted nothing more than to redefine and reinterpret its message in a contemporary context. Nor could the Democrats ignore the force of Jefferson's moral suasion. Both major political parties of the period immediately before the Civil War came to appeal to the Declaration as the embodiment of the fundamental and eternal principles of the American republic.

There could be no compromise over slavery. The argument transcended political parties to a point where views could not be accommodated even within these broad churches. So the southern states might claim that the tyranny of the northern majority would force them to accept something – abolition – which they had no wish to accept. And there was no room for manoeuvre once it was seen that this was one issue which demanded uniformity, for there was a widespread conviction, as William Seward argued in 1858, that slavery provoked 'an *irrepressible conflict* between opposing and enduring forces, and it means that the United States will sooner or later become either an entire slave holding Nation, or an entirely free labor Nation' (quoted in Cooper, 1885, bk 1, p. 74). The options were clarified: there could be no co-existence between slave states and free states, so one or the other must needs prevail.

Such discussion was clarified in the Lincoln–Douglas debates. These were part of the grand tradition of American oratory and political argument, and took place in 1858 during the campaign in Illinois for election to the federal Senate. In the opening salvoes of the contest, before the formal debates had been agreed and enjoined, both candidates staked out their political territory. Lincoln pre-empted Seward's remarks in the more often quoted statement of the need for uniformity in a speech on 16 June at Springfield: 'A house divided against itself cannot stand. I believe this government cannot endure, permanently half *slave* and half *free*. I do not expect the Union to be *dissolved* – I do not expect the house to *fall* – but I *do* expect it will cease to be divided. It will become *all* one thing or *all* the other' (Angle, 1958, p. 2).

His opponent, Stephen Douglas, argued in Chicago on 9 July that, on the contrary, 'uniformity in local and domestic affairs would be destructive of state rights, of state sovereignty, of personal liberty and personal freedom. Uniformity is the parent of despotism the world over, not only in politics, but in religion' (Angle, 1958, p. 19). It became apparent that the gulf between the candidates was so wide that arguments often slid past one another. One monologue was moralistic, the other legalistic: there were few points of contact.

Douglas insisted that there should be no limits placed on any section of the community's right to decide on its own laws: to attempt such was to threaten the basis of self-government. In contrast with Lincoln's plea for conformity, he reiterated a view reminiscent of Calhoun's, that each state, as a federal element within the Constitution, should be free to dictate and manage its own internal affairs. In his words, 'he goes for consolidation and uniformity in our government. I go for maintaining the confederation of the sovereign states under the Constitution' (Angle, 1958, p. 55). Lincoln, however, insisted that this was not the issue. During the debate at Galesburg he suggested that, 'Judge Douglas declares that if any community want slavery they have a right to have it. He can say that logically, if he says that there is no wrong in slavery; but if you admit that there is a wrong in it, he cannot logically say that anybody has a right to do wrong' (ibid., pp. 303–4). The admission was crucial to the argument: the south often could not see anything amiss in the morality of its stance.

Later Lincoln refined the point, and associated the anti-slavery cause firmly with the philosophy of the Republican party. 'I suggest that the difference of opinion, reduced to its lowest terms, is no other than the difference between the men who think slavery a wrong and those who do not think it wrong. The Republican party think it wrong – we think it is a moral, a social and a political wrong' (Angle, 1958, p. 332). So where Douglas stuck by the constructionist argument, that the federal Constitution rested on self-determination and the right of each state to decide its own laws – and its own morality – Lincoln took the view that as a whole the United States had a moral duty, if not a political obligation, to pronounce on this issue that was of concern to the entire nation.

This argument that America had to declare unanimously for or against slavery could be turned neatly on its head. Illinois was then a free labour state. But, as Douglas pointed out, at the time of the formation of the Union, twelve states had been slave-holding and only one had been free. The passion for conformity and unanimity, had it been observed in 1787, would have made slavery compulsory throughout the republic. The issue was thus whether the non-slave states 'having become the majority section', should then be able to 'enforce a doctrine on the minority, which we would have resisted with our heart's blood had it been attempted on us when we were in a minority' (Angle, 1958, p. 365). What was the legitimate sphere of majority rule in relation to the protection which had to be given to minority rights?

Douglas concluded that if the boot had been on the other democratic foot, and the north in a minority, then under the terms of Lincoln's argument it would have had to accept the extension of slavery across the nation. The heroes could not have one rule for themselves and another for the villains. And further, to enforce uniformity where it was not wanted was to compromise the basic freedom of the states to exist under the forms of the Constitution. The south should not suffer at the hands of a northern moral majority. But if this defence failed there was another more simple line of attack: racism.

Jefferson had claimed: 'all men are created equal'. Douglas, however, had no doubt that some were created more equal than others. He refused to recognize negroes or for that matter Indians as his equal in anything. There was no equivocation. Jefferson and his contemporaries, so Douglas thought, would have agreed:

> I hold that the signers of the Declaration of Independence had no reference to negroes at all when they declared all men to be created equal . . . They were speaking of white men . . . I hold that this government was established on the white basis. It was established by white men for the benefit of white men and their posterity forever, and should be administered by white men and none others. (Angle, 1958, p. 374)

Now slavery does not necessarily follow from this argument. All it suggests is that government is created by one race for its exclusive benefit. But since that is the case it is therefore up to whites to decide the nature and scope of the rights they may wish to extend to others who live under their regime.

If this observation is combined with the point about state sovereignty then the question of the privileges that should be given to negroes becomes the preserve of each state government. So inalienable rights were only for whites. And when definitions were restricted in this way, equality and liberty became things granted by God to the white man but by the white man playing God to others. The issue of slavery thus became one of politics rather than morality, because the negro was not to be judged by the same moral criteria as the white man. And, if that was the attitude, slavery was no longer open to discussion in the south in terms of the morality of the institution, since slave-holders did not recognize the legitimacy of the moral objection to it.

Lincoln met this racist argument head on. The idea that negroes were not included in the aspirations of the Declaration of Independence was rooted in white bigotry, but in any event, if accepted, it immediately robbed the slave of any chance of self-improvement, status and future citizenship in the republic. Lincoln was moderate only in his language – the racist analysis showed 'a tendency to dehumanize the negro – to take away from him the right of ever

89

striving to be a man' (Angle, 1958, p. 382). This could not have been what Jefferson and, later, the Founding Fathers had intended.

He saw in the phrasing of the Constitution things which suggested a vision of a society in which slavery had disappeared, and of a republic which instead captivated Jefferson's democratic prospect. 'Covert language' was used in the document so that in the end there would be 'nothing on the face of the great charter of liberty suggesting that such a thing as negro slavery had ever existed among us' (Angle, 1958, p. 385). By not incorporating the term in the Constitution, and by referring to the contemporary institution of slavery only obliquely, the Founders had given a clear indication that they expected that this institution would wither away.

The people were to have either a short collective folk memory or no knowledge of their own history if once slavery was gone they would forget it had existed and there would be nothing left to remind them of it in the great documents which had created the political tradition of the country. But Lincoln did have a point. The Founders, he suggested, 'found the institution existing among us, and they left it as they found it' (Angle, 1958, p. 386). There was no attempt to enshrine the word, and thus slavery itself, among the constitutional precepts and principles which constructed the framework of the nation. There would be no necessity for rewriting the substantive document once it had gone: amendments would extend existing rights rather than defining them anew.

If there was ever a dialogue on slavery, the Lincoln–Douglas debates show that it was breaking down. Those who believed in the principle of states' rights and self-determination – and who thereby condoned slavery – could not convince those who thought that slavery was a travesty of political and democratic morality that there was a case to answer. Douglas summed up the nature of the chasm separating his view from Lincoln's.

He says that he looks forward to a time when slavery shall be abolished everywhere. I look forward to a time when each state shall be allowed to do as it pleases . . . I care more for the great principle of self-government, the right of the people to rule, than I do for all the negroes in Christendom. I would not endanger the perpetuity of this Union, I would not blot out the great inalienable rights of the white men for all the negroes that ever existed. (Angle, 1958, p. 400)

For Lincoln, the limitation of slavery within the expanding Union was paramount. A healthy democratic society would have to come to terms with the fact of slavery within its midst, and ultimately that too could not be tolerated. He realized the dilemma which confronted the nation. In a letter that he wrote on the eve of the Civil War to Alexander Stephens, on the other side of the divide, he seemed resigned: 'you think slavery is right and ought to be extended, while we think it is wrong and ought to be restricted. That, I suppose, is the rub' (Van Doren Stern, 1940, p. 631). Slavery, perhaps inevitably, 'represented two entirely different understandings of the demands of Christianity, of democracy, and of progress' (Craven, 1959, p. 100). It was a matter of right versus rights.

Douglas succeeded in winning his way to the Senate in 1858. Two years later, however, in the presidential election, the divisions were evident once more. Four candidates stood in what were two more or less self-contained contests. Lincoln tackled Douglas again in the north, and John Breckenridge faced John Bell in the south. Lincoln won. He did not gain a singular popular vote in ten southern states, but the northern majority in the Electoral College was enough to give him an overall victory. The southern states could recall Calhoun's words: they were indeed 'a fixed and hopeless minority'. They threw in the towel. By the end of February 1861 seven states had left the Union, and the Confederacy, with Jefferson Davis as its president, had been formed at a convention held in Montgomery, Alabama. Madison's design, the democratic republic, the balancing acts of federalism and a separation of powers seemed an inappropriate contrivance. The Founders had confronted the problem of slavery by side-stepping it. As a result, their constitutional accommodation temporarily collapsed.

Lincoln did not give up. In the period leading up to the outbreak of the Civil War, he changed tack, arguing on the south's own terms: democracy as a political process rather than as an ethical ideal. In his inaugural address of 4 March 1861 he presented the legalistic case against secession, after it had in fact started to occur. The Union could not be dissolved unless all who had contracted into it were in agreement. 'No State upon its own mere motion can lawfully get out of the Union . . . resolves and ordinances to that effect are legally void' (Van Doren Stern, 1940, p. 650). The southern states were not being constitutionally coerced by a northern majority on the issue of slavery. There had been no law passed requiring abolition, and the south could not claim that its constitutional rights had been abrogated.

If some states seceded, however, it would spark off a constant process of replication. The precedent is powerful: minorities splitting from majorities whenever it suited them ignored the vital principle of majority rule which allowed society to exist. The conclusion was inescapable. 'The central idea of secession is the essence of anarchy.' Lincoln spelt out the argument:

> A majority held in restraint by constitutional checks and limitations, and always changing easily with deliberate changes of popular opinions and sentiments, is the only true sovereign of a free people. Whoever rejects it does, of necessity, fly to anarchy or to despotism. Unanimity is impossible: the rule of a minority, as a permanent arrangement is wholly inadmissable; so that, rejecting the majority principle, anarchy or despotism in some form is all that is left. (Van Doren Stern, 1940, p. 653)

There was no alternative to majority rule. But what Lincoln failed to recognize, or at least chose to ignore, was that it was always an argument to be deployed by those with the numbers on their side. His own election demonstrated that if the majority and minority were fixed, locked in disagreement with no point of contact or compromise between them, then the appeal to mere numbers had little force.

If both the moralistic and the legalistic attacks failed to impress the southern states, there was a last best hope: that secession was a practical impossibility. 'Physically speaking we cannot separate . . . A husband and wife may be divorced, and go out of the presence and beyond the reach of each other, but the different parts of our country cannot do this' (Van Doren Stern, 1940, p. 654). But they might. This last claim of Lincoln's borders on a pious conviction believed through desperation. In April 1861 the 'bonds of Union' finally snapped.

The Civil War was catharsis. Lincoln in the Gettysburg Address on 19 November 1863 would re-dedicate the republic to its democratic purpose.

> Four score and seven years ago our fathers brought forth on this continent a new nation, conceived in Liberty, and dedicated to the proposition that all men are created equal. Now we are engaged in a great civil war, testing whether that nation or any nation so conceived and so dedicated, can long endure. (Commager, 1951, p. 152)

The prospect remained: the idea of a republican democracy built on values and a shared sense of moral purpose. 'We here highly resolve . . . that this nation under God, shall have a new birth of freedom – and that government of the people, by the people, for the people, shall not perish from the earth' (ibid., p. 153).

On the other hand, there could be no illusions about the war and its impact on the democratic fabric of American society. Calhoun's 'Real Monument', wrote Walt Whitman, 'is the desolated, ruined south; nearly the whole generation of young men between seventeen and thirty destroyed or maim'd; all the old families used up – the rich impoverish'd, the plantations cover'd with weeds, the slaves unloos'd and become the masters, and the name of southerner blacken'd with every shame' (Whitman, 1909, p. 69). Lincoln may have recognized the moral implications of the democratic ideal, but his argument failed to carry the necessary force to persuade the south to compromise within the Union, rather than seek solace outside it.

WALT WHITMAN AND THE CULTURAL IMPULSE OF DEMOCRACY

Whitman's views on American democracy are representative of the oscillations in attitudes towards the republican experiment that were characteristic of his times. Before the Civil War he was among the first to argue for the 'democratic faith', the idea that 'we must be constantly pressing onward – every year throwing the doors wider and wider – and carrying our experiment of democratic freedom to the very verge of the limit' (quoted in Grimes, 1955, p. 195). The real world impinged. Disillusionment with the workings of republican democracy are apparent in Whitman's work as the United States slid towards Civil War. In 1856 he wrote 'The Eighteenth Presidency', described as 'one of the bitterest diatribes against the practices of realistic democracy to be found in literature of American politics' (Gabriel, 1956, p. 129). Optimism resurfaced: in *Democratic Vistas*, Whitman reiterated his call for the establishment of a new and vital democratic culture.

The 'democratic faith', which was never entirely lost, was complete and all-encompassing. Democracy should become a way of life, indeed it was the only way of life which could claim the allegiance of the free individual. Whitman thus rewrote the agenda for American democracy, or at least he added a new item to it. Jeffersonian democracy had evolved into Jacksonian democracy, expressing its faith in common humanity, and reasserting the values of equality and liberty in the 'age of the common man'. To this brew Whitman added a spiritual dimension, derived from a quasi-religious mysticism, transcendentalism.

As D. H. Lawrence pointed out: 'Whitman's democracy is not merely a political system, or a system of government – or even a social system. It is an attempt to conceive a new way of life, to establish new values. It is a struggle to liberate human beings

93

from the fixed arbitrary control of ideals, into free spontaneity'
(McDonald, 1936, vol. 1, p. 713). This extra dimension to democracy
– an individualistic faith – accentuated a broad-based humanitarian
ethic which was a common theme in the subsequent writings of the
reformers of the late nineteenth century. Whitman's work, then,
exploring new dimensions of the republican ideal, acts as a bridge
from the *ante-bellum* to the post-Appotomax world.

In the 1850s and 1860s, however, the objective reality of American
politics clouded the vision of what democracy might yet become. In
'The Eighteenth Presidency', Whitman provided an interpretation
of his contemporary political world: corrupt and manipulated by
careerist politicians. Political offices, including the presidency, were
'bought, sold, electioneered for, prostituted, and filled with prosti-
tutes'. The people had failed the democratic test – there was no
sense of republican virtue or civic responsibility among a population
which was 'credulous, generous, deferential'. The republic was
in danger of collapsing back into monarchy, for 'if this were to go
on, we ought to change the title of the President, and issue patents
of nobility' (Furness, 1964, pp. 94–5).

The poet had not lost complete faith in the rest of common
humanity. The solution was with them. Leaders should not be the
creations of a class of professional politicians, they should emerge
from the people, ordinary and amateur.

> I expect to see the day when the like of the present personnel of
> the governments, federal, state, municipal, military and naval, will be
> looked upon with derision, and when qualified mechanics and young
> men will reach Congress and other official stations, sent in their working
> costumes, fresh from their benches and tools, and returning to them
> again with dignity. (Furness, 1964, p. 93)

These people would not be corrupted by office. The new arrivals
would not be political *arrivistes*.

Even in the late 1850s, however, Whitman appreciated that there
was a negative side to the democratic prophecy. The prospect of
apocalypse then was not only before America but also before the
world.

> On all sides tyrants tremble, crowns are unsteady, the human race
> restive, on the watch for some better era, some divine war. No man
> knows what will happen next, but all know that some such things are
> to happen as mark the greatest moral convulsions of the earth. Who
> shall play the hand for America in these tremendous games? (Furness,
> 1964, p. 113)

The question was rhetorical. Whitman looked forward to the arrival of the 'Redeemer President' of the United States (ibid., p. 109). That proved to be Lincoln. The Civil War, while confirming Whitman's disillusionment with the practical workings of democracy, did at least call forth his democratic hero. Purgatory was worth it.

The poet of American democracy was confirmed in his faith. Democracy had an underlying moral purpose, as he wrote: 'according to you, dear friend, democracy is achieved if there are elections, politics, various party slogans, and nothing else. As for myself, I believe that the present role of democracy begins only when she goes farther and farther . . . Her real and permanent grandeur is her religion: otherwise she has no grandeur' (quoted in Stepanchev, 1976, p. 159). The two interpretations of democracy: process or ethical ideal, are contrasted in this statement. Yet if, as Whitman believed, that democratic faith was essentially individualistic, then the Civil War threw up a truly democratic individual. For Whitman he was 'a cosmic figure, a personification of the great soul brought to earth' (Gabriel, 1956, p. 135). Lincoln became the inspiration of the poet's democratic folklore.

So 'when we speak of Whitman the thought of Lincoln is never very far away' (Hindus, 1955, p. 20). If the president had reiterated the essential values of the democratic republic at Gettysburg, it was left to the poet to interpret the vision anew. This he did in *Democratic Vistas*. It was a restatement of his earlier concern for America to establish a genuine culture appropriate to democracy as a secular and religious faith. But now he suggested that writers and artists should accept an important creative role in the making of the American democratic myth.

The democratic experiment continued. The idea of progress was an inevitable part of this. America, for Whitman, 'counts, as I reckon, for her justification and success . . . almost entirely on the future'. The nation is 'far less important for what it has done, or what it is, than for results to come' (Whitman, 1982, p. 317). Amalgamated with this notion of progress was the sense of America's democratic mission. The United States had, uniquely among nations, the task of captivating 'the moral political speculations of ages' (ibid., p. 318), which meant establishing the republic as a society in which individuals could develop their innate abilities and capacities, as mature and self-reliant citizens. This was one vista: the transcendence of the political morality of past eras, and the striving for a democracy resting on rational self-awareness and individual republican commitment.

America could fail. The Civil War was a constant reminder. The alternatives were stark and there appeared no prospect of compromising the democratic ideal. It was all or nothing. 'The United States are destined either to surmount the gorgeous history of feudalism, or else prove the most tremendous failure of time' (Whitman, 1982, p. 318). Again, the people might not measure up to the task. How to square such lofty moral speculations and democratic political philosophy with the actual behaviour of nineteenth-century leaders and followers was a familiar dilemma. There were few Lincolns and too many Fords; yet democracy had to incorporate all talents and each capacity. Whitman tried to reconcile the ideal and the real. *Democratic Vistas* was written 'to him or her within whose thought rages the battle, advancing, retreating, between democracy's convictions, aspirations, and the people's crudeness, vice, caprices' (ibid.).

If democracy was to progress, it had to develop and create new achievements in every sphere of social existence. If this were done, it was to be hoped, the quality of its citizens would naturally improve. These achievements, moreover, should not merely overshadow past endeavours. They should obliterate them. American society had to break from the vestiges of 'feudalism, caste, the ecclesiastical traditions' which were still present in 'the very subsoil, of education, and of social standards and literature'. This is the core of *Democratic Vistas*. It amounted to a complete and irrevocable call for cultural revolution. It was essential for Whitman that America should produce 'its own forms of art, poems, schools, theology, displacing all that exists, or that has been produced anywhere in the past, under opposite influences' (Whitman, 1982, p. 320).

This democratic culture would then be appropriate to a society that had abandoned political feudalism for political democracy. Such a society, by implication, since it was suffused with democratic values, offered its citizens a morally and spiritually higher standard of life: a qualitatively superior culture eclipsing all that had existed before. Part of this was the creation of a democratic literature which embodied elements of such democratic religion and morality – the democratic faith. This literature would provide society with an image of itself which it could show to the outside world, to contemporaries and to posterity.

The key role here is assigned to authors and poets, for they inspire the myths, they are the prophets of the culture. 'The central point in any nation . . . is its national literature . . . Immortal Judah lives and Greece immortal lives, in a couple of poems' (Whitman, 1982, p. 321). So too might America. Literacy is thus no good without literature, just as the right to vote is an empty right if politics is merely process. Democracy demands more. The purpose of the democratic culture is thus to provide a focus, and a unifying and integrating force, in society. Democracy must gain 'at least as firm and as warm a hold in men's hearts, emotions and belief, as, in their days, feudalism or ecclesiasticism'. Otherwise, 'its strength will be defective, its growth doubtful and its main charm wanting' (ibid., p. 323).

The culture which Whitman planned laced together a society in which differences could be reconciled through a common commitment to democracy as a way of life. The Civil War had shown what could happen when such a consensus did not exist, and Whitman confessed that 'the fear of conflicting and irreconcilable interiors, and the lack of a common skeleton, knitting all close, continually haunts me' (Whitman, 1982, p. 324). Democracy therefore had to have this shared moral foundation, expressed in its unique culture. The material benefits supposedly conferred by the system were not enough. A democratic way of life could not be bought on the assumption of an economic system having the capacity to confer an ever higher standard of living on its population.

For Whitman it was a 'prevailing delusion that the establishment of free political institutions, and plentiful intellectual smartness, with general good order, physical plenty, industry etc . . . do of themselves, determine and yield to our experiment of democracy the fruitage of success' (Whitman, 1982, p. 325). Material prosperity would not bind the nation behind a common acquisitive purpose, as the democratic culture could inspire allegiance to a common cause. The one was superficial, the other basic to the democratic purpose.

Materialism would corrupt the democratic ideal. Already the concern to accumulate wealth was producing an American society which was 'cankered, crude, superstitious and rotten' (Whitman, 1982, p. 325). There was no doubt what was to blame. 'Money-making is our magician's serpent, remaining today sole master of the field' (ibid., p. 326). The business world, centred in urban industrial areas, was not noted for its commitment to ethics and a democratic culture, and Whitman had no illusions: 'the depravity of the business classes of our country is not less than has been supposed, but infinitely greater' (ibid., p. 325). Business practices in the accelerating industrial economy might only pay lip-service to his concept of democracy.

For the poet of democracy, then, such activity trivialized the vision. Democracy lost its purpose and 'to severe eyes, using the moral microscope upon humanity, a sort of dry and flat Sahara appears, these cities, crowded with petty grotesques, malformations, phantoms, playing meaningless antics' (Whitman, 1982, p. 327).

The danger was that a failure to live up to the wider impulse of democracy as a moral and ethical ideal would leave the way clear for commitment to a less lofty, more mundane and ultimately subversive purpose, in which the process of government, allied with the workings of capitalism, provided a materialist vision to replace the democratic vista.

The challenge, as Whitman showed, was rather to create a democratic culture which could incorporate new-found economic wealth. In *Democratic Vistas*, he recognized the place of economic development but subordinated it to the over-arching ideal, and it became a stage in the development of true democracy. Political rights, established by the Founders, were the first step, then the new material prosperity provided a secure foundation for the subsequent evolution of a democracy which blended politics and economics as part of a culture wholeheartedly committed to its ethical mission.

HENRY GEORGE, EDWARD BELLAMY, HENRY LLOYD AND THE ECONOMIC IMPERATIVE OF DEMOCRACY.

According to Whitman, 'the writers of a time hint the mottoes of its gods' (Whitman, 1982, p. 350). In the years after the Civil War many Americans worshipped wealth and found an intellectual justification for their faith in the works of the British political and social philosopher, Herbert Spencer. He captured a mood of the moment. 'His works had diffused in several hundred thousand volumes, and his tour of America in 1873 had the character of a triumphal reception' (Feuer, 1959, p. 545). Spencer's identification of the healthy society as one in which nature's 'laws of evolution' and the 'survival of the fittest' were the recipes for social and political action was admired to the extent that such concepts were taken to justify also competition, capitalism and the ethos of acquisitive materialism. Liberal capitalist democracy found in social Darwinian ideas the apologia for its creed. Nevertheless there were those who saw that the reality of economic injustices caused by industrialization and free enterprise might throttle the ideals of democracy, and who tried to build a consensus around an alternative to 'the Gospel of Wealth' in the 'gilded age'.

Henry George (1839–1897)

Henry George was among them. The republic could become a commonwealth. For that to happen, Whitman's democratic culture would have to incorporate a democratic political economy – an economic system compatible with the ideals of the Declaration of Independence and the political arrangements it had fostered. George's solution was the Single Tax. Taxing property would bring about distributive justice and equality in the economic sphere. The scheme was all that was necessary, but its necessity was paramount, for George's advocacy was made all the more compelling by his analysis of the apocalyptic consequences of existing economic practices.

His major work, *Progress and Poverty*, was published in 1879. By then it had become clear to him that:

> absolute political equality does not in itself prevent the tendency to inequality involved in the private ownership of land, and it is further evident that political equality, co-existing with an increasing tendency to the unequal distribution of wealth, must ultimately beget either the despotism of organized tyranny or the worse despotism of anarchy. (George, 1937, p. 375)

Like Whitman, George left little room for compromise. 'The civilized world is trembling on the verge of a great movement. Either it must be a leap upward, which will open the way to advances yet undreamed of, or it must be a plunge downward, which will carry us back towards barbarism' (ibid., p. 385).

The cause of such hyperbole lay in the perceived gap between progress – the dynamic force propelled by intellectual effort conceived in an atmosphere of notional political and religious freedom – and poverty caused by the distributive inequities of an economic system in which the right to property was firmly entrenched. There could be little doubt that whereas democracy was on the side of progress – indeed it was the product of that enlightened advancement – poverty was the outcome of capitalism. This 'association of poverty with progress' may have been 'the great enigma of our times' (George, 1937, p. 12), but it was the result of the incompatibility of democratic and economic theory and practice.

The answer lay in the soil. 'The ownership of land is the great fundamental fact which ultimately determines the social, the political, and consequently the intellectual and moral condition of a people' (George, 1937, p. 210). Ownership acted as a brake on progress, as it accelerated poverty. If an individual owned land – or the property built on it – then that person was in a position to exploit those who worked on such land or in such property. 'If one man can command the land upon which others must labour, he can appropriate the

99

produce of their labour as the price of his permission to labour' (ibid., p. 242). Surplus value was extracted in the form of rent. This was a violation of the law of nature; indeed, George would argue that the 'natural right' to property which Locke had suggested was abused by the development of industrial society with its patterns of ownership and methods of production. The result was the spread of poverty among those not able to enjoy the full value of their labour.

That observation was not as remarkable as the remedy: The Single Tax. George's idea was to appropriate all rent charged on land through the taxation system. Other taxes could then be discontinued. A single tax on rent would still allow private ownership of land while preventing individuals from exploiting one another. Through this mechanism, 'society would thus approach the ideal of Jeffersonian democracy' (George, 1937, p. 322). Again, 'what is it but the carrying out in letter and spirit of the truth enunciated in the Declaration of Independence?' That truth had been subverted by an economic system that was profoundly indifferent to the values of the republic. To Henry George, therefore, 'political liberty, when the equal right to land is denied, becomes, as population increases and invention goes on, merely the liberty to compete for employment at starvation wages' (ibid., p. 386). This was not the liberty upon which the republic had been founded.

The economic system had corrupted the ideal in a way that threatened the fabric of American politics and society. The inequity in the distribution of wealth was in effect but another form of tyranny and despotism, and was the contemporary consequence of America's industrialization. It was undermining the political system. Discontent caused by the inequality that resulted from capitalist enterprise would generate support for a spurious populism: the demagogue would emerge to capitalize on such a situation. It is a familiar theme, reminiscent of Cooper's concern. Henry George suggested that the only antidote was an injection of democracy into the economic bloodstream.

If this were not done, then democracy would lose all ways. Those who benefited from existing economic arrangements were not really interested in saving democracy, since 'a mere aristocracy of wealth will never struggle while it can hope to bribe a tyrant' (George, 1937, p. 376). And even if the cynical populist could be so controlled, the poverty-stricken populace was still a threat.

To give the suffrage to tramps, to paupers, to men to whom the chance to labour is a boon, to men who must beg, or steal, or starve, is to invoke destruction. To put political power in the hands of men embittered and degraded by poverty is to tie firebrands to foxes and turn them loose amid the standing corn; it is to put out the eyes of a Samson and to twine his arms around the pillars of national life. (ibid., pp. 376–7)

Democracy was that fragile. Its tendency to incorporate the masses in political processes that were largely ignored by those more concerned to accumulate wealth through exploitation meant that, if the masses were poor and the few still wealthy, society would become morally and politically bankrupt.

Without a democratic political economy based upon the Single Tax, the values that had inspired the republican idea were meaningless. What was true of America was also true elsewhere. 'The condition of the masses in every civilised country is, or is tending to become, that of virtual slavery under the forms of freedom' (George, 1937, pp. 250–1). Private ownership of land and a capitalist economy geared to the goal of rising material prosperity conspired to create a class of poor, underprivileged and spiritually deprived citizens. A new kind of servitude had arrived:

our boasted freedom necessarily involves slavery, so long as we recognize private property in land. Until that is abolished, Declarations of Independence and Acts of Emancipation are in vain. So long as one man can claim the exclusive ownership of the land from which other men must live, slavery will exist, and as material progress goes on, must grow and deepen. (ibid., p. 254)

These fundamental relationships of land ownership, wealth, progress and poverty had to be worked out in the context of a new dedication to republican values which recognized the democratic economic imperative.

We did not establish the Republic when we flung the declaration of the inalienable rights of man in the face of principalities and powers; we shall never establish the Republic until we practically carry out that declaration by securing to the poorest child born among us an equal right to his native soil! We did not abolish slavery when we ratified the Fourteenth Amendment; to abolish slavery we must abolish private property in land. (George, 1937, p. 281)

This was Henry George's utopia. 'What I stand for', he said in a speech made just before he died, 'is the equal rights of all men' (George, 1966, p. 224). Jefferson resurgent.

Edward Bellamy (1850–1898)

In the meantime, Edward Bellamy had provided another version of a democratic utopia in *Looking Backward, 2000–1887* (1888). Like George he addressed the problem of devising an economic order suitable to the democratic purpose. For Bellamy, economics just like politics had to have a secure moral foundation if it was to be styled democratic. Economic theory should at least offer the prospect of equality, and economic and industrial institutions, like their political counterparts, should be designed with ideals in mind.

Free-enterprise capitalism did not do this, but Bellamy offered an alternative which he thought could come about through permeation and social osmosis, as people realized the true nature of the existing regime. Reconstructing 'history' from the vantage of the year 2000, he predicted that 'the outcry against the concentration of capital was furious. Men believed that it threatened society with a form of tyranny more abhorrent than it had ever endured' (Bellamy, 1960, pp. 51–2). Shades of Henry George. This was because the capitalists of the late nineteenth century had pursued their own narrow self-interest at the expense of the community.

Bellamy's proposal for the transformation of this society – in effect the creation of a more democratic political economy – owed little to the individual. Instead, utopia involved a rampant collectivism, a blend of militarism and state control which some critics claimed ultimately defeated the very value of democratic liberty it sought to preserve. The future vision was constructed thus: 'when the nation became the sole employer, all the citizens, by virtue of their citizenship, became employees, to be distributed according to the needs of industry' (Bellamy, 1960 p. 57). Industrial conscription ensured the greater good.

Dr Leete, who explains the vision to his protagonist from 1887, Julian West, claims that 'now that industry of whatever sort is no longer self-service, but service of the nation, patriotism, passion for humanity, impel the worker as in your day they did the soldier' (Bellamy, 1960, p. 77). The trade-off for this apparent sublimation of individuality is that all industrial effort is geared towards the benefit of the community. It exploits itself for its own benefit. Or in Bellamy's words: 'a form of society which was founded on the pseudo self-interest of selfishness, and appealed solely to the anti-social and brutal side of human nature, has been replaced by institutions based on the true self-interest of a rational unselfishness, and appealing to the social and generous instincts of men' (ibid., p. 184). Bellamy hoped that the Madisonian idea of public virtue aided by an institutional system which held in check the infinite capacity for abuse through self-interest might be recreated in the economic sphere, as the nation employed itself in gearing self-interest to the common good.

It might appear that Bellamy is prepared to sacrifice the individual's claim to freedom of choice: that the beguiling prospect of economic equality obscures the regimentation of free will that this new industrial order apparently demands. Or have his critics often missed the point? Taking his side for a moment, the essence of his utopia is co-operation. And this necessarily involves a sense of the equality of individual worth. As Dr Leete observes, 'unequal distribution of wealth, and, still more effectual unequal opportunities of education and culture, divided society in your day into classes, which in many respects regarded each other as distinct races' (Bellamy, 1960, p. 113). This situation is the antithesis of Whitman's democratic ideal, where an integrating culture weaves society together, uniting it in a common cause. The differential in wealth and the divisions in society make the prospects of true democracy at most shaky and at least unlikely. Bellamy emphasizes the point: 'to educate some to the highest degree, and leave the mass wholly uncultivated . . . made the gap between them almost like that between different natural species, which have no means of communication' (ibid., p. 151). In such a situation social co-operation is impossible. However, once equality has been established in all facets of economic and social life, the concept of a truly democratic community is no longer a mirage.

More significantly, in this new society, 'equal education and opportunity must needs bring to light whatever aptitudes a man has, and neither social prejudices nor mercenary conditions hamper him in the choice of his life work' (Bellamy, 1960, p. 101). Here Bellamy is advocating merely the idea of positive liberty in an egalitarian society: the individual pursuing unique talent to the extent of personal ability and capacity. Moreover, the ordinary worker does have options in the industrial army. A period of apprenticeship is served, admittedly in a job dictated by the co-operative interest of the community – the sort of social service that nowadays is offered in some countries as an alternative to military conscription – but then the individual is free within certain limits to decide on a career.

The difference is that there is order in the labour market. Incentives are manipulated to make jobs attractive, principally through variation in the hours of work, so as to equalize supply and demand for labour in any particular trade. Everyone can find a job that is equally satisfying: there are no problems over wage differentials, because there are no wages. Money is unnecessary since everyone has access to what they need from national storehouses. Impractical it may be, but does this utopia destroy liberty?

What Bellamy attempted was the substitution of rational planning and maximum efficiency for what he saw as the random relationships of supply and demand created in the free-market system. If this were seen as threatening liberty, his answer might have been further questions. Under capitalism, what kind of liberty did the ordinary worker have in terms of finding work that was both suitable and satisfying? Job satisfaction could be as much of a luxury in the free-enterprise system as it might appear to be in his ideal society. In addition, was it not a spurious kind of liberty that found its mature expression in unemployment?

Bellamy did not see a threat to liberty, or indeed to individualism, in his utopian experiment. In *Looking Backward* he contrasts his future society with contemporary America. He raises the spectre of Cooper's and de Tocqueville's qualitative and quantitative tyranny of the majority. Dr Leete claims that, to his generation, 'liberty is as dear as equality or fraternity', and that 'a government, or a majority, which should undertake to tell the people, or a minority, what they were to eat, drink, or wear, as I believe governments in America did in your day, would be regarded as a curious anachronism indeed' (Bellamy, 1960, p. 129). So co-operation need not mean compulsion or conformity, and equality need not imply uniformity.

It was simply that more could be achieved through the harmony of co-ordinated economic effort than through the cacophonous competition of the market-place. 'The difference between the age of individualism and that of concert was well characterized by the fact that in the nineteenth century, when it rained, the people of Boston put up three hundred thousand umbrellas over as many heads, and in the twentieth century they put up one umbrella over all the heads' (Bellamy, 1960, pp. 110–11). Bellamy's democratic political economy is such a metaphor.

Liberty and equality in contemporary American society were, to Bellamy, vacuous values. Like Whitman he appreciated that the society which eschewed them in the pursuit of material wealth was essentially mediocre. Literature and arts were sacrificed; 'the cultured society of the nineteenth century – what did it consist of but here and there a few microscopic oases in a vast unbroken wilderness?' (Bellamy, 1960, pp. 151–2). On the other hand, the democratic political economy set the people free, and 'there ensued an era of mechanical invention, scientific discovery, art, musical and literary productiveness to which no previous age of the world offers anything comparable' (ibid., p. 116). The fault of existing democracy, such as it was, was the 'old, crude and brutal economic system' (Phillips, 1898, p. 503) which held society back from the glittering prospect of republican values in action.

Many of Bellamy's arguments echo Henry George's analysis. The central point was that republican liberty could exist only once economic equality had been established. In *Equality*, written in 1897 as a sequel to *Looking Backward*, Bellamy returned to praise Jefferson as the democratic mentor of the nation, again following George's nostalgic vision. There is no doubt, however, which Jeffersonian sentiment is accentuated. The title is a give-away. 'As we look at it, the immortal preamble of the American Declaration of Independence, away back in 1776, logically contained the entire statement of the doctrine of universal economic equality guaranteed by the nation collectively to its members individually' (Bellamy, 1936, p. 16). Equality even more than liberty is the ethical basis of the republic, which might yet become a commonwealth. 'The primal principle of democracy is the worth and dignity of the individual. That dignity, consisting in the quality of human nature, is essentially the same in all individuals, and therefore equality is the vital principle of democracy' (ibid., p. 27).

On the other side of the coin was a 'structural weakness' in the democratic system. This was the tendency, as the quality of life came to be judged in material terms, for individuals, and indeed classes, to pursue a self-interest at the expense of the community. The result was a vicious circle: inequalities of wealth exacerbating selfishness, leading to corruption. The economic structure in America after the Civil War appeared to highlight this fundamental democratic contradiction: far from proving the compatibility of the goals of Jefferson's Declaration and capitalist enterprise, it evinced an inherent distinction between notional political equality and actual economic inequality, and between the natural right to liberty and the wage-slavery of the supposedly free market, which attracted both analysis and criticism. Whitman's democratic culture could not develop without a democratic political economy. Henry George and Edward Bellamy appreciated that.

Henry Demarest Lloyd (1847–1903)

So too did Henry Demarest Lloyd. More concerned with the descriptive than the prescriptive – *Wealth Against Commonwealth* (1894) was a meticulous and systematic exposé of the business practices of the Standard Oil corporation – Lloyd too saw that true democracy demanded an economic theory different from the prevailing orthodoxy. Like George, he saw a paradox, not in terms of poverty and progress but rather in the juxtaposition of two other concerns: although liberty produced wealth, wealth was destructive of liberty. Economic individualism and the freedom of the entrepreneur may have resulted in wealth for some, but only at the expense of the liberty of others.

This balked the development of a democratic culture since such progressive concentration of wealth was an insidious force subverting republican values. As Lloyd observed: 'monopoly cannot be content with controlling its own business. The same law has always driven the tyrant to control everything – government, art, literature, even private conversations'. It was a familiar argument, since 'in all ages wealth has found that it must rule all or nothing . . . Hence we find it in America creeping higher every year into the seats of control' (Lloyd, 1936, p. 234). Once economic power could buy political influence, the victory was all but complete.

The lobbyists of the business corporation were thus active in the institutions of democratic government and were able to use wealth to 'force the nomination of judges who will construe the law as Power desires, and of senators who will get passed such laws as it wants for its judges to construe' (Lloyd, 1936, pp. 234–5). Standard Oil had done everything to the Pennsylvania state legislature except 'refine it'. The corporation had pocketed democracy.

Taking issue with such practices, Lloyd moved on to attack the theories underlying the economic orthodoxies of *laissez-faire* capitalism. 'Institutions stand or fall by their philosophy, and the main doctrine of industry since Adam Smith has been the fallacy that the self-interest of the individual was a sufficient guide to the welfare of the individual and society' (Lloyd, 1936, p. 330). Such self-interest was the equivalent of political anarchy. It was as if economic man had not advanced beyond the state of nature: the war of all against all which civilized society attempted to avoid. No economic social contract had been negotiated. To Lloyd, 'it was one of the paradoxes of public opinion that the people of America, least tolerant of this theory of anarchy in political government lead in practising it in industry' (ibid., pp. 332–3). The basic mismatch emerged between the accepted norms of the economic and the political spheres.

Henry Lloyd deliberately recast the vision of true economic democracy in the rhetoric which had inspired the political idealism of the republic. 'We got republican liberty by agreeing each with the other never to seek to become kings or lords or dukes. We can get industrial and economic liberty only by a like covenant never to let ourselves or anyone else be millionaires' (Lloyd, 1936, p. 359).

There are shades of both Madison and Lincoln in *Wealth Against Commonwealth*. The republican genius of *The Federalist* is echoed in: 'democracy is not a lie. There live in the body of the commonalty the unexhausted virtue and the ever refreshened strength which can rise equal to any problems of progress' (ibid., p. 366). And there is the reformulation of Lincoln's speech at Springfield:

> for as true as that a house divided against itself cannot stand, and that a nation half-slave and half-free cannot permanently endure, is it true that a people who are slaves to market-tyrants will surely come to be their slaves in all else, that all liberty begins to be lost when one liberty is lost, that a people half democratic and half plutocratic cannot endure. (ibid., p. 357)

The challenge remained. It was to eradicate 'corporate power and wealth and irresponsibility in the name of the commonwealth of democratic institutions' (quoted in Destler, 1946, p. 136). And it was a challenge bolstered by a faith in the inevitability of success. Social progress came in stages. Religious freedom and toleration had been a first step. Then freedom for the citizen represented through the political right of universal suffrage. Those two steps having been accomplished, the final step in the emancipation of the individual would be the attainment of economic freedom.

In an address at the Central Music Hall in Chicago on 6 October 1894, Lloyd explained that philosophy. 'No great idea is ever lost. The greatest of human ideas is democracy. It has often disappeared, but it has never been lost. We have democratized religion. We have nearly finished democratizing kings, and we are now about to democratize the millionaire' (quoted in Destler, 1946, p. 214). Such an all-encompassing vision offered the prospect of a democracy in which religious, political and economic institutions were in harmony rather than in a constant state of mutual suspicion. This 'co-operative commonwealth' would become 'the legitimate offspring and lawful successor of the republic' (quoted ibid., p. 218). For some the advance towards a democratic political economy became an act of faith. For Lloyd its achievement would be the result of a deterministic analysis of the inevitability of its success. He was essentially an optimist.

Lloyd joins George and Bellamy as representatives of a generation of social critics and commentators who appreciated that the Civil War had not brought about the abolition of slavery in all its forms. The short-term impact of their ideas was profound, even if nowadays they appear not to fit in with the dominant tradition of liberal democratic

107

thought, and their ideas tend to be dismissed as intellectual curios. George and Bellamy led a political movement – nationalism – which captured the imagination and the votes of a significant minority before it was absorbed in the larger concern of populism. Active in politics, George ran for mayor of New York in 1886 and did not come bottom of the poll. In fact he was more popular in that contest than Theodore Roosevelt (George, 1966, p. 223).

For a short time, therefore, 'nationalism', accompanied by 'socialism' and 'capitalism', was the everyday currency of political debate. In 1890 the *North American Review* suggested that after the tariff and the speakership – two issues of immediate economic and political concern – the two subjects uppermost in the public mind were 'probably Nationalism and electric lighting' (quoted in Morgan, 1974, p. 276). A new Enlightenment seemed likely. Lloyd, too, was politically influential. He inspired a generation of 'muck-rakers' who continued his journalistic investigations into the corrupt ethics of business. In the long term such practical effects dissipated: it is a self-evident truth that the republic did not become a commonwealth. Capitalism survived.

CONCLUSION

Was such criticism therefore misplaced? Were George, Bellamy, Lloyd and their supporters carried away by millenarian fervour as they argued to extend the liberal tradition of American democratic thought to embrace a socialism that was sometimes overt, sometimes inchoate? There can be little doubt that these Cassandras of contemporary democracy tended to overstate their case in an attempt to draw attention to the enormity of the challenge. It was easier to win converts by creating an atmosphere of crisis.

The recurrent theme in their writings is that American democracy was not so much in a state of malaise as facing Armageddon. If there was no democratic political economy – and by extension no democratic culture in the United States – liberty, equality, order and stability would submit to tyranny, plutocracy, anarchy and social unrest. What existed may have been mediocre, but nevertheless it was plunging towards catastrophe. Democracy had to triumph. There was no safety net across the abyss.

The prophecies proved inaccurate, for the worst did not happen. Democracy, or at least its political institutions, survived the Civil War and the developing industrial leviathan and struggled on into the twentieth century. Time made the apocalyptic arguments *passé*.

Similarly the deterministic edge to the analysis seems out-moded. A democratic culture built on political rights and material prosperity, or a democratic economy as the last part of a struggle against first religious and then political intolerance may have seemed logical progressions, but the fact remains that the republic did not become a commonwealth.

Both the belief that democracy faced a spiritual and a moral crisis, and the conviction that it might overcome it, were the product of a fundamental and shared conviction that Christian values were the basis of the true democratic ethic. Much of the rhetoric employed to argue the case was Biblical, and much of the optimism stemmed from an understanding that Christian morality would be the foundation of the new democratic order. In turn this made criticism of contemporary society all the more trenchant. For the perceived lack of morality, particularly in business practices but also in political behaviour, stood in stark contrast to the prospect of a democratic society suffused with the spirit of Christian beliefs and values.

It also meant that something had to be done. And the solutions seemed both obvious and simple once the problem had been diagnosed and analysed. Too obvious and too simple – Karl Marx denounced Henry George as '"utterly backward" in his analysis of modern capitalism' (quoted in Thomas, 1983, p. 181). George himself was moved to describe Bellamy's utopia as a 'castle in the air with clouds for its foundation' (quoted in Gabriel, 1956, p. 221). Elsewhere William Morris thought it 'a horrible cockney dream' (quoted in Parrington, 1930, vol. 3, pp. 311–12). The political, social and economic panaceas may have been mere placebos.

Did this mean that Whitman's vista of a democratic culture was equally idiosyncratic speculation? In a sense it was. But the various communitarian experiments of the nineteenth century, inspired by 'secular utopian socialists', of which Brook Farm is the best-remembered example, showed that there was a desire to construct democratic commonwealths within the republic. This strand of socialist and humanitarian thought, often imported from Britain or France, wove its way through the American democratic tradition as it became part of the republican ethos.

Thus Horace Greeley, a publicist for the ideas of the French socialist Fourier, might have been anticipating Whitman and indeed the other social critics of the late nineteenth century when he wrote in the *New York Tribune* in 1851:

> If democracy be what we believe, it must have a wider and more
> perfect application. It must create a new social as well as a new

109

political system. It must reform the relations of labor, of property, and of social life, nor stop till all servitude, all castes, all inequality of privilege have disappeared to give place to integral liberty, justice and fraternal co-operative relations. (Quoted in Lunde, 1981, p. 17)

The message survived the Civil War. If democracy was to prove itself a viable form of government, then its ethos had to permeate all aspects of social existence, and not merely the political system which was its foundation. It had to have a point.

At the same time, the attempts to rationalize the existence of slavery in the *ante-bellum* period, as well as the later justifications of industrial capitalism in terms of the material success it brought to those who benefited from its profits, demonstrated that there was a powerful climate of competing opinion. Whereas the moral implications of the democratic ideal may have ultimately won through – if only as a result of the Civil War – the dominant ethos within the American democratic tradition appeared to eschew values except as they impinged upon the political rhetoric of the republic. Democracy was confined to a political strait-jacket: a political process, an end in itself. In economic terms, equality seen in terms of an equality of opportunity, and liberty viewed in terms of free enterprise, married capitalism to democracy. Only a few argued that such an interpretation of values was at odds with what they saw to be the Jeffersonian ideal. For them, to tolerate capitalism was the moral equivalent of condoning slavery in the south. Capitalist democracy was an oxymoron.

In the end it might become a question of ideology. Henry Lloyd believed that 'socialism is true democracy', and for those who argued the ethical case the inversion that 'true democracy is socialism' might have had more force, because it certainly scared their opponents (Dombrowski, 1936, p. 131). For if the claims that democracy had a moral, cultural and economic dimension were accepted then it could appear that in looking to their own tradition – the Declaration of Independence and the subsequent course of the republican experiment – Americans were socialists despite themselves.

The first fifty years had laid the foundations. It has been suggested that:

Despite the limitations of Jeffersonian and Jacksonian Democracy, they were an important part of the environment out of which a theory of modern socialism could emerge in the United States. They provided a powerful climate of industrial opinion hostile to significant aspects of industrial capitalism and many of the elements from which a socialist theory could be built. (Harris, 1966, p. 7)

Jefferson and Jackson closet socialists? The identification of democracy with the ideology of socialism was at least controversial if not dangerous. And again it is too simple. For to promote such a case is to deny the force of that conservative 'liberal tradition' which is uniquely American. Liberty as a value cannot be ignored even if equality becomes the concern. De Tocqueville had described the dilemma. Those who look at the 'democratic faith' in ideological terms can become giddy in a theoretical maze.

The alternative idea of democracy as a useful political system avoids such ideological anguish. The notion of socialism as a foreign import rather than as a natural outcrop of America's own democratic values gained currency as the social critics failed to 'democratize the millionaire'. Indeed one of capitalism's major beneficiaries, Andrew Carnegie, in a saccharine panegyric written in 1886, and called convincingly *Triumphant Democracy*, was sure that socialist agitation could only be an unnatural and un-American activity.

> A Socialists' procession marches through the streets in Chicago, probably not an American in the array – a parcel of foreign cranks whose Communistic ideas are the natural growth of the unjust laws of their native land, which deny these men the privileges of equal citizenship, and hold them down as inferiors from their birth – and forthwith European papers alarm the timid and well-to-do masses of Europe by picturing this threatened assault upon property as the result of republicanism, the truth being that in no other country are the rights of property held so sacredly as in America. (Carnegie, 1886, p. 348)

American democracy did not require this kind of ideological overcoat.

So those who promoted the idea of the evolutionary necessity of the Gospel of Wealth had one interpretation of the nature of American democracy, and they confronted others who were inspired by a deterministic faith in a different message, backed by a religious conviction of its worth. But the two sides were not about to fight, even though the divide between them was as wide as that which had divided Douglas from Lincoln before the Civil War.

In another respect, Carnegie had a point. The European press could portray the apparent drawbacks of republicanism in action with relish. In Britain there was a tendency to deride the American democratic experiment, particularly as the Civil War seemed to confirm suspicions. In 1861 *The Times* pronounced:

> Far be it from us to dogmatize about democracy or to attribute the Civil War to republican institutions. The secession of the South is

certainly not a necessary result of any form of government. Yet it is not too much to say that the form which democracy has taken for the last thirty years, or since the Presidency of Jackson, was likely to lead to such a result. (*The Times*, 18 Oct. 1861)

Later, philosophizing on the American experience, the newspaper – part of the establishment which wanted the south to win – noted that 'every form of republican government wherever founded, has either ripened and consolidated into a constitutional monarchy, or, which is the commoner result, violently merged into absolutism. There is nothing peculiar to Americans to arrest the milder process, except a headlong leap into the worse'. (*The Times*, 2 Feb. 1863)

The implication was there. Britain was secure, for it was not then a republic. But *The Times* was wrong. The American republic did survive the Civil War. And indeed the impetus of the idea of democracy in Britain, not least because of American influence, meant that despite such lofty pronouncements the political and social establishment there had little about which to be complacent.

Part three

The democratic debate in Britain

CHAPTER 5

Preparing for Democracy: The British Constitution 1789–1832

In 1789, the year when George Washington took office as the first president of the United States, there was the start of major political and social upheaval in France. As Thomas Paine gleefully wrote, 'from what we now see, nothing of reform in the political world ought to be held improbable. It is an age of Revolutions, in which everything may be looked for' (Paine, 1969, p. 168). Towards the end of the eighteenth century, both America and France offered a republican prospect. And what of Britain? Throughout the nineteenth century the constitutional settlement there consistently denied such a vision. Despite change, the fundamental elements survived. The Crown, the House of Lords, and the House of Commons remained still to be seen through the dust of reforming activity.

The gradual development of political democracy in Britain in this period was inspired as much by a reaction against the progress of an egalitarian ethic in the United States and in Europe as by internal political pressures and events. Two ideas merged to give British democracy its characteristic nature: a dominant fear of revolutionary change on the one hand, and a complacent belief in the adaptive capacity of the 'matchless constitution' on the other. Democracy in Britain cannot be seen in isolation from the historical constitutional tradition of which, in the nineteenth century, it was so emphatically a part.

Debate about democracy became more pointed as the American and French Revolutions unfolded, and persisted through most of the following century. Arguably the discussion never died: its nature, like that of the constitution itself, merely changed. The stage was set in the 1790s, by Edmund Burke and Thomas Paine, among others. *Reflections on the Revolution in France* (1790) showed that Burke's concern was for Britain as much as it was for a European neighbour, and Paine, the itinerant peddler of revolutionary propaganda, assumed that one of *The Rights of Man* (1791–2) was the right of reply.

Polemic then gave way to philosophy. Jeremy Bentham's utilitarianism was the precursor, or at least a most formidable example, of nineteenth-century liberal rationalism, and when applied to political matters it prescribed a democratic injection to cure the diagnosed sickness of the contemporary constitutional system. The utilitarian critique of government, with James Mill its most eminent publicist, was hit by Lord Macaulay's counterblast, as the defenders of the status quo moved to the attack. Squabbling over the nature of the constitution continued, until the 1832 Reform Act gave practical point to the argument. The grounds of discussion changed. The framework of the balanced constitution and mixed government was broadly accepted by political theorists and practising politicians alike. The problem remained, however, as to the composition of its democratic element.

The nature of the British constitution in the late eighteenth and early nineteenth century was thus open to different interpretations. Yet a basic issue remains. What was this constitution about which there was so much debate? There was no document. The British constitution remained unwritten. But there were some constitutional principles, and more significantly there was a particular Whig theory of constitutional change which was based upon a conservative analysis of its historical evolution. It was in this context that the democratic idea advanced.

THE IDEA OF THE CONSTITUTION AND THE CONTINUITY OF CHANGE

It is not encapsulated in a single document. This fact alone can cause distress to students of the British constitution and to those who seek to explain it. Contrast it with America's. If Americans are tied by their democratic faith to a nostalgic vision first glimpsed in 1787, then, as one nineteenth-century British writer put it, the British constitution 'or the system and institutions under which we are governed, is a growth and not a manufacture; and consequently, more than in the case of any other nation, its history is expressive of the character and development of the people who possess it' (Medley, 1894, p. 4). The absence of a single document, however, is useful. For the idea of the constitution in this as in any period can be reinterpreted and reinvented according to the demands of the moment.

By the late eighteenth century, British constitutional theory had come to rest upon the concepts of mixture and balance, as well as upon the fundamental animating principle of parliamentary sovereignty. This meant that Parliament had become the pivot on which the constitutional system turned. In a society divided into three broad social and political strata – the monarchy, the aristocracy and the democracy – that one institution was where their functions and powers were fused and blended to achieve a vaunted and valued constitutional stability. The king in Parliament – *rex in parliamento* – was the ideal.

Although there might be a notional separation of powers between the executive and the legislature, the fact that Parliament was where those powers were melded meant that the possibility existed for the executive to dominate the legislature. Nevertheless, the Crown, the House of Lords and the House of Commons were supposed to check and balance each other in an eternal triangle of mutual control. At least that was the theory. It was a system of government which seemed enviably safe and secure, and which preserved for its citizens the value of liberty. Foreigners such as Voltaire, Montesquieu and Delolme had revelled in the merits of the British constitution (see Voltaire, 1734; Montesquieu, 1748; Delolme, 1789).

The principle of parliamentary sovereignty had not been established without a long struggle. It had competed with another doctrine, that of the divine right of the monarch to rule. The course of that contest could be charted and used to promote a major constitutional myth. This romanticized account of the past was accentuated by Whig historians as Paine's 'age of Revolutions' became infectious in Europe. The myth became the essence of a simple and convenient theory of constitutional adaptation: because change had been achieved peaceably in the past, it would be so in the future. The idea of the constitution could be expressed through a sense of the continuity of change. The strength of the adaptive capacity of the constitutional tradition, it could be argued, lay in the way in which radical departures from existing conventions were not to be seen as revolutionary shifts in direction so much as part of a continuous process of organic growth and development.

Britain's constitution changed constantly with circumstance. It was plastic, malleable, adaptable within the limits of tradition and convention. Some of it indeed was written down. It was just that it was written in various places and at various times, when exigencies of the moment demanded the codification of precedent. If it represented a historic accommodation between the king, the Lords and the Commons, the history of its evolution traced the changing nature of the relationship within the triumvirate. The Whig interpretation of that development, which found its expression in the nineteenth century

117

in such works as Macaulay's *History of England* (1848), offered an image of constitutional adaptation which could be believed with a sense of satisfaction, if not self-delusion.

For a constitutional historian who was searching for documents, Magna Carta could be a convenient find. In 1215 the monarch's power was limited as a result of aristocratic demands. Magna Carta became a symbol of the constitution's capacity to give some protection to individual liberties in the face of executive tyranny. But the royal prerogative remained and the king could claim a divine right to rule. Most of his subjects had faith in the doctrine under which potentially absolute authority could be exercised. So a contradiction emerged between the constitutional ideal of a limited monarchy which could be traced to the document – the monarch ruling with consent, through a Parliament in which Lords and Commoners found some degree of representation – and the doctrine of absolute monarchy based upon divine right. The tension between monarchs who claimed that right and other sections of the community who saw that this could impinge on their liberties could be seen in the subsequent history of constitutional development.

During the seventeenth century the constitution broke down. The doctrinal tussle between the principles of divine right and parliamentary sovereignty culminated in the Civil War. Continuity could be preserved only after severe dislocation in convention, tradition and precedent. There was regicide, republic and restoration. It was hardly an era of stability, harmony or consensus. Nor in the end did it resolve totally the dilemma at the heart of the constitution. The power of the monarchy was interrupted, not abnegated. Whig historians could emphasize the impact of the Cromwellian revolution by noting significantly that it had failed.

It was the so-called 'Glorious Revolution' of 1688 which finally resolved the issue. This:

> eliminated for ever from the English constitution the doctrines of the divine right of kings and the passive obedience of subjects. William III and his successors had a title to the throne that was merely statutory; they held their office provisionally, subject to their observance of the conditions laid down in the Bill of Rights and the supplementary Act of Settlement. (Hearnshaw, 1918, p. 138)

More documents indicated the extent of the constitutional upheaval. And more to the point the concept of parliamentary sovereignty finally supplanted the idea of the divine right of the monarch to rule. The philosophical justification was found, moreover, in such places as the works of John Locke.

For some constitutional historians, then, this period from Magna Carta to the 'Glorious Revolution' could be portrayed as an era in which fundamental changes took place within the constitution without – except for the interregnum – affecting its outward forms. The king's power was successively and successfully limited. And the restraint of the possibility of arbitrary monarchical power allowed the fulfilment of a right to individual liberty. In addition, not only was the 'matchless constitution' of the late eighteenth and early nineteenth century based upon the firm principle of parliamentary sovereignty, but a theory of constitutional change could be argued which accounted for the nation's political stability. In the climate of revolution and republicanism, the inference was clear. If the constitution was not broken, why mend it? There was no need to write it down. To do so, indeed, would be to invite catastrophe.

For Whig historians it was the 'Glorious Revolution' which had shaped the modern British constitution just less than a century before America, in reaction against the abuse of executive power it saw in Britain, rejected its colonial status and started to write its own documents. When Parliament assumed the right to decide who should occupy the British throne, the superstition that had surrounded the concept of monarchy was broken down. As Macaulay wrote in his *History of England*, this effectively placed the constitution on a firm foundation.

> For a really limited monarchy cannot long exist in a society which regards monarchy as something divine, and the limitations as mere human inventions. Royalty, in order that it might exist in perfect harmony with our liberties, must be unable to show any higher or more venerable title than that by which we hold our liberties. (Macaulay, 1967, vol. 2, p. 344)

The point about this revolution, then, was that it was a political rather than a social dislocation. It was dignified and peaceful. As Macaulay described it, it was 'noiseless' (quoted in Blaas, 1978, p. 118). It added to the mystique of continuity as it marked the triumph of one ancient precedent over another.

Certainly, to write down any more principles was unnecessary. Macaulay went on to assess the character of the achievement of the unchallenged convention of parliamentary sovereignty:

> The main principles of our government were excellent. They were not, indeed, formally and exactly set forth in a single written instrument; but they were to be found scattered over our ancient and noble statutes; and, what was of far greater moment, they had been engraven on the

119

hearts of Englishmen during four hundred years. (Macaulay, 1967, vol. 2, p. 376)

These principles, Macaulay claimed, established the individual's freedom and protection from acts of arbitrary governmental power, and they were enshrined in the basic laws of the nation. The conclusion was that 'a realm of which these were the fundamental laws stood in no need of a new constitution' (ibid.). Macaulay was writing of the seventeenth century with the nineteenth very much in mind.

He observed that 'it is because we had a preserving revolution in the seventeenth century that we have not had a destroying revolution in the nineteenth' (Macaulay, 1967, vol. 2, p. 380). In this remark is the key to an understanding of why it proved necessary to emphasize the historical weight of continuity, tradition and stability, which were taken to be the hallmarks of the constitution. By describing the adaptive ability of the constitution to meet new challenges by overturning old precedents and claiming new conventions as part of ancient traditions, historians like Macaulay attempted to find in their nation's history a defence against the incursion of new ideas such as democracy, republicanism and an equal right to liberty. If the constitution was protean, it might endure without changing its outward forms: instead merely periodically admitting a different emphasis on the relationships which existed within it.

Macaulay thus reiterated a view which had been expressed from at least the late eighteenth century onwards. There was a kind of support for the constitution which was unswerving in its admiration not only for its principles but also for the way in which change was controlled and stability maintained. In 1798 the *Anti-Jacobin Review and Magazine* was one source among many which could claim, perhaps not unexpectedly, that 'whatever scribblers may assert, England possesses the most stable, firm and best known *constitution* in the universe – *the existing law of the day*, the *res constituta*, established by the wisdom of the King and his Parliament' (*Anti-Jacobin Review*, 1798, vol. 1, p. 470). And yet the contemporary influence of new ideas was not confined to America and Europe alone.

American arguments did indeed have an impact on radical thought in Britain. The received wisdom of the Whigs' interpretation of the constitution could be challenged. Moreover, their concept of continuous adaptation in the past need not be relevant in the present. The main radical criticism had been heard across the Atlantic. Having established the principle of parliamentary sovereignty, Britain had still not developed sufficient controls over the authority of the executive – the king – in the legislature – Parliament – mainly because that institution, or at least the House of Commons, did not adequately represent the nation.

Neither was an interpretation of history an adequate philosophy of constitutional change. Peaceful adaptation through a sense of continuity with the past need not be a guide to immediate action. The culmination of tradition in the establishment of the unchallenged principle of parliamentary sovereignty could, indeed, sow the seeds of future instability. De Tocqueville argued, with a germ of insight, that once it was accepted that Parliament was sovereign the British constitution ceased to exist. The implications of that idea could be traced along a worrying line of analysis. A parliament – any parliament – had the power to reinvent and recreate the rules of the constitutional game. It alone could make the laws, and there existed no countervailing power to question their constitutional propriety. There was indeed no single document by which to measure their validity.

The paradox was clear. Although there was no formal amendment process, the constitution was in effect under threat of constant amendment as it became what Parliament said it was. There were of course notional checks: the tradition of common law, established statute, convention and precedent. All might act as constraints, but in the end the only real barrier to constitutional change was an assessment of what could be considered possible. A sense of self-discipline was essential.

The constitution's critics, not least the Americans, argued that by the end of the eighteenth century such self-discipline had broken down. The theoretical balance of the system had been disturbed. The executive, in the form of the monarchy, had come to dominate the legislature. In such a situation, there was no protection against arbitrary acts of executive power. The flexible constitution hence was brittle. The liberties of the individual were preserved only because they were not violated: not because they could not be abused if the king through Parliament so chose. And with the monarch dominating Parliament, the opportunity to threaten liberty was a temptation which was difficult to resist.

It was no good arguing, moreover, that since parliaments were composed of representatives of the people, the chance of their allowing such an infringement of liberty was unlikely: that turkeys would not vote for an early Thanksgiving in America or an early Christmas in Britain. Who represented the people? And which people were represented? During the eighteenth century the aristocracy, by virtue of their nobility, had a voice in the House of Lords, but their

121

natural instinct, it was suggested, was to side with the monarch rather than with the people. On the other hand the House of Commons was elected on a restricted franchise, in unequal constituencies, at corrupt and often uncontested elections. The issue of constitutional reform without revolution could thus be articulated best in terms of the need radically to overhaul the nation's representative system. In turn the impact of the ideal of democracy was seen in terms of the assumption of the basic right to vote.

That simple idea of participation through an extension of the right to vote was in itself a remarkable departure from constitutional tradition and convention. As there was no precedent to guide, opponents of such a reform could suggest that balance, instead of being restored, might still be disturbed if power oscillated away from the king towards the representatives of the people. If Parliament was sovereign, and the House of Commons could claim an increased legitimacy and independence within the constitutional structure through representing a wider cross-section of the community, then the representatives of the people could annex the determination of public policy. Furthermore, once the principle of an equal right to vote was conceded, then the majority of those representatives might be elected by the working classes. If they imitated the monarch, and followed a natural propensity to rule in their own interests, they might trample on the liberties of others. That was the fear in the nineteenth century.

An irony emerges. On the one hand it could be argued that a single written document was to be avoided, as it was not in keeping with the idea of the constitution and the theory of the continuity of change. Besides, to contemporaries it smacked of revolution and republicanism. On the other hand a written constitution could have guaranteed liberties which might be threatened by parliamentary sovereignty and the dominance of the executive in the legislature. It could have diluted the impact of a potential working-class government. Liberty might not be swamped by the flood-tide of egalitarianism. The rejection of the idea of a written constitution with an established amendment procedure made the problem of representative reform – the problem of democracy in Britain – infinitely more complex.

In this atmosphere, to promote the myth involved in the Whig interpretation of constitutional history was one way of defusing demands for radical change. Such an analysis was a consistent theme in nineteenth-century publications and periodicals. Macaulay's work was an important contribution. Again, also in 1848, when revolution in Europe was once more a contagious concern, Henry Rogers, writing in the *Edinburgh Review*, sounded a familiar warning:

> Abundant experience proves that it is quite a mistake to suppose that the sudden introduction of even a better constitution will necessarily carry with it that great element of all political excellence – *Stability*; . . . such stability is founded less upon ideas of theoretical perfection than upon association and habit. (Rogers, 1848, p. 367)

Tradition was to remain the only right guide to action.

Democracy thus arrived in nineteenth-century Britain within the context of a particular and unique constitutional tradition, which gave rise to a two-stage debate. The first step was to establish an idea of the constitution which emphasized the historical advantages of the continuity of change. This was to deflect the revolutionary republican impetus triggered by events in America and France. The need for a written constitution was avoided by this argument, but it left the political structure of the nation vulnerable to the potential impact of reform in the shape of an extension of the right to vote. The second step was thus to manage such change so that the historic 'balance' of the constitution, tilted in favour of the monarchy in the eighteenth century, was not overwhelmed by working-class representation in the legislature in the nineteenth. With an appreciation of that process of discussion, the initial arguments can be traced through an exposition of the views of Edmund Burke and Thomas Paine.

EDMUND BURKE AND THOMAS PAINE: REFORM AND REVOLUTION

At the close of the eighteenth century, Britain's balanced constitution and the idea of mixed government, while still commanding the respect of many of its citizens as well as that of some European theoreticians for the ingenious way it appeared to combine intellectual freedom and civil liberties with Hobbesian undertones and Lockean prescriptions, was nevertheless rejected elsewhere as a practical guide. The aim of the constitution was to dissipate a concern about the possibility of arbitrary government. But Americans had pointed to it as the abuse which had triggered their demand for independence. Constitutional critics thus argued that practice fell short of the ideal. Yet the theory and the tradition in Britain continued to incorporate a profound belief in their own superiority.

It was precisely this tradition which Burke set out to defend. The Revolutions in America and, more especially, France had destroyed existing constitutions in the name of republicanism and had attempted to recreate them on a foundation of natural rights. But liberty and equality could not be mixed or balanced with hierarchy. Burke's intention, then, was to demonstrate that 'what was done in France was a wild attempt to methodize anarchy; to perpetuate and fix disorder' (Burke, 1850, p. 495). Britain should not import the experience. Rather, the British constitution, the embodiment of the organic state, and the symbol of the historic continuity and traditions of the nation, must be preserved. Any attempt to destroy it and re-establish political society according to some rationalist presuppositions or premises of natural rights was not only mistaken. It was plain wrong.

In this way, Burke wrote:

> our political system is placed in a just correspondence and symmetry with the order of the world, and with the mode of existence decreed to a permanent body composed of transitory parts; wherein, by the disposition of a stupendous wisdom, moulding together the great mysterious incorporation of the human race, the whole, at one time, is never old, or middle aged, or young, but, in a condition of unchangeable constancy, moves on through the varied tenor of perpetual decay, fall, renovation, and progression. (Burke, 1910, pp. 31–2)

The grandiloquent prose was clearly prescriptive. Revolution remained outside the orbit of Burke's conservative planet. Democratic developments might take place within the nation, but only on terms consistent with its principles. Foreign examples should so remain.

Burke was no democrat and still less a republican. He indulged in a scathing attack on those in Britain who had suggested that the French experience might prove relevant to British domestic politics. In particular, a sermon from Dr Richard Price, delivered to members of the Revolution Society – formed to commemorate the Glorious Revolution of 1688, when the country had to some extent forgotten its commitment to tradition and continuity – drew his most damning criticism.

In castigating Price, Burke was attacking one of the more notable radical dissenters of the period. Price had been active in the cause of reform, and had established a considerable reputation abroad. He had 'won fame in Europe and America as a political pamphleteer especially in defence of the American revolutionaries in their struggle for independence and in celebration of the opening events of the French Revolution' (Thomas, 1977, p. vii). Posterity has been as kind to Price's reputation as Burke was – a reflection, perhaps, of the impact of the latter's book and its denouncement of the radical case.

Price's assertions – that the people had the right to choose who governed them, that governers might be held accountable by the governed, and that the people could choose the form of government they wished – while eminently democratic, amounted according to Burke to 'a new and hitherto unheard of bill of rights'. Such a charter could be taken to undermine one bastion of constitutional practice: the hereditary monarchy. The monarchy, for Burke as for others, was the living manifestation and the enduring source of the stability of the British constitutional and political system. The concept of succession – despite what had been achieved in 1688 – was paramount. There could be no right to elect kings, as succession ensured continuity, and on the certainty of the hereditary principle 'the unity, peace and tranquillity of this nation doth, under God, wholly depend' (Burke, 1910, pp. 14–17). Monarchs were essential not least because they remained at the pinnacle of a social pyramid in the secular world, as God remained the ultimate arbiter in the spiritual one. Both the Deity and the monarchy inspired a deference, which thus became evident throughout the nation's hierarchy. 'We fear God; we look up with awe to kings; with affection to parliaments; with duty to magistrates; with reverence to priests, and with respect to nobility' (ibid., p. 83).

Decapitating the body politic would destroy such a neat definable order and so disrupt the essential balance. Equipoise was everything. Burke assured the British people that 'we are resolved to keep an established church, an established monarchy, an established aristocracy and an established democracy, each in the degree it exists and in no greater' (Burke, 1910, p. 88). Democracy on its own was not to be recommended, as the Greeks had correctly advised. 'If I recollect rightly, Aristotle observes, that a democracy has many striking points of resemblance with a tyranny' (ibid., p. 121). That was to be avoided. France was pursuing an inappropriate path and would be better advised to import British political practices than export a revolutionary tendency. Burke at least was in no doubt: 'I wish my countrymen rather to recommend to our neighbours the example of the British constitution, than to take models from them for the improvement of our own' (ibid., p. 243).

The extent to which Burke castigates not only the supporters of the French in Britain but also the revolutionaries themselves gives some indication of the seriousness with which he viewed the problem. America had adopted a republican constitution. France had pursued a revolutionary one. Britain might not be far behind. As Burke had suggested in a parliamentary speech made on 9 February 1790, there was a concern lest Britain might be induced 'through an admiration of successful fraud and violence, to an imitation of the excesses of an irrational, unprincipled, proscribing, confiscating, plundering, ferocious, bloody, and tyrannical democracy' (quoted in Thomas, 1977, p. 313).

The defence, then, was both necessary and appropriate, but it merely served to stir the controversy. For some, America and France remained captivating visions of what might be achieved elsewhere. Their self-appointed spokesman was Thomas Paine. He replied to Burke, and tried to set fire to the 'matchless constitution'. *The Rights of Man* was a charter for republican democracy. Whereas Burke excoriated republicanism, Paine expatiated on its merits. But more especially he argued that the people had every right to break with the past, to reconstruct their political world afresh and to deny that continuity and tradition which Burke had seen as so important. 'Every age and generation must be as free to act for itself, *in all cases*, as the ages and the generations which preceded it. The vanity and presumption of governing beyond the grave is the most ridiculous and insolent of all tyrannies' (Paine, 1969, pp. 63–4).

If the people wanted a republic now, they should not feel constrained by atavistic affection for monarchy. Paine's world was immediate, the past and the future irrelevant. Nothing was fixed, and constitutions could be reconstituted. In this way, 'a law not repealed continues in force not because it *cannot* be repealed, but because it *is not* repealed: and the non-repealing passes for consent' (Paine, 1969, p. 66). This view must naturally lead to the conclusion that 'as the present generation of people in England did not make the Government, they are not accountable for any of its defects' (ibid., p. 153). And the most immediate defect was the very institution which Burke had triumphantly defended – the monarchy.

Paine hated monarchs. He thought, moreover, that the institution which had inspired America to fight a revolutionary war had been shown by the French to be *passé*. 'What is this metaphor called a crown, or rather what is monarchy? . . . It appears to be a something going much out of fashion, falling into ridicule, and rejected in some countries both as unnecessary and expensive' (Paine, 1969, pp. 146–7). There was an alternative, based on a philosophy of natural rights, a belief in rationalism and, most obviously, the example of America. 'The independence of America, considered merely as a separation from England, would have been a matter but of little importance, had it not been accompanied by a revolution in the principles and practice of governments' (Paine, 1969, p. 181).

Republican government, involving the democratic principles of election and representation, had successfully replaced government by hereditary succession. The former was based on reason, the latter on ignorance. To Paine the choice was clear: 'government on the old system, is an assumption of power, for the aggrandisement of itself; on the new, a delegation of power, for the common benefit of society' (Paine, 1969 p. 193). Given the chance, as they had been given it in America and in France, the people should adopt the republic on the grounds of reason, liberty and justice.

The broad outline of this controversy over constitutions is thus clear: suspicion of radical change versus a principled case for it. According to Burke, 'rage and phrensy will pull down more in half an hour, than prudence, deliberation, and foresight can build up in a hundred years' (Burke, 1910, p. 164). According to Paine, 'when we survey the wretched condition of man under the monarchical and hereditary systems of Government . . . it becomes evident that those systems are bad, and that a general revolution in the principle and construction of Governments is necessary' (Paine, 1969, p. 165).

Reflections on the Revolution in France was published in London on 1 November 1790, and 'created something of a sensation in the literary and political world'. Not surprisingly, given the general drift of its argument, George III was reported to have suggested that every gentleman should read it. It sold 7,000 copies in the first week of publication (Fennessy, 1963, p. 1). *The Rights of Man*, published in two parts in 1791 and 1792, made a similar impact in different circles. It has been described as 'one of the most influential pieces of political journalism that ever was written in English. It brought politics to the people at a moment when the people were ready to come to politics' (ibid., p. 244). The importance of Paine lay in the way in which he mobilized public opinion, particularly among the working classes.

They did not necessarily have to agree with his point of view – deference was a deeply ingrained habit of mind – but at least they might talk about it. *The Rights of Man*, it has been suggested, 'did not, indeed, bring about a revolt of the workers, but it served the workers well as a sort of elementary political text-book which they could use as a basis for discussion, and a starting point of their political education' (Fennessy, 1963, p. 247). Despite this, in practical terms, Burke's view prevailed. There was no attempt to imitate the French revolution in Britain, nor was there any serious effort to recast contemporary government and the constitution on the principles which Paine argued were at the heart of the French and American revolutionary experiences.

At least, that was the case as far as the 'political establishment' was concerned. It is necessary, however, not to underestimate the force of sympathetic sentiment in favour of the French Revolution, which contributed to extra-parliamentary agitation. The Society for Constitutional Information, which Burke had dubbed a 'poor charitable club', was active in its support for the principles of revolutionary constitutional change, along with other organizations such as the London Corresponding Society. The king, as well as the government under the younger Pitt, thought that such francomania went beyond the pale: the papers of both societies were seized in 1794, and they were investigated in both Houses of Parliament by committees concerned with seditious practices.

These Societies were attempting nothing less, it was alleged, than 'the subversion of the established constitution'. Among strands of evidence adduced in support of this allegation was the fact that the Society for Constitutional Information had recorded its approval of 'the intention of publishing a cheap edition of the first and second parts of the Rights of Man' (*Parliamentary History*, 1794, vol. 31, col. 476). Republicanism was in the air. The government became jittery and acted to suspend habeas corpus and quash the plot. Pitt himself had no doubt that the principles outlined by Paine lay behind the supposed sedition.

> This whole system of insurrection would appear . . . to be laid in the modern doctrine of the rights of man; – that monstrous doctrine, under which the weak and ignorant, who are most susceptible of impression from such barren abstract positions, were attempted to be seduced to overturn government, law, property, security, religion, order and everything valuable in this country, as men acting upon the same ideas had already overturned and destroyed everything in France, and disturbed the peace and endangered the safety, if not the existence, of every nation in Europe. (ibid., cols. 498–9)

In the House of Lords debate on the Habeas Corpus Suspension Bill the idea of the rights of man was again the ghost at the feast. The Societies 'began their operations by endeavouring to corrupt the minds of the lower classes of the public, by disseminating pamphlets, containing the whole of their system'. Paine's cheap edition was among such agit-prop and 'here was the foundation of that system which had since ripened into treasonable practices by subsequent proceedings' (*Parliamentary History*, 1794, vol. 31, col. 576). There was intense suspicion of the potential of these subversive ideas to capture the minds of the people. It had happened elsewhere, and Britain was even prepared to fight a war with France on the pretext that it might put its adversary back on the path of sane constitutional practice, and stop the contagion from spreading.

At least that was how Pitt presented the case in the debate in Parliament in May 1794 following hard on the heels of the suspension of habeas corpus, when Fox suggested that the French war should be ended. Pitt argued, 'we have no desire to conquer France: we wish only to free it from a system of tyranny equally oppressive to itself and dangerous to its neighbours' (*Parliamentary History*, 1794, vol. 31, col. 648). This appears as an antediluvian Truman doctrine, incorporating a sense of constitutional self-righteousness with a suspicion of France as an eighteenth-century domino.

Hence Paine's case was viewed with abject disdain whereas Burke's sentiments undoubtedly struck a responsive chord in Parliament. In the second report of the secret committee of the House of Lords respecting seditious practices, the case against radicalism was forcefully put, in terms which Burke had previewed. To introduce a system of government based on the rights of man:

> necessarily implies the overthrow of all subordination in the state, the abolition of the established form of parliament, together with the destruction of hereditary monarchy, and the subversion of every safeguard which the wisdom of ages has established in this happy country for the peace and welfare of society, for the encouragement of industry, morality, and religion, for the protection of innocence and the punishment of vice, and for the secure enjoyment of property, of liberty, and of life itself. (*Parliamentary History*, 1794, vol. 31, col. 894)

Burke won the argument for the establishment. He 'deliberately provided the English with a political image of themselves which they could contemplate with satisfaction' (Fennessy, 1963, p. 252). The image could encourage complacency. Burke may have stood against a tide of rationalist revolutionary fervour, but he did so on a rock of carefully argued conservative logic. Paine was less rigorous. His idea that one generation could not bind another to any particular form of government lacked both sophistication and depth. There is no way of deciding the divisions between generations: history admits no artifice. More graphically, as one contemporary critic pointed out, 'the generations of men are not like crops of wheat or potatoes' (Elliot, 1791, p. 17). Paine was attempting to impose a freeze-frame on a continuous reel of experience – that very continuity which Burke had argued was natural, inevitable and ever-present.

More significantly, despite his contemporary impact, Paine remains relatively neglected in discussions of the development of British representative government. He should not be. His views, however misguided some may have been – and others retain an intuitive plausibility – were and are significant. For Paine, more than Burke, reflected the intellectual climate of his time, even if he remained a stranger to the dominant interpretation of British constitutional history. Burke did not share the common eighteenth-century belief that a new order could be imposed on society by the advance of individual reason. It was this rationalist ideal that continued to inform the philosophical tradition and provided the context for the evolution of liberal democratic theory in Britain, despite continued efforts to argue against its case. The constitutional debate between Burke and Paine becomes part of a continuing dialogue. The utilitarian reason of Jeremy Bentham provides another, no less important, strand.

JEREMY BENTHAM, JAMES MILL AND THE UTILITARIAN ALTERNATIVE

Bentham, utilitarian guru, wrote in the preface to his *Fragment on Government* published in 1776, as discontented Americans contested British rule, that there was a 'fundamental axiom'. '*It is the greatest happiness of the greatest number that is the measure of right and wrong*' (Bowring, 1962, vol.1, p. 227). Utilitarianism thus sought to examine the implications of that basic principle in the context of a moral and ethical framework that was all-encompassing, and in which politics and appropriate systems of government were but elements in the grander design. They were important parts. In Bentham's own writings the encroaching idea of democracy is pronounced. From the *Fragment on Government*, in which reforms within the contemporary constitutional context are suggested, he progressed, via the *Plan of Parliamentary Reform* (1827), to the *Constitutional Code* (1830) and the full-blooded embodiment of his 'ideal republic' (ibid., vols. 3, 9).

At first sight the 'greatest happiness' principle does not appear as a necessary and sufficient justification for democracy. The principle of utility, applied to politics, merely sets out criteria by which government might be assessed. The object of government becomes the promotion of the greatest happiness of the greatest number in the community, and its success or failure is decided according to its perceived ability to meet that objective. There is nothing inherently democratic in this. Each adherent to the principle of utilitarianism could maintain, at least in theory, that one or another form of government was in fact most suited to achieving the target of greatest happiness. An enlightened despotism, as long as it was committed to the utilitarian ideal, might be just as appropriate to it as a representative or a direct democracy. On the other hand, utilitarian principles came to be associated emphatically with notions of democracy, particularly after Bentham had been persuaded of the intellectual case in favour, and had become more and more convinced of the need to reform the 'matchless constitution'.

The *Fragment on Government* was a critique of Blackstone's *Commentaries on the Laws of England*. It was published in the same year that the Americans promulgated their Declaration of Independence. This is not to suggest, however, that Bentham rejected the foundations of British constitutional theory in favour of a transatlantic substitute, at least, not at this stage. Bentham 'regarded the American Declaration of Independence as so much "jargon" ' (Stephen, 1950, vol. 1, p. 289). The theory of natural rights left him cold. The idea, which Richard Price had taken up, that one such right was liberty, expressed in terms of self-government, appeared less than persuasive. Price had coined the slogan 'every man his own legislator', a piece of propaganda which irritated Bentham enough for him to reject the American case for self-determination entirely. As with Burke over France, Price succeeded in alienating Bentham over America. Bentham later observed: 'Dr. Price with his self-government made me an anti-American' (Hart, 1982, p. 61).

Price, again, and Thomas Paine figured in the demonology which influenced Bentham's attitude towards the French Revolution. But it was the trauma of the event itself which had the biggest impact on him. He observed the Revolution, and, as the violence it sponsored became ever more clear, 'it is not too much to say that he was frightened out of his wits. Like Burke and Wordsworth, he came, as Leslie Stephen said, to see the glare of hell in the light which others (Richard Price and Tom Paine among them) took to herald the dawn of the millennium' (Hart, 1982, p. 69). However, despite his antipathy to revolutions elsewhere, the insistent nagging of utilitarian logic led Bentham to adopt a democratic perspective on government. That, coupled with the evolution in America of a form of democracy that appeared stable, and seemed, despite the adoption of almost universal manhood suffrage, to secure the safety of property, brought about a *volte face*. America became the example.

In his *Plan of Parliamentary Reform*, written in 1809 but published eight years later, Bentham's vitriolic is reserved for the British constitution, while his plaudits are given to the United States. He inveighed against political inertia in Britain, which found it easier to resist changes – be they in prison design or constitutions – than encourage them. America proved his case:

Propose anything good; the answer is at hand: – wild, theoretical, visionary, Utopian, impracticable, dangerous, destructive, ruinous, anarchical, subversive of all governments – there you have it. Well, but in America there it *is*; and no such evil consequences – nothing but what is good, results from it. Aha! and so the United States government is your government, is it? – You are a republican, then, are you? – what you want is to subvert this constitution of ours; the envy of nations! the pride of ages! – matchless in rotten boroughs and sinecures! (Bowring, 1962, vol. 3, p. 437)

It was easy to mock. But changes, even if they were to occur within the existing constitutional order, still had to be justified. The utilitarian alternative, then, was closely argued, and it is simply expressed. The basic problem of government is to ensure that, in keeping with the 'fundamental axiom', it pursues the greatest happiness of the greatest number of its citizens. The solution is to create an identity of interest between government and governed. Government, like the individual, is self-interested. It may harm the general good when it appears to be in its own interest to do so. Only if the government and the communal interest are tied together can harm be avoided: logically the government is bound to pursue the public interest.

The issue then becomes: how can this identification of interest be achieved? Popular elections are necessary: the electoral constraint is powerful. Elections should also be frequent, possibly annual, to give full force to this sanction. Universal suffrage becomes a key idea: a government tethered by the electoral halter needs to pursue the interests only of those who have the vote. The case is made. In addition, Bentham argues, in order to make the best use of the power of the ballot, people should have free access to, and fullest publicity about, the various institutions of government. Popular and annual elections, universal suffrage and freedom of information were thus utilitarian prescriptions to promote an identity of interest between government and the people. That was utilitarian democracy.

It was emphatically not the form of the contemporary British system of representation. Hence change was necessary. In the utilitarian analysis can be detected the stirrings of a democratic liberal conscience. Even though Bentham, in 1809, did not seek to overturn the existing constitution his views still gave other constitutional theorists a headache. The need, as he perceived it, was for the establishment of a 'democratic ascendancy'. Given the tendency for the monarchy and aristocracy to ally for their own purposes against the people, the democratic element in the constitution had to be strengthened sufficiently to become an effective counter-weight. Reform should aim to give to the House of Commons the political capability to stand its ground opposed to the other branches combined.

> [W]ithout any outward and visible change in the forms of the constitutions . . . have the two separate, partial and sinister interests – viz the *monarchical* and the *aristocratical*, – obtained over the *democratical* interest (which is no other than the *universal* interest) not only an *ascendancy* – but an ascendancy so complete that, under the outside show of a mixed and limited monarchy, a monarchy virtually and substantially absolute is the result. (Bowring, 1962, vol. 3, p. 446)

Utilitarian reforms could remedy this. They were necessary on both theoretical and practical grounds. And to critics who might think his proposed changes excessive, Bentham's new slogan 'Look to America' offered a more extreme example of what he sought to achieve, with no worse effects. 'There, all is democracy: all is regularity, tranquillity, prosperity, security: . . . All, all is democracy: no aristocracy: no monarchy: all that dross evaporated' (Bowring, 1962, vol. 3, p. 447). The utilitarian reforms were far more circumspect, and could come about within the framework of the existing constitution. Bentham, in 1809, was no revolutionary.

If Bentham provided the bald outline of the moderate utilitarian case for democracy, before moving to the more extreme republicanism of the *Constitutional Code*, it was James Mill who was the best publicist for utilitarian ideas on government, and he has remained so. In a sense, Mill's was the more authoritative version, and it attracted at least equal obloquy. Encyclopedias are not usually meant to be controversial. Yet the supplement to the Encyclopedia Britannica which came out in 1820 contained Mill's *Essay on Government*, which was just that.

Even if the argument was familiar it need not have bred contempt, but critics were still not persuaded, and some nine years later Macaulay's reply to Mill's analysis was an attack on the whole rationale behind the utilitarian intellectual position. There is no denying, however, that Mill argued his position cogently, and presented the utilitarian version of democracy in a more accessible form than Bentham had: there is more than an appropriate filial admiration in John Stuart Mill's opinion of his father's essay, that it was regarded 'by all of us as a masterpiece of political wisdom' (Mill, 1873, p. 104).

James Mill naturally defined the object of government in terms of the 'greatest happiness' principle, but again to envisage an end was one thing, it was another to design a form. Mill thus devotes part of the *Essay on Government* to a discussion of various forms of government and the drawbacks inherent in each. He adopts a classic Aristotelian typology – the one which lies behind traditional British constitutional theories of mixed government and balance – in order to analyse such different structures in terms of how they might measure up to the utilitarian goal.

The magic number is three. Mill considers what he refers to as the democratical, the aristocratical and monarchical forms of government – the usual utilitarian nomenclature. Democracy in its pure sense is a practical impossibility since the community as a whole cannot constitute the government in itself. Some form of representative government is inevitable. Exit Rousseau. The community has to 'choose a certain number of themselves to be the actors in their stead' (Lively and Rees, 1978, p. 59). The aristocratical form of government, government 'by any number of persons intermediate between a single person and the majority' (ibid., pp. 59–60), is also open to criticism. Whereas the community cannot have an interest opposed to its own – since, by tautological definition, the community interest is the general interest – the aristocracy can. If given power, they may use it for their own ends and 'they will thus defeat the very end for which Government was instituted' (ibid., p. 61).

Monarchical government is open to a similar objection: Mill rehearses the familiar argument first advanced by the Greeks that there is always the temptation to pursue the private interest rather than that of the community as a whole. Monarchy is potentially corrupt to the extent that human nature is basically conditioned by the idea of self-interest. Government, indeed, is needed to arbitrate between and exercise control over self-interested individuals. As Mill suggests,

> whenever the powers of the Government are placed in any hands other than those of the community, whether those of one man, of a few, or of several, those principles of human nature which imply that Government is at all necessary, imply that those persons will make use of them to defeat the very end for which Government exists. (Lively and Rees, 1978, p. 61)

It is the classic dilemma of government: one faced by the Founders in America as well as utilitarians in Britain.

All three forms of government, as described by Mill, are imperfect. Following Bentham, he rejects the idea that the existing blend in the balanced constitution purges their defects while retaining their benefits. The balanced constitution is a myth. 'The Monarchy and the Aristocracy have all possible motives for endeavouring to obtain unlimited power over the persons and property of the community.' They conspire. Instead of being a merry-go-round, the constitution was a tug-of-war on quicksand, dragged down by the combined weight of monarchs and aristocrats pulling the community after them. 'The balance, therefore, is a thing, the existence of which, upon the best possible evidence, is to be regarded as impossible' (Lively and Rees, 1978, p. 72).

If the forms of government standing on their own have drawbacks, and if the union between them also retains imperfections, Mill's objective of good government appears to trickle away like so much constitutional dust through the fingers. Is government to achieve utilitarian ends thus impossible? Mill remains optimistic by following the utilitarian orthodoxy of the 'democratic ascendancy'. The House of Commons could become a constitutional counter-weight, if it were truly representative, elected frequently on the basis of a wider franchise.

Mill, like Bentham, advocated an extension of the right to vote. In the *Essay on Government* he argued against a favourite scheme of some reformers, who wanted to see the representation of classes in Parliament: this would merely lead to a 'motley aristocracy' (quoted in Stephen, 1950, vol. 2, p. 80). Instead he urged purely and simply that more people should have the right to vote, and his defence of this point of view offers an important insight into another aspect of utilitarian thought: the utility of education. One of the principal arguments against increasing the suffrage, apart from the general fear of giving the working class political power, was that the masses were, on the whole, too ignorant to exercise their right to vote. Mill accepted that argument but thought something could be done about it.

Ignorance is curable. There is no intrinsic reason why the people should not be trusted to judge for themselves in politics. Education is the antidote to ignorance: again rationalism is at the heart of the utilitarian case, but more especially clear is the link between democracy and reason – argued, too, in an implicit form by Paine. Mill considered that any difference between classes of men was ultimately due to differences in education, by which he meant socialization or the 'whole action of the "environment" upon the individual' (Stephen, 1950, vol. 2, p. 82).

There were four main elements in such education – domestic, technical, social and, finally, political education, 'the keystone of the arch' (quoted in Stephen, 1950, vol. 2, p. 82). Blended together, these elements opened the way for progress and for the responsible use of political power: 'teach the people and let them vote freely and everything would follow' (ibid., p. 83). There was thus no danger in the universal franchise, particularly when the education argument was linked to a further idea: the capacity of the middle class to act as exemplar and guide. The *Essay on Government* thus ends with a eulogy to the middle class.

'It is to be observed', Mill wrote, 'that the class which is universally described as both the most wise and the most virtuous part of the community [is] the middle rank.' Members of the middle class could promote utilitarian values. They contributed most to science, to art and to government itself. If the right to vote was extended, then 'of the people beneath them, a vast majority would be sure to be guided by their advice and example' (Lively and Rees, 1978, pp. 93–4). Mill concluded his essay with this panegyric, and retained the optimistic belief that it was among the middle class that the leaders and guides would be found to instruct the less fortunate in the ideals of representative government. Democracy would thus find its natural leaders among the educated and the intelligent – the two not being in every case synonymous.

LORD MACAULAY AND THE DEFENCE OF BALANCE

Mill had claimed that the *Essay on Government* would not be controversial. It was. The rejection of the idea of the balanced constitution, the criticism of the representation of interests or classes – a thinly veiled attack on the concept of 'virtual representation' – and above all the recommendation of a 'democratic ascendancy' and universal male suffrage all appeared alarming. Those opposed to the utilitarian argument stood their ground on a firm acceptance of the status quo, and could suggest that there was little to be gained from tilting at constitutional windmills.

They believed that the balanced constitution was not a myth, and if it was not a myth, if there was an acceptable equilibrium, then there was no need to establish a democratic ascendancy: it would not restore balance, it would disrupt it. In addition, if all was well with the constitution, little was to be gained from extending the right to vote. To do so might be to become hostages to the caprice of the lower class. The middle class might not be in control. There was the possibility that the ignorant would continue to ignore it, and that it would be 'swamped' as a result of giving the vote to the masses. Critics who had opposed Bentham's *Plan of Parliamentary Reform* thus found new allies hostile to Mill. The most notable attacks inevitably came from the Whigs, the most notorious from Lord Macaulay in the March 1829 issue of the *Edinburgh Review*.

According to Macaulay, Mill's theory 'rests altogether on false principles, and . . . even on those false principles he does not reason logically' (Lively and Rees, 1978, p. 99). The argument was essentially methodological. Politics was not, as Mill had assumed, deductive science, and the utilitarian approach on this basis was little more than ethereal musing, divorced from any understanding of the real world. Rationalism was highly suspect, as Burke had pointed out, and like him Macaulay placed faith in practical experience as a guide to political action. Of the *Essay on Government* he wrote, 'We have here an elaborate treatise on Government, from which, but for two or three passing allusions, it would not appear that the author was aware that any governments actually existed among men' (ibid., p. 101).

What Mill had done then was to assume that human nature exhibited certain qualities – in particular, self-interest – and from such initial premisses he had derived his political argument, oblivious to empiricism, and what actually occurred in the world outside the theoretical abstraction. Macaulay argued, on the other hand, that deductions based on *a priori* assumptions could not be applied to the study of governments, and indeed Mill was faced with a problem when empirical observation conflicted with professed belief and logic. Macaulay caught him out. Mill had observed that in Denmark the people had thrown out a government dominated by the aristocracy and had substituted an absolute monarchy, and were 'as well governed as any people in Europe' (Lively and Rees, 1978, p. 101). Yet he did not allow that fact to detract from his utilitarian theory, leaving him open to Macaulay's jibe that 'to believe in a theory *because* a fact contradicts it is what neither philosopher nor pope ever before required' (ibid., p. 102). Mill was thus too dismissive of empiricism because he was too committed to inductive theorizing.

The essence of Macaulay's criticism of Mill, however, goes beyond exploitation of faulty method. Rather, he is concerned to refute the idea that the balanced constitution is a myth. Monarchy and aristocracy do not always combine for sinister purposes. If the interests of the king are opposed to those of his people, it does not follow that they are identical with those of the aristocracy. Historically, Macaulay claims, there have been cases when sovereigns have allied themselves with the people against the aristocracy, and when the nobility has been at one with the people against the monarch. 'In general when there are three parties, every one of whom has much to fear from the others, it is not found that two of them combine to plunder the third' (Lively and Rees, 1978, p. 113). The notion of balance implies a constant jockeying for political power between the three elements of the constitution. Utilitarian theory locks two of these forever in constant opposition to the third. It is wrong on this point. 'That broad line of distinction which Mr. Mill tries to point out between monarchies and aristocracies on the one side, and democracies on the other, has in fact no existence' (ibid., p. 115).

Macaulay also disagreed with Mill on the fundamental question of who should have the right to vote. He thought that to extend the franchise would be 'to give the poor majority power over the rich minority' (Lively and Rees, 1978, p. 119), and that this would open the way for the poor to 'plunder' the rich. This whole argument implied that parliamentary power was irresistible, and as such it could be used for proper purposes, if retained in the hands of those who already controlled it, or improper ones, if it was let slip into the grasp of the people. There could be no justification for undermining the existing pattern of authority. Even if the 'greatest happiness' principle was applied, in which case, looking at the issue in purely quantitative terms, it might be suggested that the rich few should concede to the less prosperous many, Macaulay still argued that the intensity of suffering which is inflicted, as well as the number of sufferers, must be taken into account.

It is not enough, therefore, to justify a measure such as universal suffrage according to the ready-reckoner criterion of the greatest happiness of the greatest number: there is a qualitative impact which must also be recognized. In addition, the utilitarians fall into a similar pit as Paine, in assuming that the 'greatest happiness' principle can be applied to a single instant and a single generation. It cannot be shown that the interest of every generation is identical with the interest of all or any succeeding generations. It is a mistake to give the lower orders the vote for these reasons. To do so would be to invite them to abuse such power and 'plunder' the rich, and this would be unjust both on the grounds of intensity – the pips would really squeak – and because it might unfairly affect the fortunes of future generations.

CONCLUSION

By the beginning of the nineteenth century the idea of the British constitution had been rocked, first by the prospect of revolution ushering in a republican government, and then by the demand for political democracy in the shape of an extension of the right to vote. Critics attacked the inheritance of constitutional tradition as a hindrance to rational reform. On the other hand the cause of political stability was emphatic in its support for the constitution. So, when argument was joined, a radical and a conservative line of attack and defence were established.

Paine may have been optimistic about the prospects for revolution in Britain, given his experiences elsewhere, but Burke found comfort in the constitutional myth which proved the wisdom of the concept of change in continuity with the past. Bentham and Mill pursued a line of philosophical inquiry which rationalized reform within the existing structure of the constitution, but even this met with the scorn of those who had inherited the myths of the past and accepted them as a necessary part of the creation and maintenance of political stability.

Macaulay, like Burke, appreciated the importance of continuity, but also like Mill he had much esteem for the middle class. However, where Mill had looked to the middle class to train the lower orders in the arts of responsible government, Macaulay saw its members as joining an exclusive club. The vote stopped there. This was because 'the higher and middling orders are the natural representatives of the human race. Their interest may be opposed, in some things, to that of their poorer contemporaries, but it is identical with that of the innumerable generations which are to follow' (Lively and Rees, 1978, pp. 122–3). The assertion rests on nothing but an ingrained prejudice of class superiority, and a complacent belief in the enduring effectiveness of the existing political settlement. Indeed, in this light, the whole of Macaulay's critique appears soon to shade into a rationalization of the status quo, and certainly it did the cause of democratic government little service.

In the same way, Burke's theory of 'virtual representation' – the idea that interests in society which did not find a voice in Parliament could still be identified with similar interests elsewhere which did have that privilege – betrayed the innate conservatism of his disposition. The fundamental problem remained. The logic of democracy, as it implied an extension of the right to vote, could lead to political power moving from its traditional centres towards those who were seen by many in the nineteenth century as ill fitted to exercise it. British democratic theory had to respond to the challenges posed by the political illiterates of the working class.

The utilitarians, in recommending a 'democratic ascendancy' and a wider suffrage, were discriminating positively in favour of the advancing ethic of egalitarianism, to say nothing of liberty, and so became targets for intellectual abuse. Macaulay rounded off his attack on 'the barren theories of the utilitarian sophists' by commenting that such speculation 'hurts the health less than hard drinking and the fortune less than high play: it is not much more laughable than phrenology, and is immeasurably more humane than cock-fighting' (Lively and Rees, 1978, p. 129). Later, however, it could be pointed out that 'phrenology was felt to be a democratic science, since bumps were no respecters of class divisions' (Thompson, 1955, pp. 315–16). The problem of democracy, then, could not be dismissed so lightly.

CHAPTER 6

A Grudging Acceptance of the People's Right to Vote

The scope of the constitutional debate which had been enlarged as a result of the American and French Revolutions narrowed in the early years of the nineteenth century. Paine had offered a revolutionary prospect in response to Burke's defence of the existing constitution, but Bentham's utilitarian reforms were proposed within the contemporary structure, to plaster the cracks that had appeared in the facade of mixed government and balance. James Mill and Lord Macaulay were representatives of this more parochial debate. However, the matter of constitutional change assumed a more immediate relevance with the passage of the 1832 Reform Act. That Act, the first extension of the right to vote in the nineteenth century, was one of the signposts pointing the way in which democracy began to develop in Britain.

The discussion of the constitution had not taken place in a vacuum of abstraction, and the agitation for reform had built up a head of steam sufficient to make the 1832 measure look, in retrospect, an inevitable outcome, given the mood of the time. Had there been no concessionary reform, Paine's wish for more radical change might have been realized. According to Lord Grey, one of the architects of that first Reform Act, 'the principle of my Reform is to prevent the necessity for revolution' (quoted in Brock, 1973, p. 336). In saying this, he was pointing to perhaps the most important precedent set in 1832: the practical resolution of the idea that constitutional change could occur within the context of existing institutions, through parliamentary rather than revolutionary means.

At the same time, those who framed this limited extension of the right to vote were concerned not to pave the way for further alterations in the structure of representation. Democracy should be contained. Contemporary politicians appreciated that the Reform Act involved an 'obvious effort "to afford sure ground of resistance to further innovation" ' (quoted in Moore, 1976, p. 189).

The essentially conservative change, then, was to prove sufficient initially to defuse the political and social tensions of the period, but it was not ultimately a convincing settlement. Rather, it was tailored to the needs of the time. One contemporary radical politician, John Bright, summed up the 1832 Reform Act: 'it was not a good Bill, but it was a great Bill when it passed' (quoted in Brock, 1973, p. 332).

The Reform Act granted what might otherwise have been taken by force: the right of a wider section of the community to find representation in parliament. With hindsight it can be seen as an important first stage in the controlled evolution of democracy, even if at the time it was viewed as a means of revitalizing the traditions of the constitution and burying demands for further reform. One thing it did not do was effectively to establish a 'democratic ascendancy'. It was essentially a holding operation for the aristocracy. Agitation for reform continued, therefore, and in a separate and conflicting way the Chartist agitation which grew in the aftermath of the 1832 Reform Act also set the tone for the journey towards representative democratic government.

By mid-century the case for further reform became practically irrefutable. Disraeli's conservative government grasped the nettle, and proposed a further extension of the right to vote. This measure was designed to incorporate a greater cross-section of the community – principally a proportion of the working class – within the representative structure of the nation. The prospect alarmed both liberals and conservatives, and numerous proposals were made which were designed to mitigate the perceived impact of this democratic development. A representative selection of the arguments can be seen in the works of John Stuart Mill, Walter Bagehot and Matthew Arnold. In their separate ways each was anxious to preserve what he appreciated as the peculiar genius of the British constitutional and political system from the threatening impact of the democratic idea. The outcome of reform in the nineteenth century provides an indication of the success of their suggestions.

A PEOPLE'S MAGNA CARTA

Chartism focused attention on the potential social and political instability which could result from change. The 1832 Reform Act had redefined the criteria governing the right to vote, changing the rules which decided who might be included in the suffrage. If the rules had been changed once, they might be altered again in the face of renewed agitation and a measure which drew a line between those who were allowed to vote and those who were not, the voters and the voteless, was bound ultimately to increase the political, if not the class consciousness, of the latter. The more the have-nots appreciated what they did not have, the more concerned they were to have it.

Prior to 1832 it had appeared that elements of the middle class were prepared to enter into a pact of convenience with sympathetic leaders of the working class in order to push for political reforms. Afterwards, as the middle class had gained some of what it required, it regained and retained a determination not to share it around, and not to allow the lower orders a greater influence in politics. It was some years before working-class people realized that they could expect little from the reformed House of Commons – although legislation such as the Poor Law Amendment Act of 1834 might have given a heavy hint – and out of the political, social and economic environment of the 1830s emerged the Chartist movement. It was an extra-parliamentary pressure group operating outside the traditional mould, and at the same time it was an effort towards democracy and greater social equality.

The idea of a 'People's Charter' was rooted in the mythology surrounding Magna Carta, which was held to be a document incorporating a statement of popular rights and limiting the arbitrary authority of the king. In demanding such a Charter, the agitators of the 1830s had spotted one of the major technical problems of attempting radical change of the constitution. It was all very well to proceed by stealth, relying on custom and practice to create and maintain constitutional convention. But if there was to be a fundamental shift in the balance, or a different alloy in the mixture, then it became necessary to write down precisely the new powers of government and the changed status of the individual. That was what the Americans had done in their Constitution and Bill of Rights, and it was such a statement which was required by the Chartists. Some had indeed looked to the 1832 Reform Act as a new Magna Carta, and regarded it as something akin to a new Bill of Rights, but the failure of that Act to be such in practice prompted working-class radicals to demand a true Charter of their own.

Chartism centred mainly in the burgeoning industrial areas: it was indeed as much a product of the Industrial Revolution as democracy itself was of the American and French Revolutions. In May 1838 the so-called People's Charter was published, and was accompanied by an address containing some statements vaguely reminiscent of the American Declaration of Independence and also echoing sentiments which had been expressed on the Continent. 'Suffice it to say, that we hold it to be an *axiom in politics* that *self-government, by representation, is the only* just foundation of political power – the only true basis of constitutional rights – the only legitimate parent of good laws' (quoted in Rosenblatt, 1916, pp. 95–6).

In so far as it represented an overt example of working-class radicalism, Chartism was a force which served to provoke the fears of the middle class, reinforcing the obsessive concern with the consequences of extending the franchise which dominated political discussion in the nineteenth century. The more so, because the political demands of the movement were backed up by the ever present possibility of working-class violence. The tyranny of the majority might be matched by the tyranny of the mob.

A glimpse of the country as it appeared in 1839 makes the point: 'in truth the aspect of Great Britain in these days was sufficiently terrifying. From Bristol to Edinburgh and from Glasgow to Hull rumours of arms, riots, conspiracies and insurrections, grew with the passing of the weeks' (Hovell, 1918, p. 136). The excesses of Chartism were largely controlled, but the name of the movement still became associated with the idea that elements of the working class were intent on something like class warfare. This explains the Chartists' failure to achieve much reform of a practical nature. It was only when Chartism ceased to be a name inspiring terror that the process of giving effect to its programme was taken up by the middle-class Parliaments of the later nineteenth century (ibid., p. 302).

In June 1839 Chartists presented the National Petition, signed by about one and a quarter million people, and re-stating the basic demands of the movement, to Parliament. It achieved nothing. The debate on the Petition in Parliament is interesting, however, mostly because it allowed Benjamin Disraeli, who was to be the architect of the second Reform Act in 1867, to put forward his views on extra-parliamentary political activity and the constitution. Disraeli had a conception of the British constitution which was based on a kind of idealized Toryism. To him, the 1832 Reform Act had been disastrous, in that it had destroyed the basis of that constitution and so had given birth to Chartism. Prior to 1832 a small portion of the nation had been given political rights on the understanding that they should protect the civil rights of the rest of society.

In 1832, according to Disraeli, Parliament 'had transferred a great part of that political power to a new class whom they had not invested with those great public duties' (quoted in Hovell, 1918, p. 162). Chartism was not purely the result of economic causes or political concerns but rather the outcome of a situation in which the peculiar merits of society before 1832 no longer existed. The notion of each class taking an interest in the welfare of others may have been the consequence of a nostalgic not to say romanticized idea of feudal society, but it was an ideal common among supporters of the old constitutional system. Not only Disraeli but also *The Times* subscribed to it. As the newspaper pointed out, 'the old English system was to govern the working classes and to take care of them' (*The Times*, 29 Dec., 1840). Only through the honouring of such obligations could deference be preserved, since deference had to be merited if it was to be maintained. After 1832, it was thought, the system had broken down: a wide section of the middle class had gained political power without responsibility. The result was working-class discontent and middle-class suspicion. The expression of it was Chartism and the measures taken to control it.

Chartism, then, was an important aspect of the movement for reform after 1832. It was a practical demonstration, moreover, that the idealized constitution preached by Disraeli was an anachronism in a society in which an industrial working class now co-existed with other social groups. The Chartists represented a new departure, at odds even with the era of the 1832 Reform Act, for they accepted as fundamental what few people in parliamentary circles, with the exception of rare radicals, had come to terms with: the idea of a vote simply as a 'right'.

JOHN STUART MILL AND THE PROBLEM OF A WORKING-CLASS DEMOCRACY

In the context of extra-parliamentary Chartist agitation, and during the period when the legislature had settled back into a comfortable post-reform complacency, the publication in Britain of de Tocqueville's *Democracy in America* had a profound impact. Depending on the point of view it was taken to confirm, the book provided either the prospect or the warning of what was to come. The advance of the egalitarian ethic was inevitable, and democracy was not to be denied. The phrase 'tyranny of the majority' now became a political mantra for those who were concerned that, in sweeping all before it, the democratic idea might flatten everything around. De Tocqueville's work, therefore, was extremely influential in once more shifting the ground of the constitutional debate.

As John Stuart Mill commented in a critique of the first volume of *Democracy in America*, 'not to determine whether democracy shall come, but how to make the best of it when it does come' was de Tocqueville's concern (Himmelfarb, 1963, pp. 174–5). It was a problem that was troubling Mill as well, as he increasingly questioned the utilitarian legacy of his father and Bentham. The liberal rationalist strand of utilitarian thought on democracy thus became intertwined with other influences, not least that of de Tocqueville, to give the younger Mill new insight into the concept, and a more subtle appreciation of the difficulties of representative government.

Mill's ideas on democracy were not strictly the product of utilitarian education. They were both eclectic and variable reflecting a constant search for the essence of the ideal and the practical form it might take. Democracy involved values, not least liberty, and should promote not stifle them. It was a complex issue, particularly after Mill had come to believe that the qualities of human nature were variable rather than absolute, and that because of such malleability different aspects of character might be shown at various stages in human development. It followed that different forms of government were appropriate at different times according to the prevailing conditions of society.

Democracy could be culturally and temporally specific. For Paine and the utilitarians the case in favour of democracy had been unequivocal, either through an appeal to the 'Rights of Man', or by argument derived from the greatest happiness principle. John Stuart Mill, on the other hand, thought that democracy might indeed be a beneficial form of government but was only an appropriate one when a particular stage of political development had been reached. Democracy, moreover, came in different varieties.

In an article entitled 'Democracy and Government', published in the *London Review* in 1835, Mill was able to draw a distinction between mass representative democracy, a form of government definitely not suited to that time, and what he termed a 'rational democracy'. In this, the people retained the ultimate control in that they were able in the last resort to dismiss the government, but it was still necessary to retain 'the government of the wisest and these must always be the few' (Williams, 1976, p. 182). What Mill advocated here was government by 'an enlightened minority, accountable to the majority in the last resort' (ibid., p. 183). It was a view of democracy that would certainly have been difficult to square with some of Bentham's more radical pronouncements on the subject, and it also seems somewhat removed from the paternal *Essay on Government*.

It was a reflection of Mill's growing concern with the issues of the extension of the suffrage and the risks involved in giving the working class the vote. If democracy did indeed mean majority tyranny, then, however admirable the ideal, the practice threatened not only a fundamental shift in political power but a change for the worse. Mill's suspicion of such consequences was confirmed by his reading of de Tocqueville, whose influence on his subsequent attitude to democracy was direct, dramatic and unmistakable.

Mill wrote reviews of both volumes of *Democracy in America* for the *Westminster Review*. In the first critique, he pointed out that de Tocqueville had not only provided an introduction for the British reading public to the practical experiment of democracy in the United States but had also, in approaching the subject from an almost deterministic angle, effectively rewritten the agenda for discussion. The traditional arguments were redundant. As Mill observed: 'America is usually cited by the two great parties which divide Europe, as an argument for or against democracy. Democrats have sought to prove by it that we ought to be democrats; aristocrats, that we should cleave to aristocracy, and withstand the democratic spirit' (Himmelfarb, 1963, p. 174).

If the advance of democracy was, as de Tocqueville suggested, inevitable, that choice was no longer relevant. 'We have it not in our power to choose between democracy and aristocracy . . . But the choice we are still called upon to make is between a well and an ill-regulated democracy; and on that depends the future well-being of the human race' (Himmelfarb, 1963, p. 182). It was a matter of some concern, as de Tocqueville had rightly pointed out, but at root, Mill believed, the question of democracy was a question of attitude. If people could accept the 'rational democracy' argument and defer to the educated and intelligent, then the prospect of tyranny receded. Responsibility in government was important, and in this way 'the people ought to be the masters, but they are masters who must employ servants more skilful than themselves' (ibid., p. 195).

Government by the wisest – the few – should be accountable to the people, but even in advocating this Mill still adhered to a very Burkean concept of representation. It was essential to good government that the uninstructed masses should be guided by their more educated peers. They should not interfere, so 'making their legislators mere delegates for carrying into execution the preconceived judgment of the majority' (Himmelfarb, 1963, p. 196). Indeed, 'the substitution of delegation for representation is therefore the one and only danger of democracy' (ibid., p. 197). Burke, the author of the *Address to the Electors of Bristol*, would undoubtedly have endorsed such sentiments. In that speech Burke had presented forcefully the argument that members of parliament were elected, not delegated, representatives: following their own ideas of what was best for the nation, rather than carrying out the instructions of their constituents.

In his review of the second volume of *Democracy in America* which appeared in 1840, Mill seemed relatively sanguine about the progress of democracy in Britain (Himmelfarb, 1963, pp. 214–67). The wave of egalitarianism, so strong in the United States, had been dispersed by the breakwater of the British constitution. Democracy was still under control, and it was certainly not the working class that had benefited from any trend towards more populist government. 'The passion for equality of which M. de Tocqueville speaks, almost as if it were the great moral lever of modern times, is hardly known in this country even by name.' Mill recognized that this situation might not remain the same, and was prepared to admit that: 'the power of the higher classes both in government and society is diminishing, while that of the middle and even the lower classes is increasing and likely to increase' (ibid., p. 224). Mill, at his most paternalistic and patronizing, was still confident that the threat from an extension of the right to vote had been overstated.

Universal suffrage is never likely to exist where the majority are *prolétaires*; and we are not unwilling to believe that a labouring class in abject poverty, like the greatest part of our rural population, or which expends its surplus earnings in gin or in waste, like so much of the better paid population of the towns, may be kept politically in subjection, and that the middle classes are safe from the permanent rule of such a body. (ibid., p. 227)

Situations change. By the 1850s a further extension of the right to vote seemed not only inevitable but also imminent. The 1850s and 1860s, however, were a graveyard of unsuccessful Reform Bills. *Festina lente* was the order of the day. In part this was a reflection of the inability to agree on the extent to which the suffrage should be widened, and in part it was due to the continuing fears about the dangers of the numerical majority. To give the vote was one thing, the concern endured: what if the power of the ballot was the precursor of real political influence? William Rathbone Greg, writing in the *Edinburgh Review* in 1852, pointed to the dilemma. To enfranchise the working class 'would not merely admit them to a share, and a large share in the representation, but would throw the entire or the preponderating control over that representation – in other words the supreme power of the State, into their hands'

(Greg, 1852, pp. 460–1). Universal suffrage could lead to the 'most ruinous and pestilential tyranny' (ibid., p. 469).

In 1859 Whitwell Elwin, editor of the *Quarterly Review*, sounded a similar warning: 'Let the middle classes of this great country, the manufacturers, the respectable tradespeople, the farmers – all, in short, who employ labour and pay wages – pause before they put themselves and their property under the dominion of their men' (Elwin, 1859, p. 274). De Tocqueville was correct in pointing to the inevitability of the democratic advance, but as the nineteenth century wore on, although progress towards democratic representative government continued, the force for change was met by a fear of change. The debate as to how to cope with the perceived threat of the 'tyranny of the majority' thus remained the essential context within which further extensions of the right to vote took place.

In 1861 Mill re-entered the discussion with the publication of *Considerations on Representative Government*. By now, his suspicion of the numerical majority as the unchecked force of democracy was acute. The 'class tyranny' theory was concisely put:

> One of the greatest dangers, therefore, of democracy, as of all other forms of government, lies in the sinister interest of the holders of power: it is the danger of class legislation; of government intended for (whether really effecting it or not) the immediate benefit of the dominant class, to the lasting detriment of the whole. (Mill, 1886, p. 51)

It is the utilitarian suspicion of combination against the interests of the community, couched in the rhetoric of class. To overcome both the quantitative and the qualitative drawbacks of an extended franchise – the threat that the majority decides not only political questions but also sets cultural standards with no reference to the views of the minority – a mechanism was required to allow the voices of the educated and the intellectual to be heard.

Again, it was a re-iteration of de Tocqueville's thesis, in a slightly different form.

> The natural tendency of representative government, as of modern civilization, is towards collective mediocrity: and this tendency is increased by all reductions and extensions of the franchise, their effect being to place the principal power in the hands of classes more and more below the highest level of instruction in the community. (Mill, 1886, p. 59)

Mill was confident that such democratic conundrums might be solved. Institutions could be constructed in such a way as to allow

149

minorities to find representation, while the majority's right to rule was accepted

Minority representation was the key. Those who disagreed with majority sentiment should at least be able to find advocates for their views within the legislative assembly. The majority should not be allowed to predominate. 'It is an essential part of democracy that minorities should be adequately represented. No real democracy, nothing but a false show of democracy, is possible without it' (Mill, 1886, p. 55). Such representation would stand as a bulwark against the encroaching tyranny of the majority. Mill thus favoured institutional changes which might ultimately result in the development of an adequate system for the representation of minorities.

In particular he was drawn to electoral reform. Thomas Hare's scheme for 'voluntary constituencies' became a central plank in his proposals to promote democracy and safeguard it against the tyranny of the class majority. This plan was a complicated effort to achieve the representation of minorities. Moving away from the concept of territorial constituencies, Hare proposed that voters should list candidates in order of preference, and be allowed to vote for anyone standing for election. A mathematical quota necessary for election would be established, and once a candidate achieved this, any surplus votes would be transferred to others listed on the ballot. Voters thus would join together 'voluntarily' in support of their preferred candidate. For the system to work, each ballot would be signed by the voter so that successful candidates would know whom they supposedly were to represent.

Mill wrote to Hare after his discovery of the latter's system:

> it is the only representative mechanism which is capable of fulfilling all the demands of principle. Every other is a mere rough piece of botching compared with it; and this character of the plan stands out so prominently when once it is understood, that it has a fair chance, if sufficiently promulgated, of being widely and enthusiastically taken up by the elite of the nation. (Mincka and Lindley, 1972, p. 606)

Mill was over-optimistic. 'Of all prominent men', he wrote, William Gladstone, the liberal leader, was 'the likeliest to appreciate' the scheme (Mineka and Lindley, 1972, p. 612). He did not. A government report on a similar electoral system in use in Denmark was published in 1864 but made little impact on politicians and public alike. Mill persevered in his advocacy, and tried to press Hare's scheme in Parliament in an amendment to the 1867 Reform Bill. He was roundly defeated. The idea was flawed by being too esoteric to catch the imagination of a still relatively unsophisticated electorate, and by being less open to control by politicians than were alternative methods. Discussing Mill's amendment speech, *The Times* observed that 'such a House as that imagined in this scheme would be a Babel, a Lilliput, a Chaos and nothing more' (*The Times*, 1 June, 1867). The press, among others, remained unconvinced.

Hare's scheme remained a catalyst for those who considered that such institutional contrivances could be a safeguard against the threatened expansion of the electorate, and was at the centre of discussions of proportional representation after 1867. In its translated form – as the single transferable vote – it subsequently became a principal method of proportional representation to be advocated in Britain, but its perceived complexity has hitherto worked against it.

When Hare had been challenged that his ideas were not in keeping with British constitutional traditions, he had commented somewhat tartly: 'it would be as well if we could have some definition of the "old English principles and notions of representation" which deserve to be called "good", that we may discover whether there be in them anything inconsistent with the proposed method' (Hastings, 1867, p. 202). On the other hand such principles and notions were held to exist, and as the second Reform Act took shape there was evidence that a nostalgic attachment to them remained. An article in the *Edinburgh Review* in 1867 felt able to assert that:

> the immense majority of the nation are opposed to any measure which would overthrow the balance of the Constitution; and substitute the preponderance of the class, the most powerful in numbers, but the weakest in political experience and education, for the union and adjustment of forces, by which the Constitution has for ages been maintained. (Dodson, 1867, p. 282)

In this sense there were those who, unlike Mill, were not prepared to give democracy a chance. Mill's commitment to the ideal was anchored in a belief that such a system of government could, with appropriate safeguards, promote through education and participation the development of a more rational 'democratic citizenship'.

Others were not so sure. They could take comfort, however, in Paine's observation that 'there are two ways of governing mankind. First by keeping them ignorant. Second, by making them wise' (quoted in Del Veccio, 1956, p. 98). If Mill favoured the latter approach he was defending an ethically sound yet practically porous position. The opposing belief was that in reality education and participation merely threatened stability and the status quo. This view, encapsulated in Paine's first option, rationalized a form of democracy resting on different values from those which Mill wanted to promote.

WALTER BAGEHOT AND THE PROSPECT OF A DEFERENTIAL DEMOCRACY

The apotheosis of ignorance as a method of democratic control forms the basis of Walter Bagehot's work. Whereas John Stuart Mill interpreted democracy in a radical form, advocating education and participation as a necessary part of realizing an ideal, Bagehot expressly considered that the strength of British government lay in the fact that the people on the whole were naive and apathetic, and should remain so. So 'one of Walter Bagehot's most characteristic political ideas was his appreciation of what he called *stupidity*, and the importance he attached to it as a pre-requisite of political stability' (Stevas, 1959, p. 49). His consistent concern revolved around the problem of how fundamental constitutional changes might take place without disturbing the social equilibrium in which the fortunate few were relatively unaffected by the demands of the bovine many.

While he was prepared to admit that change was inevitable, Bagehot believed that it should nevertheless occur gradually, and that most importantly it should come about in an intelligible and controlled manner. In *Physics and Politics*, published in 1872, he wrote in praise of the 'gift of "conservative innovation" – the gift of *matching* new institutions to old' (Bagehot, 1900, p. 81). In many ways it was with this that his earlier, most famous work, *The English Constitution* (1865) had been concerned. If reform was irresistible, it was because existing institutions were becoming arthritic: a problem particularly evident in the legislature. Bagehot provided an analysis of parliamentary reform in an article written in 1859 as an aperitif to the 1865 oeuvre.

In this article Bagehot isolated two major roles played by the House of Commons after 1832. First he referred to the 'ruling function': the ability of the government to make and pass laws. Then there was the 'expressive function': the capacity of the House to represent a variety of classes, interests and views. If the nature of the ruling function was determined by the broad constitutional settlement, the expressive function was a direct reflection of the system of representation. That system was biased, not only in favour of the landed interest but also towards the counties at the expense of the borough constituencies. The representative system did not adequately represent the community.

One section especially missed out. As Bagehot observed, 'we do not provide any mode of expression for the sentiments of what are vaguely but intelligibly called the working classes. We ignore them' (Stevas, 1959, p. 434). At this stage, however, he merely pointed out the problem. He could not commit himself to the democratic idea that parliamentary representation should be based on a wider suffrage. Rather, in an argument reminiscent of Mill, Bagehot suggested that democracy need not be an absolute ideal resting on 'an obscure conception of abstract right', and that fitness to govern was not an inherent human quality. 'That fitness is relative and comparative: it must depend on the community to be governed, and on the merits of other persons who may be capable of governing that community' (ibid., p. 441). If there are undertones in this view of John Stuart Mill's 'rational democracy', they are in a minor key. Bagehot dismissed the utilitarian legacy as a 'fiction of philosophers' (ibid., p. 440). He did not admire the Mills.

Although Bagehot accepted the idea that government by the educated over the uninstructed was appropriate, this was easily translated not into a demand for greater participation to encourage 'democratic citizenship' but into an appreciation of the need to maintain a social hierarchy. The higher orders of society must rule the lower, simply because *a priori* they had the capacity and were better able to govern. The working class must hence know their place, 'they must always be subject – always at least be comparatively uninfluential' (Stevas, 1959, p. 441).

The basic dilemma which emerged from this attitude was how to give the working class the vote yet not admit it to a share of political power. Mill's preferred option of minority representation was no real solution. It would merely bring into a House of Commons elected by the working class a few representatives of the wealthier classes, whereas what Bagehot wanted was 'a Parliament generally agreeing with the wealthier classes and containing special representatives for the lower' (Bagehot, 1859, p. 27). Mill was wrong.

Bagehot returned to this theme in *The English Constitution*. He regarded electoral reform as a surrender to the new electorate, which would destroy the basis of middle-class rule by shifting the locus of political power from Parliament to the constituencies. Such constituency-based government, 'the government of immoderate persons far from the scene of action', would therfore replace parliamentary government, its antithesis (Bagehot, 1963, p. 161).

All electoral reform was bad. Hare's 'voluntary constituencies' were 'inconsistent with the necessary prerequisites of Parliamentary government' (ibid., p. 166). They would mandate the representatives who were the product of this voluntary association, and this idea was 'inconsistent with the extrinsic independence as well as with the inherent moderation of a Parliament'. 'Compulsory constituencies are necessary, voluntary constituencies destructive'; 'the optional transferability of votes is not a salutary aid but a ruinous innovation' (ibid., p. 170). Bagehot was both convincing and convinced.

So much for Mill and Hare. They were prepared to submit to majority rule and retreat to the defensive stockade of minority representation. Bagehot, however, continued to search for a means of overcoming the threatening tyranny of working-class majority. *The English Constitution* was thus in some ways a reply to and a refutation of Mill's *Considerations on Representative Government*. In his book Bagehot set out his answer to the conundrum of working-class suffrage, and by approaching the subject from a different angle he was able to show how an illusion of democracy could be constructed, making it unnecessary to resort to elaborate electoral reforms and other institutional manipulations.

He observed the contemporary constitution and discovered its 'efficient secret', a secret so well hidden that it had escaped Mill. Effective political power was exercised by the 'efficient' means of Cabinet government controlling Parliament. This was done in a society which was politically quiescent and above all deferential. The other 'dignified' institutions, the most obvious of which was the monarchy, were crucial to the inspiration of deference. So, if the middle class could preserve the actual secret of political power then the dignified parts of the constitution remained as a sop to the working-class voter, who had absorbed the political values of a deferential society.

The monarchy could abdicate its political role in the balanced constitution – or at least submit to the sovereignty of parliament – but it could not neglect its ultimate responsibility in helping to sustain the hierarchical society. The analysis endures; cosmetic significance survives. As Bagehot observed, 'a royal family sweetens politics by the seasonable addition of nice and pretty events'. These become the nineteenth-century equivalents of a photo-call. One ritual in particular stands out: 'no feeling could seem more childish than the enthusiasm of the English at the marriage of the Prince of Wales. They treated as a great political event, what, looked at as a matter of pure business, was very small indeed' (Bagehot, 1963, pp. 85–6). Remember 1981.

The core of Bagehot's analysis lies in the way in which he describes party government in Parliament, or more specifically in the House of Commons, as central to a system of constitutional control. In the House of Commons he found a fusion between the dignified and the efficient and 'the dignified aspect of the House of Commons is altogether secondary to its efficient use'. More than this, 'the House of Commons needs to be impressive, and impressive it is: but its use resides not in its appearances but in its reality. Its office is not to win power by awing mankind, but to use power in governing mankind' (Bagehot, 1963, p. 150). Although he stressed the importance of the development of the Cabinet within the institutional structure, the real instrument of government was the political party. 'Party organisation is the vital principle of representative government' (ibid., p. 159). It was essential to preserve the position of parties within the House of Commons as agencies which could be relied upon to carry out the functions of government according to the traditions of the constitution irrespective of representative reforms.

Bagehot's solution to the threatening extension of the right to vote thus rested on the construction of a democratic illusion. A wider suffrage was acceptable if those who were given the vote were channelled into support of a political system which appeared democratic but in which privilege was safeguarded against the possible incursions of a working-class majority. It was a symbolic and deferential democracy, but the symbols were rooted in substance: myth became the mortar binding theory and practice, and the reality underpinning the democratic illusion was a recognition of the role played by political parties.

Viewed in this way, *The English Constitution* was as much prescriptive as descriptive. Reform was still a gamble. In the introduction to the second edition of the book, Bagehot wrote:

> we have not enfranchised a class less needing to be guided by their betters than the old class: on the contrary, the new class need it more than the old. The real question is, Will they submit to it, will they defer in the same way to wealth and rank, and to the higher qualities of which these are the rough symbols and common accompaniments? (Bagehot, 1963, p. 272)

The odds on a positive answer might be shortened if 'our statesmen' came to realize not only their opportunity but also their obligation. 'They have to guide the new voters in the exercise of the franchise: to guide them quietly, and without saying what they are doing, but still to guide them' (ibid., p. 274). The extension of the right to vote forced politicians and their parties to organize beyond the confines of Parliament, but in a controlled and purposeful manner.

Bagehot warned that parties should not simply compete for working-class support. Deference should not be inverted. It would be the ultimate folly if the newly enfranchised came to control party policy, or if the parties constructed policies designed to buy off the working-class vote. The tradition of the House of Commons as part of the parliamentary institution which was, as Burke had suggested, the 'deliberative assembly of the nation' should not be delivered over to class interest. '*Vox populi* will be *Vox diaboli* if it is worked in that manner' (Bagehot, 1963, p. 277).

On the other hand there was an equally significant alternative consideration. If no attention was paid to working-class voters, they might be inclined to form their own party, in which case the course was again set for a numerical class tyranny. 'In all cases it must be remembered that a political combination of the lower classes, as such and for their own objects, is an evil of the first magnitude' (Bagehot, 1963, p. 277). The party system therefore treads a tightrope. It must neither submit to the working-class voters nor alienate them.

Where Mill relied upon institutional mechanisms to resist an encroaching prospect of working-class tyranny, Bagehot thus offered an interpretation of British attitudes, habits and style of government which afforded encouragement to the belief that reform could be controlled within existing constitutional structures. It was a sociological analysis, revealing in its insight and appreciation of the workings of the mid-nineteenth-century British political system. It was not, however, the only alternative offered to Mill's critique of the problem of the extension of political democracy. Many wrote on this issue of paramount concern. And among the other contributions to the debate was Matthew Arnold's discussion of the relationship between culture and democracy.

MATTHEW ARNOLD AND THE PROMISE OF A CULTURED DEMOCRACY

Walt Whitman once described Matthew Arnold as 'one of the dudes of literature', a cultural snob (quoted in Raleigh, 1957, p. 61). The transatlantic attitude is interesting. For where Whitman thought that a democratic culture was a necessary part of the vista, Arnold saw culture as an antidote to the supposed deficiencies of democracy. '*Culture and Anarchy* – culture *or* anarchy': the choice is clear (Trilling, 1965, p. 252). Arnold saw that the old order was changing. Religious beliefs were less secure, and new ideas were threatening.

> The Sea of Faith
> Was once, too, at the full, and round earth's shore
> Lay like the folds of a bright girdle furl'd.
> But now I only hear
> Its melancholy, long, withdrawing roar,
> Retreating to the breath
> Of the night-wind, down the vast edges drear
> And naked shingles of the world. ('Dover Beach', Arnold, 1913, p. 402)

Society was in flux while democracy gained political strength. That was the worry, and Arnold's concern was like Mill's and like Bagehot's: to channel the change – not so much through institutional reforms or constitutional interpretations, as via the conduits of a new set of cultural standards.

In an essay entitled 'Democracy', Arnold concluded that the power of the aristocracy had been eroded. 'The time has arrived . . . when it is becoming impossible for the aristocracy of England to conduct and wield the English nation any longer' (Arnold, 1879, p. 7). This was because democracy was 'trying to *affirm its own essence*; to live, to enjoy, to possess the world, as aristocracy has tried, and successfully tried, before it' (ibid., p. 8). But that essence might involve the relentless pursuit of the mediocre – the familiar charge and repeated complaint – for 'the difficulty for democracy is, how to find and keep high ideals' (ibid., p. 26). Arnold tried to find a solution to this difficulty, professing a commitment to democracy, while retaining a belief in the merits of the few, and remaining nervous about the ignorance of the many.

Arnold realized that a society which rested on an ethos of egalitarianism had more to offer than one in which hierarchy imposed order, if not stability. This indeed was the view which R. H. S. Tawney was later to quote approvingly at the beginning of his book *Equality* (1931). In his essay on democracy, Arnold argued for a concept of equality as the basis of a healthy society.

> Can it be denied, that to live in a society of equals tends in general to make a man's spirits expand, and his faculties work easily and actively; while, to live in a society of superiors, although it may occasionally be a very good discipline, yet in general tends to tame the spirits and to make the play of the faculties less secure and active? (Arnold, 1879, pp. 10–11)

There was no such equality in Britain.

157

In another essay, called simply 'Equality', Arnold wrote: 'when we talk of equality, we understand social equality: and for equality in this Frenchified sense of the term almost everyone in England has a hard word' (Arnold, 1879, pp. 49–50). Everyone, that was, who might suffer as a result of an injection of social egalitarianism. Such inequality confined society in a way which affected each stratum of the class system it produced. 'Our inequality materialises our upper class, vulgarises our middle class, brutalises our lower' (ibid., p. 92). Again, as Tawney was also to observe, it was the educational system which was one of the most powerful social influences sustaining inequality. Arnold, inspector of education, did not miss the point. He demonstrated 'the aristocracy's control of the administration of the state through their control of the public schools . . . an insight into the instruments of power unequaled in his day except by Bagehot's' (Lippincott, 1938, p. 96). Not what was taught but where it was learnt became the crucial issue in the attempt to maintain the tradition of inegalitarian hierarchy.

In 'Democracy' Arnold saw that hierarchy breaking down. And the sentiments of 'Equality' might be taken as those of a democrat committed to that ideal, or at least prepared to worry about its absence. Arnold seems to assume the role of an advocate of egalitarian democracy – indeed a prototypical socialist. But he was more ambivalent than that. For he was concerned about the impact of a more democratic order on the quality of life in British society.

Like Mill, he looked for ways of preserving excellence under a system which valued the common person. In this sense, 'the unifying purpose of the writings of both Arnold and Mill was to prepare their culture for its imminent democratization' (Alexander, 1965, p. vii). Both appreciated 'that the great problem of modern life is the preservation of the ancient humanistic ideal of culture in a democratic society' (ibid., p. 12). *Culture and Anarchy* (1869) was an attempt to explore the implications of that issue. In doing so, however, Arnold had to examine the concepts of equality and liberty, and to adopt elastic definitions for these ideas in the context of the over-arching theme of 'culture'. He thus becomes a democrat very much on his own terms.

'It is so much a counsel of perfection that it becomes a counsel of despair' (Trilling, 1965, p. 252). Prompted, like so much nineteenth-century British analysis of democracy, by concern at the likely consequences of the 1867 Reform Act, *Culture and Anarchy* was Arnold's most formidable contribution to the debate. Unlike Whitman, born in a democracy and seeking to perfect it, Arnold was faced with a potentially damaging phenomenon and was casting around for appropriate barricades. He found one in the state. The argument of his book is a justification of a philosophy which imbues the state with the authority to control the democratic experiment. Arnold looked to a group of cultured altruists to take on the responsibility and power of the state. In this respect he was at odds with an established strand of liberal theory which looked upon an over-mighty state as inimical to individual liberty.

He claimed to be among them. 'I am a Liberal tempered by experience, reflection, and renouncement, and I am, above all, a believer in culture' (Arnold, 1965, p. 88). What, then, was culture? For Arnold, it was 'properly described not as having its origin in curiosity, but as having its origin in the love of perfection: it is a *study of perfection*. It moves by the force, not merely or primarily of the scientific passion for pure knowledge, but also of the moral and social passion for doing good' (ibid., p. 91). Britain was a long way from subscribing to this ideal. The ethos of the industrial age did not incorporate a sense of morality and social altruism.

> The idea of perfection as an *inward* condition of the mind and spirit is at variance with the mechanical and material civilization in esteem with us . . . The idea of perfection as a *general* expansion of the human family is at variance with our strong individualism, our hatred of all limits to the unrestrained swing of the individual's personality, our maxim of 'every man for himself'. Above all, the idea of perfection as a *harmonious* expansion of human nature is at variance with our want of flexibility, with our inaptitude for seeing more than one side of a thing, with our intense energetic absorption in the particular pursuit we happen to be following. So culture has a rough task to achieve in this country. (Arnold, 1965, p. 95)

Yet for Arnold it was the only hope.

Culture set standards. Democracy needed ideals: culture supplied them. Not so much the abstract ideals of equality and liberty, to be sure, but aesthetic, spiritual, even religious targets, which were to be the basis of a new morality – the next wave to come in on Dover Beach. The connection between democracy and culture was made. 'The idea which culture sets before us of perfection . . . is an idea which the new democracy needs far more than the idea of the blessedness of the franchise, or the wonderfulness of its own industrial performances' (Arnold, 1965, p. 109). Culture supplied democracy with those ideals which could not be found through mere reliance upon existing virtues.

Arnold argued that loss of standards went together with a misplaced faith in what have more recently been rediscovered in Britain as 'Victorian values'.

> The English reliance on our religious organisations and on their ideas of human perfection just as they stand, is like our reliance on freedom, on muscular Christianity, on population, on coal, on wealth, – mere belief in machinery, and unfruitful; . . . it is wholesomely counter-acted by culture, bent on seeing things as they are, and on drawing the human race onwards to a more complete, a harmonious perfection. (Arnold, 1965, p. 104)

Such values may have been relevant to the past, and even to contemporary British society, but culture looked to a future where a new ethos was necessary for the coming democratic age.

Culture depended on the nurturing of a free intellect, and those who could help liberate society from stereotyped argument and ways of thought helped to promote an egalitarian rationalism which could form the basis of a truly democratic society. So 'men of culture are the true apostles of equality' (Arnold, 1965, p. 113), who might guide society towards such a democratic future. The advantage of culture as a basis of intellectual hegemony was that its claim to superiority was based upon the commitment to reason. A proper democratic society was founded on such rationalism, a sense of intellectual equality imbued in the concept of culture.

The interpretation of liberty in this rational cultured society was more open to debate. For in advocating the positive action of the state to promote culture at the expense of anarchy, Arnold effectively inveighed against the ideal of negative liberty. As a 'liberal of the future' he was at odds with some contemporaries. The discussion in *Culture and Anarchy* on 'doing as one likes' was a challenge to the arguments which J. S. Mill had presented in *On Liberty* (1859). For Mill, liberty was a value and an object in itself. But for Arnold, the interpretation was a little different. 'Our prevalent notion is . . . that it is a most happy and important thing for a man merely to be able to do as he likes. On what he is to do when he is thus free to do as he likes, we do not lay so much stress' (Arnold, 1965, p. 117). The free individual in society still needed standards and values, and liberty in itself was not enough.

Mill might argue for the paramount importance of liberty – it was the essence from which all else could be derived but Arnold believed in guidance. Although he agreed that 'the central idea of English life and politics is the *assertion of personal liberty*' he saw the danger in the unlimited application of the principle (Arnold, 1965, p. 117). For if the working class were now to be incorporated in the life and politics of the country, and were to assert its equal right to liberty, the result would be anarchy. Arnold's underlying fear was that if the working class were free to do what it liked it might not like the other classes in society, and might impinge on the liberty which had previously been the exclusive preserve of others. And the problem with the masses remained the same. There were more of them.

So the commitment to liberty could lead to trouble in the new democratic age. 'For a long time . . . the strong feudal habits of subordination and deference continued to tell upon the working class. The modern spirit has now almost entirely dissolved those habits and the anarchical tendency of our worship of freedom in and for itself . . . is becoming very manifest' (Arnold, 1965, pp. 118–19). The mere value of freedom was not enough, since liberty exercised irresponsibly – and Arnold did not consider the working class to be particularly responsible – promoted social instability.

Re-enter culture. It implied 'right reason', a sense of using liberty 'responsibly' which stood opposed to the anarchic strand of liberty – doing as one liked with no sense of moral responsibility – by providing a notion of authority. The agency which could promote this idea of liberty interpreted in the context of culture was once more the state. A question, however, remains. Who controls the state? Or rather who should control it?

In a class-based society, each class might have competing claims and different champions. Aristocracy, the middle class and the working class had their advocates. But which of these classes, if any, could claim to be cultured: to be the repository of rational authority, the 'apostles of culture'? None. Neither the Barbarians, nor the Philistines, nor the Populace, as Arnold styles them, could be exclusively entrusted with the responsibility of state power. 'We want an authority, and we find nothing but jealous classes, checks and a dead-lock.' Luckily, the ubiquitous concept could help here as well, since 'culture suggests the idea of *the State*. We find no basis for a firm State-power in our ordinary selves: culture suggests one to us in our *best self*' (Arnold, 1965, p. 135).

If individuals discover their 'best selves' they can be trusted with the power of the state. And there is some hope, since within each class there are those who can respond to the altruistic demands of a rational culture.

When we speak of ourselves as divided into Barbarians, Philistines, and Populace, we must be understood always to imply that within each of

161

these classes there are a certain number of *aliens*, if we may so call them,
– persons who are mainly led, not by their class spirit, but by a general
humane spirit, by the love of human perfection; and that this number
is capable of being diminished or augmented. (Arnold, 1965, p. 146)

It is on these 'aliens' that society must rely: democracy must be
guided by the exceptional altruistic individuals that exist within each
class.

Culture and Anarchy offers another solution to the problem of
democracy, a solution which relies on aesthetic sensibility, spiritual
regeneration, moral awareness and above all an appreciation of
rationalism as necessary to the interpretation of the values of equality
and liberty. The antithesis is clear. On the one hand 'we have found
that at the bottom of our present unsettled state . . . lies the notion of
its being the prime right and happiness, for each of us, to affirm himself, and his ordinary self: to be doing freely and as he likes' (Arnold,
1965, p. 176). On the other 'the very framework and exterior order
of the State, whoever may administer the State, is sacred: and
culture is the most resolute enemy of anarchy, because of the great
hopes and designs for the State which culture teaches us to nourish'
(ibid., p. 223). Arnold offered the British liberal tradition a way out
of the threatening incursions of democracy, through a philosophical
justification of state authority. 'Through culture seems to lie our way,
not only to perfection, but even to safety' (ibid., p. 222). Culture
provided the context for a form of equality and liberty to co-exist
with a principle of authority. Arnold had performed the democratic
conjuring trick: incompatible values accommodated in harmony.

So he wanted a democracy. But on his own terms, interpreting
values in a different way. The concept of culture acted as an
intellectual filter, offering a refined concept of democracy which
was at odds with many contemporary interpretations. Mill may have
argued for a rational democracy but not an authoritarian one, and
Arnold's interpretations of the ideas of equality and liberty were
not the same as those of Americans such as Jefferson, Madison, or
more significantly Whitman – the apostle of an American culture.
Thus some of Arnold's views seem, even within the context of his
times, decidedly undemocratic, even as he professed his belief in the
concept. This is particularly evident, moreover, when his attention
is focused on an example of contemporary democracy in action: the
United States.

For Americans he became 'both a fad and a myth' (Trilling, 1965,
p. 395). Opinion divided. Arnold was 'both a morbid sceptic, who
made gratuitous criticisms of the United States; but he was also a

vigorous social reformer who wrote "lofty" poetry' (Raleigh, 1957, p. 50). He was interested in the country, appreciating that it had escaped some of the problems associated with Britain's 'religion of inequality' and rigid class structure, but nevertheless tending to regard it as hopelessly middle-class in the pejorative *petit-bourgeois* sense of the term. In 1883 he risked his prejudices by travelling there, as a guest of Carnegie, whose book *Triumphant Democracy* Arnold described ingenuously as 'a most splendid picture of American progress' (Jones, 1944, p. 396). In turn, Carnegie praised him as his 'guide in religion as Herbert Spencer was his guide in philosophy' (Trilling, 1965, p. 391). Arnold's lectures in America, and his writings on American democracy were such, however, that in many ways the American industrialist was merely feeding the hand that bit him.

Arnold's idea of Americans, like his concept of the state, was Burkean in origin. 'I adhere to my old persuasion, the Americans of the United States are English people on the other side of the Atlantic. I learnt it from Burke' (Arnold, 1974a, p. 2). But Americanism was a threatening consequence of democracy that stood opposed to the possibilities presented by culture. As de Tocqueville had pointed out, and as Arnold readily accepted, Americanized democracy was mediocre, bland, vulgar and in sum, uncultured. Despite this, prior to his visit Arnold assumed that it might be possible to spread the message of culture there. Not all Americans could be Philistines: the very size and population of the country was enough to make him optimistic.

> This is a case where the question of numbers is of capital importance. Even in our poor old country . . . there are to be found individuals . . . lovers of the humane life, lovers of perfection, who emerge in all classes, and who, while they are more or less in conflict with the present, point to a better future. Individuals of this kind I make no doubt at all that there are in American society as well as here. (ibid., p. 5)

He set out to discover them.

And he was disappointed. His ideas on democracy did not mesh well with the interpretation most Americans placed on the essential values expressed in the Declaration of Independence. For Jefferson had said nothing about culture there. Arnold thought this an oversight.

> And the American middle class, or rather the whole American nation, which was middle class, though it possessed such virtues as industriousness and religiosity, was, he firmly repeated, without culture, that is without that 'type of civilization combining all those powers which

163

go to the building up of a truly human life – the power of intellect and knowledge, the power of beauty, the power of social life and manners, as well as the great power of conduct and religion, and the indispensable power of expansion' – Arnoldesc for liberty and equality. (Jones, 1944, p. 395)

American democracy was emphatically not Arnold's democracy.

He lectured America about it. One of his offerings was called 'Numbers: or the Majority and the Remnant', and it was 'as pretty a little piece of anti-democratic propaganda as one can possibly find, even today' (Jones, 1944, p. 398). Arnold criticized the whole rationale of majority rule in a democracy. He set up the majority as a target, at which he then lobbed a large intellectual and philosophical brick.

It may be better, it is better, that the body of the people, with all its faults, should act for itself, and control its own affairs, than that it should be set aside as ignorant and incapable, and have its affairs managed for it by a so-called superior class, possessing property and intelligence. Property and intelligence cannot be trusted to show a sound majority themselves: the exercise of power by the people tends to educate the people. But still, the world being what it is, we must surely expect the aims and doings of the majority of men to be at present very faulty, and this in a numerous community no less than in a small one. (Arnold, 1974b, p. 145)

American democracy needed friends like Arnold, for he had the solution. If the majority was unreliable, then at least there was the 'remnant', the enlightened section of the minority. The remnant were the 'aliens' from *Culture and Anarchy*, who could, if their numbers were sufficient, save the majority from inevitable ruin. Using historical examples, evidence culled from 'philosophers and prophets', Arnold showed that the majority was fatally unsound. Even in the United States the case could be made: perhaps especially in the United States:

Where is the failure? . . . I suppose that in a democratic community like this, with its newness, its magnitude, its strength, its life of business, its sheer freedom and equality, the danger is in the absence of the discipline of respect: in hardness and materialism, exaggeration and boastfulness; in a false smartness, a false audacity, a want of soul and delicacy. (Arnold, 1974b, p. 162)

But at least America had potential. By virtue of numbers, the chances of a 'remnant' existing with the strength to correct the deficiencies of the majority were greater than elsewhere. Ironically, this was a case of an advantage conferred by numbers. 'What a remnant yours may be, surely! A remnant of how great numbers, how mighty strength, how irresistible efficacy!' There was none the less no room for complacency. For numbers might not after all be enough. The Assyrian and Roman empires, suggested Arnold, had been populous too but had failed to find within their borders an adequate remnant. Luckily the United States added another dimension to the quest. Like the English, most Americans were of Germanic stock. 'You come, therefore, of about the best parentage which a modern nation can have' (Arnold, 1974b, p. 163). This, allied to the Puritan tradition and a sense of discipline, gave American society hope.

Culturally arrogant, racially supremacist, and dismissive of an entire tradition of American intellectual thought, Arnold was hardly a democrat in the sense that most of his audience might have understood the term – even had they been able to hear him. The lecture did not go down well. Whitman summed up the general feeling. 'I insist upon the masses . . . they are our best, they are preservative: I insist upon their integrity as a whole – not, of course denying or excusing what is bad. Arnold is all wrong on that point: it is good, not bad that is common' (quoted in Jones, 1944, p. 403). Press comment was critical, sensing that this idea of culture incorporated some un-American ideas about the democratic faith.

Such a suspicion was confirmed, as Arnold's whole attitude towards the American democratic experiment became one of condescension. In an interview he gave to the *Boston Herald*, he suggested that 'the Americans are a commercial people, with the intellectual limitations of such . . . Business absorbs the time and powers of the men as it does not in Europe: consequently there is in America no class of gentleman as in England, although everywhere there are individuals equal to any gentleman in the world' (Arnold, 1974c, p. 248). Perhaps he was merely canny. He appreciated that there was a pretension among the middle-class American entrepreneurs that he met to be accepted in a world of culture.

As an outsider in the United States, Arnold could afford to shock. But his American trip does nevertheless offer an angle on his views of democracy in action. From his attitude to the American people, it can indeed be claimed that 'the smooth surface of the doctrine of "culture" has drawn attention away from the deep distrust of the people upon which it rests' (Jones, 1944, p. 405). His idea of the 'remnant' endorses that impression. The American tour places *Culture and Anarchy* in perspective.

America confirmed Arnold's prejudice. Democracy could be the enemy of culture, even though culture was to be the saviour of democracy. In a final comment on civilization in the United States, Arnold admitted it.

> What really dissatisfies me in American civilisation is the want of the *interesting*, a want due chiefly to the want of those two great elements of the interesting, which are elevation and beauty. And the want of these elements is increased and prolonged by the Americans being assured that they have them when they have them not. (Arnold, 1977, p. 368)

Only his alien remnant of Germanic stock might provide the prospect of a democratic culture – but there again such a culture would require novel interpretations of liberty and equality, and a basic appreciation of the limitations of majority rule.

Arnold, then, emerges as a powerful critic of contemporary notions of negative liberty, a concerned commentator upon social conditions and democracy, and an idiosyncratic analyst of American democracy in action. He was an innovative, if somewhat convoluted thinker, who fashioned another solution to the pressing problem of political reform. What he recommended was difficult: a change of attitudes, aspirations and ideas of epic proportions. But he had no doubt. 'Unless we are transformed, we cannot finally stand, and without more light we cannot be transformed' (Arnold, 1974d, p. 240). Otherwise democracy might be no more than a power cut.

CONCLUSION

Americans might prefer Walt Whitman's idea of a democratic culture to Matthew Arnold's, for the one was part of their existing democratic tradition whereas the other was alien to it. In Britain Arnold's was but one suggested means of absorbing the force of political democracy without too much damage to the social structure. Like Bagehot, he did not see institutional reform as necessary, but where the author of *The English Constitution* placed his faith in existing attitudes as an antidote to an extension of the right to vote, Arnold did not. In the end, though, the conservatism of a Bagehot might have defused his liberal concern.

In the same way, Bagehot's view of democracy prevailed to the extent that supporters of John Stuart Mill's concern for electoral reform were out-numbered. The dominant opinion in mid-nineteenth-century Britain was that if sufficient faith were maintained in the workings of existing institutions, notably the party system, the problems of enfranchising the working class could be both met and overcome. This controlled development of political democracy implied a particular settlement. The working class were not to act as a cohesive unit, and thus as an unstoppable majority; rather class solidarity had to be dissipated in support of existing party organizations.

That this could happen was not an especially heroic assumption. Glimmers of hope had already been seen. Just prior to the 1867 Reform Act, an article in the *Edinburgh Review* pointed out that the concept of working-class solidarity might prove to be illusory. 'What evidence is there that this class of voters is constantly to vote *as a class* with undivided strength, when every other class in the community is divided by the influence of party and of opinion? ' The working-class conservative voter – the 'angel in the marble' – had already been glimpsed. 'It is then a fallacy to suppose that the admission of a more numerous body of voters from a lower class in society tends necessarily to throw their unanimous weight on the popular or democratic side' (Reeve, 1866, p. 587). If the working class was divided, a quantitative tyranny of the majority was unlikely, and Mill's qualitative concern that democratic society was culturally mediocre was not sufficiently shared to warrant consideration of schemes of minority representation.

The influence of party came to pervade the emerging democratic polity in nineteenth-century Britain. Party organization, which had been haphazard and intermittent prior to 1867, became more methodical and permanent. The image which emerges is of politicians in existing parties realizing that something could be done to dissipate the potential impact of the working-class vote, and beginning to follow two major strategies. The first was to organize not only their traditional support in the constituencies but also support among those who had only recently acquired the right to vote. Secondly, as part of this, and whatever the strictures of Bagehot, they started to make overtures to the working class either in the form of legislation, or promises of it, or by the formation of institutions in which the new voters might find representation within the party. These steps initially avoided and then retarded the creation of a separate working-class party.

In addition, other factors contributed to the initial success of the existing parties in channelling the support of the new electorate. It has been pointed out that in the nineteenth century 'general elections were not general. Only about half the seats were contested by both parties' (Hanham, 1964, p. 91). If there was no contest in a constituency, those who now had the right to vote still had no need to use it. In effect the contemporary political parties colluded:

the electorate was presented with no choice between competing candidates. Where contests did take place, moreover, entrenched parties could contribute to the healthy level of corruption which influenced results in their favour, at least until the Corrupt Practices Act of 1883 cut down the amount of expenditure allowed at elections.

Other barriers were raised against the creation of a party exclusively representing the working class. Members of Parliament remained unpaid: a subtle deterrent to those who did not have an adequate independent source of income. In 1868 an audience of working men was left in no doubt as to this. 'Though Representation is open to us, we cannot understand too soon, that the House of Commons, like the London Tavern, is open only to those who can pay the tariff' (G. J. Holyoake, quoted in Hanham, 1964, p. xii). It also became evident that in the initial period after 1867 the working class, or at least its leaders, was content to remain in support of the existing party framework. As late as 1881 Engels felt bound to admit that the working class in Britain had become the 'tail of the great Liberal Party' (quoted in Pelling, 1965, p. 7). All these things contributed to and even enhanced the capacity for control.

A further extension of the right to vote in 1885 did not depart from inherited practice. Indeed the controlled move towards more representative democratic government demonstrated in the earlier reforms could be seen once more in the negotiations between the established political parties over the arrangements for the redistribution of parliamentary seats which accompanied the alteration in the franchise. The heart of the matter may have been the right to vote, but, as John Bright had pointed out in 1859, 'the question of distribution is the very soul of the question of reform' (quoted in Noble, 1884, p. 1). It was realized that drawing the boundaries of parliamentary constituencies and deciding on the number of representatives which each should return to the House of Commons could have a profound impact on the outcome of elections, and on which party formed the government. When, in 1885, the electoral system in its modern form was settled by negotiation between the party leaders of the time, Gladstone and Salisbury, the strategy of democratic control was all but complete. The distribution of parliamentary seats was determined by those who ultimately stood to benefit from the agreement.

Democracy in Britain could thus have opted for either a radical or a conservative road. In practice it chose safety and stability. The Reform Acts and the Chartist agitation were signposts on the way. Walter Bagehot struck a more responsive chord than either John Stuart Mill or Matthew Arnold. Fear of working-class power remained an animating spirit for a philosophy of control. In this context, it is irrelevant to debate whether the concept of class can be considered an explanation of British politics in the nineteenth century, since for contemporaries its significance was assured. The political language of the nineteenth century was articulated in terms of class. The political literature of the new industrial society was replete with references.

There was, then, a profound concern at the possibility of a working-class 'tyranny of the majority'. The rhetoric of class determined the dimensions of debate. The fear was paramount. It structured the response of politicians and philosophers alike. As the twentieth century dawned, it could be observed that the British system of representation was 'an accumulated patchwork, composed partly of a little conviction, partly of a little concession and partly of a little cowardice' (Hansard, series 4, vol. 166, col. 624). The same comment might sum up the history of the evolution of political democracy in Britain in the nineteenth century. As a result it had, and still has, its critics.

CHAPTER 7

Democracy's Critics: Outsiders Looking On

One such critic was Thomas Carlyle. He might be overlooked by some, since 'Carlyle, in his substance and his spirit, is now seen to represent a position so extreme that we wonder at the number of Victorians who, albeit briefly, believed themselves to be his followers' (Alexander, 1965, pp. 6–7). Nevertheless, his attitude to the new democratic, industrial and social order that was emerging in nineteenth-century Britain was influential in informing the views of others. He established a strand of criticism that can be traced in its intellectual and spiritual descent through John Ruskin to William Morris. All three articulated a powerful critique of British society as it grappled with the problems of the new democratic and industrial age.

Walt Whitman admired Carlyle, and it is useful to compare the two, particularly as they highlight an essential difference between American and British critics of democracy. Whereas criticism of American democracy emerged from within the republican democratic tradition – and was indeed committed to that tradition – as part of the constant effort to interpret the ideas of the Declaration and the philosophy of the Constitution, in Britain social critics were often hostile to the idea of democracy itself. They were commentators on a political and social order on which a version of democracy had been imposed, rather than one which incorporated the concept as a fundamental belief.

So Carlyle 'was never at any stage of his life a democrat', even though the logic of his incisive critique of contemporary society might have led him to advocate democracy as a remedy (Le Quesne, 1982, pp. 40–1). Instead he found the democratic prospect horrible. To an extent, the same could be said of Ruskin. And in Morris the defence of democracy is on particular ideological grounds, by implication rather than by design. Yet it is significant that these British commentators often mirror in their work, and sometimes anticipate, the charges made by the generation of social critics of democracy in America after the Civil War. They even offer similar solutions.

There was a convergence of ideas such that the intellectual heritage to which Morris was an heir incorporated a democratic faith reminiscent of an American vision, exploring the economic dimensions of the term and concluding that true democracy is co-operation, Christian fellowship and socialism. Not everyone agreed on the mechanics of reform, but like Americans, British writers could be drawn to utopian speculation to publicize their ideas. And Morris's *News from Nowhere* (1890) was a direct riposte to Bellamy's *Looking Backward*. The issues they confronted were the same – the quest for a democratic political economy. It is thus illuminating to compare these Anglo-American critiques, from inside and without, for these British commentators, unlike their American counterparts were outsiders looking on.

THOMAS CARLYLE (1795–1881)

Carlyle's work was first published in America. 'Emerson set an example of American pioneering in Carlyle studies when he saw to it that *Sartor Resartus* [1836] appeared as a book in Boston before it did in Britain' (Fielding and Tarr, 1976, p. 42). Already the themes were apparent: an attack on contemporary social conditions and on the idea of universal suffrage, and the beginnings of a fascination with the hero. But the attraction of the work for Emerson and American transcendentalists lay in the rejection of the ethos of nascent industrialism, materialism and *laissez-faire* economics. It was not so much the outlook of a democratic as of one who 'saw the real greatness of a nation in the intensity and depth of its moral life and its intellectual achievements and not in its political aspirations' (Cassirer, 1946, p. 222).

A contemporary American reviewer, generally unsympathetic to the transcendentalist movement, was nevertheless won over by the elegance of Carlyle's style in *Sartor Resartus*.

What we chiefly prize in it is its philosophic, spiritual, humane cast of thought. It is in thorough opposition to the materialism and mechanisms of our grooved and iron-bound times. It resists the despotism of opinion seeking to rule by crowds and suffrages and machinist's devices. It soars away far beyond the theories of Utilitarian calculators. It spurns everything shallow. It expands and lifts itself above everything

171

contracted. It places us at a free distance from the turmoil of vulgar and selfish life. It exposes many an abuse and illusion of the passing ages. It is spirit. (Seigel, 1971, p. 43)

Proselytizing ideas that those who looked on democracy as an ethical ideal could find sympathetic, from the perspective of a confirmed anti-democrat, Carlyle assumed a curious intellectual position. He was among democrats but not of them.

He was a democratic camp-follower. His writings in the 1830s were on subjects – the French Revolution and Chartism – that assumed a significant place in the democratic demonology. His concerns were topical, in that revolution was discussed not as an abstract possibility in Britain during that decade but as a potentially imminent reality. Carlyle's *French Revolution* thus 'reflected both that fear and the rising moral disquiet' of an intellectual establishment recognizing the inequities of the prevailing social order but concerned at the consequences of any radical change (Le Quesne, 1982, p. 43).

Carlyle continued to worry at the theme. He defined Chartism, in his work of that title published in 1839, as the outcome of 'the bitter discontent grown fierce and mad, the wrong condition therefore or the wrong disposition, of the Working Classes of England' (Carlyle, 1905a, p. 119). And he saw that there was a need to do something: the intellectual strait-jacket of *laissez-faire* could no longer be applied to political problems in the same single-minded way that some felt it ordered the economic sphere. Given the fact that 'the Working Classes cannot any longer go on without government; without being *actually* guided and governed', and that the country 'cannot subsist in peace till, by some means or other, some guidance and government for them is found', the ineluctable conclusion was that 'in regard to the lower orders of society . . . the principle of *Laissez-faire* has terminated, and is no longer applicable at all . . . Not misgovernment, nor yet no-government; only government will now serve' (ibid., pp. 155 and 157).

But not democratic government. The Chartists may have de-manded a new constitution, but Carlyle was no fellow-traveller. He thought that democracy '"self-government" of the multitude by the multitude is . . . everywhere passionately clamoured for at present'. It was 'by the nature of it a self-cancelling business; and gives in the long run a net result of *zero*'. True democracy was a democracy of work where everybody had an equal chance of finding useful employment. That was impossible in Europe. The economic pre-conditions did not exist as they did in America, where, 'with its boundless soil, every man being able to find work and recompense for himself, democracy may subsist'. Instead of that, 'not towards the impossibility, "self-government" of a multitude by a multitude; but towards some possibility, government by the wisest, does bewildered Europe stagger' (Carlyle, 1905a, pp. 158–9). So the only hope for the old world was to submit to the guidance of those most fit to govern, who could make the best decisions in this era of limited possibilities.

In common with other contemporaries, Carlyle had a profound mistrust of democracy as a form of government. This was not so much because he feared the political power of the mob. He merely thought they were incompetent. If given free rein, they would make bad social conditions worse. By a different route, therefore, he reached a conclusion similar to that of writers like John Stuart Mill who pressed the case for a 'rational democracy' in which the best – 'the wise' – should govern. Yet Mill at least believed that the government should be accountable to those it governed. Carlyle was not concerned with such technicalities.

Rather he looked to a *deus ex machina* to solve the problem of government and democracy. The hero could do it. 'The medieval form of hierarchy was changed into the modern form of "hero-archy". Carlyle's hero is, indeed, a transformed saint, a secularized saint' (Cassirer, 1946, p. 192). If Mill looked for ordered government within a theory of democracy, Carlyle's approach was radically different. The people do not figure in his reckoning. They do not elect the hero who is to govern them: they merely recognize his presence and acquiesce to his perceived superiority. Superman comes on to the open market.

This statement in *Heroes, Hero-Worship and the Heroic in History* (1841) sums it up:

> Find in any country the Ablest Man that exists there: raise *him* to the supreme place, and loyally reverence him: you have a perfect government for that country; no ballot-box, parliamentary eloquence, voting, constitution-building, or other machinery whatsoever can improve it a whit. It is in the perfect state; an ideal country. (Carlyle, 1904, p. 197)

This doctrine of the nineteenth-century leviathan, so at odds with the 'spirit of the age' could not be taken seriously for long. Hero-worship and the need to follow the edicts of an autocrat, with the loss of individual choice and liberty which it implied, was not worth the sacrifice for the supposed reward of an alleviation of social and political miseries. Nevertheless, the failure of the doctrine of the hero to gain widespread support should not invalidate the other side of Carlyle's analysis: a mordant criticism of contemporary society

173

– a society that had lost all sense of moral integrity and religious commitment.

Such criticism was explored in *Past and Present* (1843). The very title invites a comparison. But it is not so much an American-style exercise in nostalgia as a brutal indictment of contemporary life.

> There is no longer any God for us! God's laws are become a Greatest-Happiness Principle, a Parliamentary Expediency: The Heavens over-arch us only as an Astronomical Time-keeper: a butt for Herschel-telescopes to shoot science at, to shoot sentimentalities at: – in our and old Jonson's dialect, man has lost the *soul* out of him; and now, after the due period, – begins to find the want of it! This is verily the plague-spot; centre of the universal Social Gangrene, threatening all modern things with frightful death. (Carlyle, 1897, pp. 136–7)

Carlyle's Dover Beach. There is more. He despairs. 'There is no religion; there is no God; man has lost his soul, and vainly seeks antiseptic salt. Vainly: in killing Kings, in passing Reform Bills, in French Revolutions, Manchester Insurrections, is found no remedy' (ibid., p. 137). Once belief is eroded, society drifts into disorder. The industrial age has no answers.

The materialism of contemporary society is at odds with Carlyle's concern for moral values rooted in religious conviction. He is contemptuous of 'this Mammon-Gospel, of Supply-and-demand, Competition, Laissez-faire, and Devil take the hindmost, . . . one of the shabbiest Gospels ever preached; or altogether the shabbiest' (Carlyle, 1897, p. 183). And he is equally critical of those he calls the 'Idle Aristocracy', 'the Owners of the Soil of England; whose recognized function is that of handsomely consuming the rents of England . . . and as an agreeable amusement . . . dilettante-ing in Parliament and Quarter-Sessions for England' (ibid., p. 178). If the sentiments might be those of a socialist, *Past and Present* could still be described as 'in a real sense an essay on fascism', while the doctrine of the hero has been taken as an ideological precursor of twentieth century totalitarianism (Lippincott, 1938, p. 26). Carlyle can be quarried by ideologues of all persuasions.

Sometimes he sounds like Henry George. 'Liberty, I am told, is a divine thing. Liberty when it becomes the "Liberty to die by starvation" is not so divine!' (Carlyle, 1897, p. 212). He recommends the hero – not the democratic hero, the 'Redeemer President' of Whitman – but an autocrat. He also has ideas for industrial organization – 'industrial regiments' – which pre-empt Bellamy's *Looking Backward*. Unlike the American critics, however, he does not see equality or co-operation as the essence of a healthy society. Instead, his hero will lead the industrial regiments away from the miseries of unemployment towards a life in which work rather than profit is a common value and goal. Work is an index of moral superiority. Organization solves unemployment. Carlyle's society is efficient, not democratic.

His antipathy towards contemporary society was such that the invective of the *Latter-Day Pamphlets* (1850) was greeted with a 'universal howl of execration' from his own contemporaries. Ever eclectic, his targets included not only

> Democracy, Aristocracy, Monarchy, Political Economy, Protectionism, Mammon-worship, and such other recognized interests and social entities as we have already been more or less accustomed to be girded at; but other interests and entities that thought themselves safe and consecrated from attack by the high guardianship of universal opinion, have found themselves ridiculed and made a mock of. (David Masson, Seigel, 1971, p. 339)

The *Pamphlets* were like that: the 'work of a man who is turning his back on the world in despair' (Le Quesne, 1982, pp. 79–80).

For Carlyle, 1848 was the cathartic year: 'one of the most singular, disastrous, amazing, and, on the whole, humiliating years the European world ever saw'. Revolutions, Irish problems, social distress and the apparent triumph of democracy, 'monstrous, loud, blatant, inarticulate as the voice of Chaos', gave a new edge to his fears (Carlyle, 1907, p. 5). He struggled to make sense of the new conditions. 'Whence comes it, this universal big, black Democracy; whither tends it; what is the meaning of it?' (ibid., p. 9). Like John Stuart Mill, Walter Bagehot, Matthew Arnold and others, Carlyle saw that the advent of democracy placed new demands on those who exercised political power and influence, and that there was little room for manoeuvre.

'If we can find the right meaning of it, we may, wisely submitting or wisely resisting and controlling, still hope to live in the midst of it; if we cannot find the right meaning, if we find only the wrong or no meaning in it, to live will not be possible' (Carlyle, 1907, pp. 9–10). But submission was not his style. He rejected the idea of democracy both as an ideal and as a process of government. Others might be fooled into thinking that democracy was a benign system, and not a challenge or a threat to the social order. They might consider that the outward forms of democracy – the right to vote, competitive elections – were a good idea. But not Carlyle.

175

The example of a democracy in action, America, was dismissed in terms more forthright than those used by de Tocqueville, Cooper or Arnold, but the sentiment was the same. Democracy in America had produced a nation of stunning mediocrity.

> They have doubled their population every twenty years. They have begotten, with a rapidity beyond recorded example, Eighteen Millions of the greatest *bores* ever seen in this world before, – that hitherto is their feat in History! – And so we leave them, for the present; and cannot predict the success of Democracy, on this side of the Atlantic, from their example. (Carlyle, 1907, p. 21)

Democracy in Britain might take a different shape, but Carlyle's suspicion remained acute.

In his view, moreover, democracy ran counter to the universal order. Despite his social – almost socialist – conscience, he was a religious conservative. Democracy was impossible since 'the Universe itself is a Monarchy and Hierarchy . . . The Noble in the high place, the Ignoble in the low; that is, in all times and in all countries, the Almighty Maker's Law' (Carlyle, 1907, pp. 21–2). If God was not a democrat, humanity had little chance of creating an earthly democracy that reflected any divine sense of purpose. It was against the religious – and natural – order of things.

Here then is the essential bifurcation of Carlyle's thought, which led him in different directions when he considered democracy on the one hand and industrial and social conditions on the other. Religious belief forced him to genuflect to the natural hierarchy associated with the perceived laws of his universe. But this same spiritual conviction and concern for moral welfare, which was affronted by his observation of the values of the emerging industrial society, resulted in his criticism of contemporary social conditions.

His social conscience could not make him a democrat, because his religious beliefs would not allow it. So democracy could never be a solution. Rather, running counter to the universal law, it could only exacerbate what was already a grim situation. The result of the mingling of these ideas was a political doctrine in which the autocratic hero would restore order and hierarchy in a society threatened by egalitarian democracy. Furthermore, a belief in the work ethic – almost puritan in its intensity – as a source of moral and spiritual regeneration acted as an antidote to the social distress associated with *laissez-faire* and the materialism of the industrial age.

Such a political position was coherent enough if Carlyle's premises were accepted. It was assessed in an article that appeared in the

Fortnightly Review in 1879. The point was made that 'in the social speculations of Carlyle, it is not therefore surprising to find that the prominent idea is a Rule of Real Rulers – added to which is found the so-called Gospel of Work. For Work is the only criterion of Worth, while Worth is the one indispensable characteristic of the Real Ruler' (Courtney, 1879, pp. 819–20). These political ideas set Carlyle apart. No democrat, no egalitarian, and certainly not seduced by the appeal of liberty, he was a maverick in the self-assigned role of prophet.

'The powerful liberal establishment was shocked by his hostility to democratic beliefs and tended to regard him, in Arnold's current phrase as a "moral desperado" ' (Goldberg, 1976, p. 131). Little wonder when, in the *Latter-Day Pamphlets* he pronounced thus on liberty: 'For British Liberty we live over poisonous cesspools, gully-drains, and detestable abominations; and omnipotent London cannot sweep the dirt out of itself. British Liberty produces – what? Floods of Hansard Debates every year and apparently little else at present' (Carlyle, 1907, p. 30). Whereas others attempted to defuse the ethical idealism of democracy by planning procedural concessions – Reform Acts extending the right to vote – Carlyle saw that this would have little impact on underlying social problems. He looked to government to intervene: to fuss about democracy was to miss the point.

In the long run he saw the state becoming 'what it is actually bound to be, the keystone of a most real "Organisation of Labour" ' (Carlyle, 1907, p. 159). Political reformers, in attacking the wrong issue, only made the situation worse.

> If the constitutional man will take the old Delolme–Bentham spectacles off his nose, and look abroad into the Fact itself with such eyes as he may have, I consider he will find that reform in matters social does *not* now mean, as he has long sleepily fancied, reform in Parliament alone or chiefly or perhaps at all . . . A Parliament, any conceivable Parliament, continuing to attempt the function of Governor, can lead us only into No-Government which is called Anarchy: and the more 'reformed' or Democratic you make it, the swifter will such consummation be. (ibid., p. 233)

The only government which made sense was one committed to social reform – active, interventionist, rejecting *laissez-faire* and the power of 'the market' – rather than one which was merely writing its own epitaph through constitutional tinkering in the pursuit of an impossible democracy.

Carlyle was intemperate. Others were appalled. The *Latter-Day Pamphlets* damaged his reputation. According to one review, Carlyle, 'to the utter discomfiture of his former admirers . . . manifests a truculent and ultra-tyrannical spirit, abuses the political economists, wants to have a strong coercive government, indicates a decided leaning to the whip and the musket as effectual modes of reasoning, and, in short, abjures democracy!' (Seigel, 1971, p. 324). The condemnation was as forthright as the *Pamphlets* themselves. 'These pamphlets, take them altogether, are about the silliest productions of the day; and we could well wish, for his sake, that they had never been compiled' (ibid., p. 332). The *North British Review* weighed in with the opinion that 'never before, probably, was there a publication so provocative of rage, hatred and personal malevolence' (ibid., p. 337). Carlyle was out on an intellectual limb. But the reaction to his criticism indicated that he may have struck a disquieting chord even if his proposed solutions were at odds with prevailing opinion.

He was confirmed as a maverick: his standing difficult to assess. One contemporary admitted that 'it will not be easy for the future historian of our time to put Carlyle into right perspective in a picture of the modern age' (Courtney, 1879, p. 817). True, although even in the nineteenth century there was the concern that 'the influence of the thoughts of Carlyle over the modern intelligence already threatens to be an evanescent one' (ibid., p. 818). In his *Autobiography*, John Stuart Mill gives a useful vignette and a comparison.

> I felt that he was a poet, and that I was not; that he was a man of intuition, which I was not; and that as such, he not only saw many things long before me, which I could only, when they were pointed out to me, hobble after and prove, but that it was highly probable that he could see many things which were not visible to me even after they were pointed out. (Mill, 1873, p. 176)

For Mill, there was no doubting Carlyle's stature as a social philosopher.

Poetic intuition, however, smacked of the impractical, and that remained the criticism of Carlyle's political ideas. The *Fortnightly Review* took issue with the notion of the hero: not a figure – like Whitman's Lincoln – who emerged from the community, but 'a wholly exceptional and fortuitous personage, whose origin and cast of thought can be in no way explained by reference to the laws of heredity or the general contemporaneous condition of society' (Courtney, 1879, p. 822). On the other hand, Carlyle could not be totally dismissed.

> If in some parts of his political theory we find that the magnificent Idealist needs to be confronted with the diminutive personage of practice and experience; if we require to supplement the *Latter-Day*

Pamphlets – say with Bagehot on the *English Constitution*, or Mill on *Representative Government* – we are but true to the irony of history. Prophets, in the wise arrangements of Nature, always find effective contrast in the presence of Empiricists. (ibid., p. 828)

In the end, then, there was a place for him.

But not among liberals. His views on liberty ensured that, and indeed his idea of 'industrial armies' marked him out to some as more a socialist than anything, and not a very original socialist at that. His 'analogy of a military organization' to bring coherence to the industrial world of *laissez-faire* and its resultant unemployment was 'a conception of modern Socialism' which had been advanced by European socialists such as Charles Fourier (Seigel, 1971, p. 346). There was little new in it as an idea. It was, moreover, anathema to those who believed in the notional liberty conferred by the existing economic order.

The warning from liberals was clear. 'Let but his notion of Industrial Regiments of paupers be carried out, and he would probably regard it as a matter of indifference whether they should be called State-serfs, or by some name more flattering and honourable' (David Masson, quoted in Seigel, 1971, pp. 348–9). That was the difference. Where Bellamy in America looked to such organization to foster egalitarianism, co-operation and true democracy, for Carlyle it was a pragmatic response to the need to alleviate social distress. It was an imposed solution, not a democratic nor a socialist remedy. Just as his criticisms might have placed him with the democrats though he was not of them, so his solutions might have found favour with some socialists but he cannot be counted among them. Carlyle's greatest strength and his biggest problem was that he defied conceptual pigeon-holes. An eclectic, he remained a source of inspiration to an audience which could come to his work from a variety of angles, with divergent ideas and social beliefs.

He was liked in the United States. The transcendentalism of his early works did not appeal only to Emerson. In 1847, Thoreau wrote of him that 'for fluency and skill in the use of the English tongue, he is a master unrivaled. His felicity and power of expression surpass even any of his special merits as a historian and critic' (Seigel, 1971, p. 280). Yet Carlyle mocked America. It was not a model democracy, and whatever precedents he could find there contributed to his sense of impending chaos. His pronouncements on the Civil War in *Shooting Niagara and After?* (1867) show a staggering lack of understanding of the issues behind the conflict if taken at face value, although as a warning against the consequences of the 1867 Reform Act in Britain they do make some kind of sense.

Dismissing the concept of equality, and indeed the whole question of slavery, his concern now was more with the consequences of civil disorder. His view of equality was simple: to some it meant everyone was the same. Impossible – ' "the equality of men", any man equal to any other: Quashee Nigger to Socrates or Shakespeare: Judas Iscariot to Jesus Christ' (Carlyle, 1905b, p. 4). Similarly the matter of slavery was trifling. 'Essentially the Nigger Question was one of the smallest; and in itself did not much concern mankind in the present time of struggles and hurries' (ibid., p. 5). The Civil War only mattered, then, in so far as it served as a warning of the consequences of too much democracy.

A continent of the earth has been submerged, for certain years, by deluges as from the Pit of Hell: half a million (some say a whole million, but surely they exaggerate) of excellent White Men, full of gifts and faculty, have torn and slashed one another into horrid death, in a temporary humour which will leave centuries of remembrance fierce enough: and three million absurd Blacks, men and brothers (of a sort), are completely 'emancipated'; launched into the career of improvement, – likely to be 'improved off the face of the earth' in a generation or two! (Carlyle, 1905b, p. 7)

It was an allegorical statement. Carlyle was writing about America with Britain very much in mind. Fear of the 1867 Reform Act and the political emancipation it implied led him to look at the tangential precedent: the breakdown of the experiment of American democracy and the slide into disorder that culminated in the Civil War.

Nevertheless, *Shooting Niagara* was a direct attack on America, and Walt Whitman was provoked to reply. Carlyle had been introduced to Whitman's work by Emerson but had tended to dismiss him as 'the fellow who thinks he must be a big man because he lives in a big country' (Traubel, 1961, vol. 3, p. 15). Whitman incorporated a response to Carlyle's diatribe in the material he later revised as *Democratic Vistas*. His tone was at first as vitriolic as Carlyle's, but by the time that *Democratic Vistas* was published in 1871, he had mellowed to a point where in a footnote he admitted:

'Shooting Niagara'. – I was at first roused to much anger and abuse by the Essay from Mr. Carlyle, so insulting to the theory of America – but . . . I have since read it again . . . with respect, as coming from an earnest soul, and as contributing certain sharp-cutting grains, which, if not gold or silver, may be good hard, honest iron. (Quoted in Paine, 1939, p. 557)

In spite of the attack Whitman was a big enough poet to recognize fellow genius. Carlyle's style tended to carry him through even when the substance was at its most intemperate. If he criticized America and the idea of democracy that animated that country's political vision, Carlyle was equally at odds with the intellectual establishment in Britain. His solutions were dismissed as strange and impractical. Let Whitman, though, have a final word.

> To speak of the literature of our century with Carlyle left out would be as if we missed our heavy gun: as if we stopped our ears – refused to listen: resenting the one sure signal that the battle is on. We had the Byrons, Tennysons, Shelleys, Wordsworths: lots of infantry, cavalry, light artillery: but this last, the most triumphant evidence of all, this master stroke: this gun of guns: for depth, power, reverberation, unspeakably supreme – this was: Carlyle. (Quoted in Traubel, 1961, vol. 3, p. 70)

JOHN RUSKIN (1819–1900)

John Ruskin was likewise no democrat. The notions of equality and liberty were anathema to him. But so too was the condition of contemporary society. And his vision – a society based on Christian fellowship, co-operation, community, and a rejection of industrialism and materialism – was one that elsewhere might well have been called democratic. Again, then, his views could be interpreted as an endorsement of a philosophical and political position which their author would have rejected. Ruskin may well have 'probed the economic and intellectual foundations of the industrial system that made possible the Victorian age with more acuteness than any other writer in the century save Marx', and he may have 'insisted that capitalism must be abandoned and co-operation replace competition, and that industry must be made honest and responsible' (Lippincott, 1938, p. 2). Like Henry George and Edward Bellamy, he may have discovered the solution: a new political economy. In the end, however, unlike the American social critics, he could not bring himself to style it democratic: and in crucial respects it was not.

Ruskin could not abandon the concept of monarchy in favour of a notion of egalitarian democracy. As a conservative he had 'a most sincere love of kings, and dislike of everybody who attempted

181

to disobey them' (quoted in Anthony, 1983, p. 29). Indeed, he considered the idea of equality impossible. He wrote in *Unto this Last* (1860): 'my continual aim has been to show the eternal superiority of some men to others, sometimes even of one man to all others; and to show also the advisability of appointing such person or persons to guide, to lead, or on occasion even to compel and subdue, their inferiors according to their own better knowledge and wiser will' (Ruskin, 1905a, p. 74). He had learnt that from Carlyle.

Similarly, the idea of individualistic liberty underlay the doctrine of *laissez-faire*: a gospel of selfishness and an endorsement of an economic free-for-all that was at odds with any sense of community. 'Government and co-operation are in all things the Laws of Life; anarchy and competition the Laws of Death' (Ruskin, 1905a, p. 75). Ruskin's quarrel with these ideas, however, did not mean that, like so many of his contemporaries, he was scared of democracy. Rather he rejected it as a viable form of government and ignored it from there on.

His was a two-fold attack on contemporary society. First, Ruskin argued that the real problem facing industrial society was its misconception of the nature of its prime source of motivation: work. Secondly, he analysed critically the existing economic theories which promoted this erroneous view of work, as well as the system of industrial organization in which the mistake was condoned. He was more akin to American social critics than to those British writers who tried to predict the potential consequences of democracy in the abstract or in effect. He perceived the reality of a corrupt industrial society. His arguments are similar to some of those advanced by the supporters of the 'Social Gospel' in America, even if his conclusions led him in a different direction.

Ruskin believed in the dignity of work. Its essentially ennobling character had been changed as a result of industrialization. Work was no longer of intrinsic worth: the free expression of an individual's – and society's – inventive capacity and creative ability. It had become a process, a means to an end, a way to satisfy materialist ambition. This dehumanization of work, he suggested, was the real cause of social unrest rather than any concern with an abstract ideal such as democracy. That was merely the symptom.

In his chapter on 'The Nature of Gothic' in *The Stones of Venice* (1853), he argued the case. 'It is verily this degradation of the operative into a machine, which, more than any other evil of the times, is leading the mass of the nations everywhere into vain, incoherent, destructive struggling for a freedom of which they cannot explain the nature to themselves' (Ruskin, 1904, p. 194). The contemporary 'universal outcry' at uneven distribution of wealth and at those of superior social status was not wholly the result of hunger or a sense of social frustration. This had ever been the condition of humanity. So:

> it is not that men are ill fed, but that they have no pleasure in the work by which they make their bread, and therefore look to wealth as the only means of pleasure. It is not that men are pained by the scorn of the upper classes, but they cannot endure their own; for they feel that the kind of labour to which they are condemned is verily a degrading one, and makes them less than men. (ibid., p. 194)

Ruskin interpreted industrial society's prospect. It demanded mass-production, and the nature of factory organization (the very word 'factory' came to imply an institution which failed to encourage individual creativity, producing only uniformity) made his case. The individualism of *laissez-faire* rested on the degradation of work for the masses. The point then was whether this had the consequences which Ruskin believed it had.

His argument was strengthened by his allied analysis of contemporary economic theory. For that, too, neglected the human dimension. Capitalism was the result of a partial economic vision, based on abstractions which had no underlying assumptions of morality, and were thus neutral in arbitrating between good or bad. The 'dismal science' taught only materialism, the gospel of mammon. It pontificated as to how the economy worked without asking basic questions as to the impact of its 'laws' on society as a whole. In this way, Ruskin was unequalled 'in showing the moral defects of capitalism in general. No one could match him in showing the materializing effect of the profit motive or the degrading effect of the assumption of self-interest' (Lippincott, 1938, p. 54). His 'morality was rooted in two things: religion and imagination', neither of which, he thought, was present in the discipline of economics (Abse, 1980, p. 12).

Others had pointed to the moral bankruptcy of capitalism. But in seeing also that the result of industrialization had been the substitution of the work ethic for the ideal of ethically constructive work, Ruskin drew attention to a more subtle problem. In the end, it was not enough merely to undermine the logic of capitalist economic theory. So long as work remained degrading and dehumanizing, things could not improve, irrespective of whether economic reforms promoted equality or even liberty. It was the entire ethos of industrialism which must be rejected: there must be a change in attitudes rather than in distribution of wealth or arrangements for welfare.

Where Henry George and Edward Bellamy attacked capitalism on the ground that it denied equality and liberty, Ruskin criticized it from a different angle. Capitalism was morally wrong not because it was unconcerned with those values but because it was degrading to the worker. It is a fine distinction, but it makes Ruskin's view consistent with a rejection of economic and political democracy. Democracy was not an option. Instead:

> order, reverence, authority, obedience, these words are always on his lips, these ideas always present in his mind . . . Liberty and equality he scornfully repudiates as the negation of order and government. 'No liberty, but instant obedience to known law and appointed persons; no equality but recognition of every bitterness and reprobation of every worseness'. (Hobson, 1899, pp. 185–6).

It followed that Ruskin saw little of worth in America. In *Mulnera Pulveris* (1863) he commented that it was America's economic system that had failed the country, rather than its republican commitment. *Laissez-faire* capitalism had been refined to the point where 'there you may see competition and the "law of supply and demand" . . . in beautiful and unhindered operation . . . Lust of wealth and trust in it; vulgar faith in magnitude and multitude, instead of nobleness' (Ruskin, 1905b, p. 246). More generally, American attitudes annoyed him. In *Time and Tide* (1867) he wrote:

> the Americans, as a nation, set their trust in liberty and in equality, of which I detest the one, and deny the possibility of the other; and because, also, as a nation, they are wholly undesirous of Rest, and incapable of it; irreverent of themselves, both in the present and in the future; discontented with what they are, yet having no ideal of anything which they desire to become. (Ruskin, 1905c, p. 432)

He never visited the country. The United States continued to confirm his view of the damaging impact of liberalism and its assorted institutions upon society.

Ruskin had little time for contemporary liberal theory. It was superficial and pious in its view of humanity.

> The follies of Modern Liberalism, many and great though they be, are practically summed in this denial or neglect of the quality and intrinsic value of things. Its rectangular beatitudes, and spherical benevolences, – theology of universal indulgence, and jurisprudence which will hang no rogues – mean, one and all of them, in the root, incapacity of discerning, or refusal to discern, worth and unworth in anything, and

least of all in man; whereas Nature and Heaven command you, at your peril, to discern worth from unworth in everything, and most of all in man. (Ruskin, 1905, p. 247)

At the same time his good society was to be created not by the state – although that had a place in it – but by the hero of liberalism: the individual. Ruskin asked his audience to 'note, finally, that all effectual advancement towards this true felicity of the human race must be by individual, not public effort' (Ruskin, 1905a, p. 111). The emphasis on individualism, however, accentuated a belief in the superiority of the spiritual over the material, and the moral and religious over utilitarian notions of happiness. That was Ruskin's difference.

If he looked to individuals, he did not have too high an opinion of the mass of them. Again, he rejected democracy as a prospect since problems could only result if you gave 'vote to the simple, and liberty to the vile' (Ruskin, 1905d, p. 248). He had no confidence in the masses, degraded and dehumanized as they were by the nature of their work. And he was apprehensive enough about the threat to stability should the multitude seek political power. He admonished them not to try, stressing the futility of grabbing at political influence through the ballot box. If the working class obtained a majority of representatives in the House of Commons, it would prove impossible for them to make economic or industrial reforms 'broadly contrary to that now established by custom'. To pass class-based legislation would have disastrous consequences, for 'the only result would be that the riches of the country would at once leave it, and you would perish in riot and famine' (Ruskin, 1905c, p. 328).

So 'he rejected both pure Democracy and abstract Equality, and stood by the old world institutions of Property, Government, and Church' (Harrison, 1902, p. 107). If he could not adopt a democratic perspective, moreover, neither was he about to adhere to a socialist view of society. This might pose a dilemma, for:

> though instinctively he abhorred any threat to the established patterns of society and shrank from current radical opinions, he could not but be aware – his own experience, his reading of Carlyle, and his contact with the Christian Socialists had made him so – that tremendous wrongs, in themselves a threat to stability, were being perpetrated on the poorest and least privileged human beings. (Abse, 1980, p. 113)

Blaming it on the misconceived attitude to work offered a way out. Ruskin could criticize; he could provoke. But he did not have to make the formal leap over the divide, as William Morris was about to do.

He *was* critical and provocative. *Unto this Last*, his first real attack on the morality of industrial society and capitalism, made a stir. The *Saturday Review* greeted the publication of Ruskin's essays in the *Cornhill Review* with an attack which was as intemperate as it was personal. Ruskin should have stuck to criticizing art.

> It is intolerable that a man whose best performances are deformed by constant eruptions of windy hysterics should be able to avail himself of the pages of one of our most popular periodicals for the purpose of pouring out feminine nonsense, in language which women would have far too much self-respect to employ, upon so grave a subject as political economy. (Bradley, 1984, p. 274).

Totally dismissive, the review pronounced that 'it is an act of condescension to argue at all with a man who can only write in a scream' (ibid., p. 275).

Frederic Harrison, who wrote a biography of Ruskin, observed that 'vehement language was with [him] a literary intoxication rather than a moral fault' (Harrison, 1902, p. 95), but that language, that style, and the gist of Ruskin's comment ran counter to much mid-nineteenth-century opinion. As Carlyle wrote to him, he was 'in a minority of two at any rate' (quoted in Hunt, 1983, p. 275). It was an understatement. His ideas were influential. It was left to William Morris to make the inevitable connections and to take the inexorable step.

WILLIAM MORRIS (1834–1896)

'I am "one of the people called Socialists" ', claimed William Morris in his lecture 'Art under Plutocracy' given at Oxford in 1883 (Morris, 1915b, p. 172). With John Ruskin presiding, Morris announced his 'conversion'. It was a leap of imagination and an act of faith that had not occurred to Ruskin, but Morris's lecture was the first in which 'Ruskin's aesthetic and human message was closely linked with his own socialist convictions' (Meier, 1978, vol. 1, p. 122). Morris recognized a debt to Ruskin's ideas as in turn Ruskin had leant on Carlyle, and indeed 'it is customary in most studies to establish a spiritual descent Carlyle–Ruskin–Morris' (ibid., p. 112). But on the crucial issue of the nature and ideal of democracy Morris disagreed with his spiritual forebears.

His socialism implied an ethical subscription to ideals of equality and liberty that was essentially democratic. Vehemently anti-authoritarian, mistrustful of regimentation, and believing that 'it was possible for the values of the past to come to fruition in a democratic way in the future' (Stansky, 1983, p. 12), Morris went off at a tangent. So although in his essay 'How I Became a Socialist' (1915g) Morris acknowledged Carlyle and Ruskin as two critics of the prevailing economic and intellectual ethos – which he called 'Whiggery' – he defined his creed in a different fashion. It was 'the realization at last of the meaning of the word COMMONWEALTH' (Morris, 1915g, p. 277). And an idea of democracy was behind it.

From Carlyle came the critique of capitalism, and from Ruskin conceptions of art and work. If 'it is in Carlyle's disgust at the reduction by capitalism of all human values to cash values that his greatness lies: it is this which exercised most influence over Morris, and – while it ran underground awhile – found full and constant expression in his later years' (Thompson, 1955, p. 61). This was when Morris pointed out the results of capitalism – he preferred the term 'commercialism' – and its impact upon society: materialism, profiteering, poverty and social distress.

More critical still in the development of his ideas was Ruskin's view of work and its relationship to art. For Ruskin, industrial society robbed work of its creative potential, dehumanized it and thus destroyed its connection with art. As Morris put it in his Oxford lecture, 'ART IS MAN'S EXPRESSION OF HIS JOY IN LABOUR. If those are not Professor Ruskin's words, they embody at least his teaching on this subject.' He agreed with Ruskin that the processes of industrial society robbed work of any sense of joy, and that it was thus based on a misconception of the nature and value of labour. 'The chief accusation I have to bring against the modern state of society is that it is founded on the art-lacking or unhappy labour of the greater part of men' (Morris, 1915b, p. 173). But where Ruskin thought that the degradation of work was the function of industrial processes which were sustained by the theory of capitalist economics, Morris's analysis was slightly different.

It was the ethos of capitalism that was wrong. It was capitalism which demanded that the proper ideal of work should be sacrificed to the demands of commerce and profit. Ruskin blamed industry. He argued that a new society could be built on the essential dignity of work, eschewing capitalism as an economic theory. Such a society might still rest, however, on authoritarianism and a political order based on hierarchy. In condemning capitalism itself, Morris's criticism was at once more trenchant and further-reaching in its implications. For Morris, then, 'art had become a particular quality of labour. Delight in work had been widely destroyed by the machine-system of production, but, Morris argued, it was the system,

187

rather than the machines as such, which must be blamed' (Williams, 1958, p. 158). In shifting the accent from industry to capitalism as the dehumanizing agency, Morris grasped at a fundamentally different concept to that which Ruskin had appreciated.

He argued the point in the Oxford lecture. Once capitalism imbued society with the acquisitive spirit of the materialist ethos, work became a means to an end rather than an end in itself. Society was enslaved by the structure it had created. 'Machines and railways and the like, which do now verily control us all, might have been controlled by us, if we had not been resolute to seek profit and occupation at the cost of establishing for a time that corrupt and degrading anarchy which has usurped the name of Society' (Morris, 1915b, pp. 180–1). It was not the reform of industry that was the issue so much as the abolition of commercialism. Machines used responsibly were fine: factories merely creating profits for some, without value for society, were useless.

It was a socialist message, but Morris's socialism was of a particular, if familiar kind. It rested upon ideals: liberty and equality among them. He adopted the values which Carlyle and Ruskin had explicitly disowned. Equality of condition was a premiss upon which his concept of society rested. It was linked to ideas of co-operation and humanitarianism. 'I believe that as we have even now partly achieved LIBERTY, so we shall one day achieve EQUALITY, which, and which only, means FRATERNITY, and so have leisure from poverty and all its griping sordid cares' (Morris, 1915a, p. 26).

Liberty could not exist under the prevailing economic regime. Morris made the same connections as critics in America: 'true political freedom is impossible to people who are economically enslaved' (Morris, 1915c, pp. 71–2). Looking to reform within the existing system was a waste of effort. The problem was the system.

> You cannot abolish the slums of our great cities; you cannot have happy villagers living in pretty houses among the trees, doing pretty-looking work in their own houses or in the pleasant village workshop between seed-time and harvest, unless you remove the causes that have made the brutal slum-dweller and the starveling field-labourer. (Morris, 1915f, p. 353)

Morris's reforming socialism did not encompass only politics. Rather that socialism – that democracy – extended to economic and other aspects of social life.

It followed that mere political and institutional changes of the kind advocated by some 'democrats' would leave the basic concerns untouched. Morris identified the enemies. 'The real tyrants of the people are the Landlords and the Capitalists' (Morris, 1915d, vol. 23, p. 30). His argument dismissed political democracy as a sham, and his case was made by the familiar scape-goat: the United States.

> Will you think the example of America too trite? Anyhow, consider it! A country with universal suffrage, no king, no House of Lords, no privilege as you fondly think; only a little standing army, chiefly used for the murder of red-skins; a democracy after your model; and with all that, a society corrupt to the core, and at this moment engaged in suppressing freedom with just the same reckless brutality and blind ignorance as the Czar of all the Russias uses. (ibid., pp. 30–1)

Political democracy could mean nothing unless accompanied by economic democracy – an insight grasped, according to Morris, by socialists if not by democrats. The democratic debate had to accommodate this. 'No, it is not Absolutism and Democracy as the French Revolution understood those two words, that are the enemies now: the issue is now deeper than it was; the two foes are now Mastership and Fellowship' (Morris, 1915e, p. 122). The ideals of liberty and equality were no longer the exclusive preserve of democracy. Morris was among those who helped to hijack them for socialism.

He recognized, however, another strand of socialist opinion, which could again be derived from the writings of non-socialists, such as Carlyle and Ruskin and even Matthew Arnold, which looked to the creation of the paternal and benign state. This was what he believed the advocates of political democracy were really after. 'There is, generally speaking, amongst Democrats a leaning towards a kind of limited State Socialism, and it is through that that they hope to bring about a peaceful revolution, which, if it does not introduce a condition of equality, will at least make the workers better off and contented with their lot' (Morris, 1915d, p. 31).

Morris stepped outside that tradition. What he took from Carlyle and Ruskin was their critique rather than aspects of their cure. His solution was education. 'I say that our work lies quite outside Parliament, and it is to help to educate the people by every and any means that may be effective; and the knowledge we have to help them to is threefold – to know their own, to know how to take their own, and to know how to use their own' (Morris, 1915d, p. 38). Education is not only the basis of a democratic society, it is also the underlying force of Morris's socialist ideal.

He rejected Fabianism. When the *Fabian Essays in Socialism* edited by George Bernard Shaw were published in 1889, he took

189

issue with their promotion of the idea that capitalist society could be reformed with guidance from a bureaucratic elite, and their comparative neglect of the values on which their better society was to be built. But it was an American import which really concerned him. He hated *Looking Backward*. Bellamy threatened to win British converts to an idea which Morris found appalling. He took issue with it, such that:

> it is probable that, if the vogue and influence of Bellamy were less extensive and less deep in Britain than in America, part of the reason was the stand made by Morris, and not only this stand, which only affected a limited circle, but still more the publication of *News from Nowhere*, which was its direct result. (Meier, 1978, vol. 1, p. 73)

Looking Backward tipped a balance. The Fabians had annoyed Morris. Bellamy enraged him.

> This reformist gradualism and this theory of spontaneity, while they provoked Morris's indignation and encouraged him to broaden and sharpen his attacks against the Fabian ideology, would not have been sufficient to provoke the violent reaction whose direct consequence was the writing of *News from Nowhere*. The thing that drove him to fury was Bellamy's picture of future society, primarily its regimentation. (Meier, 1978, vol. 1, p. 80)

Morris's reading of Bellamy's society was as a vast authoritarian centralism, a *dirigiste* regime which denied values such as creativity and self-expression in work. In doing that it effectively negated liberty as well.

Bellamy had not read his Ruskin. His workforce could not have been concerned with labour as art. Instead, it would consist of 'mechanical toilers' under different masters. In addition, Morris found Bellamy's sanitized account of social change absurd. Capitalists would not surrender power through an altruistic recognition of the folly of their activities. It would have to be seized. *News from Nowhere* was thus a polemical response of the kind that Bellamy's work invited from socialists who disagreed with the virtues of a centralized planned economy.

Morris was not alone in recoiling in horror from the future prospect of Bellamy's America. A contemporary British review of *News from Nowhere* expresses a similar reaction.

> Not long past, there was published a book, of an ugliness so gross and a vulgarity so pestilent, that it deserved the bonfire and the hangman,

the fate of no worse books in a bygone age. The book has been bought by tens of thousands, and by hundreds of thousands in England and America; clubs and societies have been called after its author's name. That book is *Looking Backward*. It purported to give us an insight into the perfected society of the future; and what we saw was a nightmare spectacle of machinery dominating the world. (Faulkner, 1973, p. 339)

It was that vision which Morris took the lead in disputing. In doing so he may well have moved to an opposite extreme. 'We are aware that his opposition to *Looking Backward* led him to wilful exaggeration, more than once, on the other side' (Thompson, 1955, p. 803). But he did offer an alternative, and tried to place the same ideals that had been Bellamy's concern – equality and liberty – in the context of a different society: a democracy without the state.

So *News from Nowhere*, in rejecting all notions of authoritarianism, paternalism and regimentation, necessarily considers the state as an inconsequential inessential. If people are educated, humane and co-operative, and if a recognition of equality is the vital essence of society, then the coercive power of the state is irrelevant. 'It is true that man no more needs an elaborate system of government, with its army, navy and police, to force him to give way to the will of the majority of his *equals*, than he wants a similar machinery to make him understand that his head and a stone wall cannot occupy the same place at the same moment' (Morris, 1912, pp. 75–6).

Majority rule still ordered Morris's future society, where necessary, but it was majority rule based on consent rather than on legal or constitutional mandate. Morris removed the sanction of the state as the ultimate arbitrator in matters of social concern. Free and equal individuals learnt to live without it. Government backed by the powers of the state had never been very effective. 'The government by law-courts and police, which was the real government of the nineteenth century, was not a great success even to the people of that day, living under a class system which proclaimed inequality and poverty as the law of God and the bond which held the world together' (Morris, 1912, p. 77). Majority rule was not a problem in an egalitarian utopia.

In a socialist democracy such as Morris describes, suffused with the ideal of equality and the appreciation of liberty, the citizen does not need much direction, guidance or government. Admittedly, some communal decisions must be made, and then

the majority must have their way; unless the minority were to take up arms and show by force that they were the effective or real majority; which, however, in a society of men who are free and equal is little likely to happen; because in such a community the apparent majority

191

is the real majority, and the others, as I have hinted before, know that too well to obstruct from mere pigheadedness; especially as they have had plenty of opportunity of putting forward their side of the question. (Morris, 1912, p. 87)

In this future society everybody plays by the rules and no government need enforce them.

The political system in *News from Nowhere* is thus 'very like democracy' (Morris, 1912, p. 89). Morris recognized the limitations of a representative system and used it sparingly, but there is no doubt that the ethos of his utopia was based on the democratic idea of an equal right to liberty. What he was more concerned to establish, however, was the case against the regimentation and concentration of state power which he saw in Bellamy's work. This was not the vision of a humane, democratic, or even socialist future. For Bellamy, the individual good was in a sense sacrificed to the communal good: public virtue replaced private vice, and people recognized the benefits of pursuing communal interests. Morris, on the other hand, believed that a society could exist in which *a priori* private and public virtue were the same.

Here, then, there was no need for an external agency to promote the value of equality: it was an integral part of the utopian condition. Bellamy needed the state; Morris did not. For equality was a moral force which could hold society together, 'that aspiration after complete equality which we now recognise as the bond of all happy human society' (Morris, 1912, p. 178). Bellamy's equality could almost be counted a by-product of his industrial organization, whereas to Morris that value was the inspiration of socialist life and society.

In Morris's work, then, there is once more the criticism of contemporary British society, and contempt for *laissez-faire* economics and capitalist industrial organization. His opinions, however, remain outside the mainstream of nineteenth-century British attitudes, which tried to accommodate existing structures to new demands. His comments on the nature of an ideal democracy are to be found obliquely in his political and social analysis. Unlike Carlyle or Ruskin, Morris did not look to the state to cure the problems of contemporary Britain. In a sense, indeed, he was a democrat in an American mould.

If the disagreement over means is ignored, therefore, Morris at least looked to the same ends as Bellamy and others in the United States. His socialism was democracy: a democracy seen in terms of a commitment to the values of equality and liberty. Bellamy, writing from within a tradition which took these values from the Declaration, thought that the failure to realize them could be remedied by the action of the state. But Morris, who was the product of a society which had no such charter of expressed ideals, looked on the achievement of democracy in a different way: it was not to be imposed by the state; rather it was part of a shared ethos which became a common ideology – a form of humanitarian, anti-statist socialism. *News from Nowhere* was his Declaration of Independence.

CONCLUSION

Replying to a jibe from Ruskin which accused him of 'preaching the gospel of steam engines and factories' (quoted in McGee, 1931, p. 96), the positivist philosopher Frederic Harrison, author of *Order and Progress* (1875) and believer that scientific analysis and reason could make sense of the world, admitted that 'the times are somewhat out of joint. Steam engines and beauty do not form a happy match; and the making of the modern omelette does need a most horrible smashing of eggs' (Harrison, 1876, p. 104). However, Harrison continued, as Ruskin tried to fuse the social critique of Carlyle with the aesthetic sensibilities he would pass on to Morris, he was in danger of missing the point.

'It is not the artist who can tell us whether the world is going into its grave, or whether the sun is going out in heaven. Not the artist – but the philosopher. And yet more; it is not art that is going to regenerate life and thought and society. Not so: but it is these which are going to regenerate art' (Harrison, 1876, p. 104). Nevertheless, Harrison was later to write a biography of Ruskin which attempted to show him as a positivist fellow-traveller – although Ruskin, like his mentor Carlyle, resists such type-casting.

If they were intellectual mavericks within the context of their times, both Carlyle and Ruskin nevertheless contributed to a nineteenth-century debate in Britain on the nature and essence of the good society. This society was not, according to them, to be democratic. Carlyle mistrusted the masses; Ruskin dismissed the values on which democracy might rest. Between them they show the extent to which democracy as a cause was of but limited concern in nineteenth-century Britain, confined to the political arena and arguments about the extension of the right to vote. But their social criticism could not be overlooked as it contained more than a germ of truth. As Frederic Harrison admitted of Ruskin, 'you . . . are truly so far right, that science without religion *is* materialist, immoral, inhuman; modern life *is* in many ways chaotic and brutal; industry *is* often cruel; and progress *is* something of a scramble' (Harrison, 1876, p. 100).

In the end, running through their critiques is a strand of opinion which, as the century progressed, became influential in structuring a particular socialist attitude, rooted in a type of Christian humanitarianism. Ruskin's work *Unto this Last*

> joined such fundamental texts as the Bible, Paine's *Rights of Man*, Carlyle's *Past and Present*, in the collection of works which influenced those English socialists, many of them manual workers, whose political beliefs sprang from idealistic ideas of human brotherhood and co-operation rather than from conviction of the historic inevitability of class conflict. (Abse, 1980, p. 178)

They helped to stamp a hallmark on an aspect of the British socialist democratic tradition. Carlyle and Ruskin were in that sense with the socialists but not of them. It was true too that they 'might create Sparta, but never Athens' (Lippincott, 1938, p. 90).

They might, but they did not intend to do so. As outsiders, they were not involved in promoting their ideas except by articulating them. Others could use them as political capital. Carlyle remained the trenchant observer that no intellectual could ignore, even if he might generally disagree. And 'whatever influence his words were to have on others, Ruskin himself, unlike William Morris, his greatest disciple, rejected ordinary political action. The good society, he believed, had to be rooted in personal effort and example not in political mechanisms which he had consistently abhorred' (Abse, 1980, p. 238).

The culmination of their critique of industrial society and call for moral and spiritual regeneration was William Morris's socialist and democratic vision. Where Ruskin had attempted the 'reconciliation of political economy and Christian morality' (unsigned review, quoted in Bradley, 1984, p. 291), Morris gave the message an ideological dimension. For him, values mattered. Liberty and equality could not be peripheral concerns; they should be the animating principles of a society which thus incorporated a sense of democracy in its widest dimension. And true democracy was socialism.

Morris provided the link to the wider debate. Observing British society at the end of the nineteenth century, he recast the essential values of democracy in the context of socialist ideology. The collision between the ideals of liberty and equality which had inspired fears of a working-class tyranny of the majority could be avoided through a reconciliation of those concepts in association with the development of his interpretation of a socialist society. This resurgent idealism ran counter to the continuing effort to control the perceived threat to constitutional stability which might result from any extension of the right to vote.

In America as the nineteenth century drew to a close, a similar case had been made. The emergence of industrial society demanded, some argued, a broad redefinition of the democratic idea, if that idea was to make any sense at all. It remains, therefore, to connect democracy, values and ideology as a concluding stage of this survey of the development of the nineteenth-century democratic tradition in both countries.

Part four

Conclusion

CHAPTER 8

Democracy, Values and Ideology

As the nineteenth century ebbed away, so too did some of the interest in the idea of democracy defined in terms of values, or seen in a wider framework than the purely political. In America, a writer such as E. L. Godkin could suggest that '"Ideal government", as it is called, such as is described in Plato's "Republic", or More's "Utopia" or Bellamy's "Looking Backward", is interesting to read about, as the play of an individual mind, but no one considers any of these books very helpful to those who are actually contending with the problems of today' (Godkin, 1966, pp. 281–2). He had a point. What was the use of arguing over what democracy ought to be when the 'real world' demanded solutions to problems of a less speculative nature? Progressivism, with its underlying philosophy of pragmatism, cast a cold eye on idealistic democracy.

In Britain, conservatives argued a similar case. For Henry Maine, democracy had developed an unwarranted mystique. 'There is no word about which a denser mist of vague language, and a larger heap of loose metaphors, has collected.' Why all the fuss? 'Although Democracy does signify something indeterminate, there is nothing vague about it. It is simply and solely a form of government' (Maine, 1976, pp. 79–80). Description retreated from prescription. The case for democracy in terms of values came to be expressed in both countries largely in rhetorical terms.

Lord Bryce's massive account of *The American Commonwealth* (1888) was symptomatic of the trend. Another outsider, he observed the American democratic experiment at the end of the nineteenth century, but not from the perspective of an earlier critic. He confessed that 'the book which it might seem natural for me to take as a model is the *Democracy in America* of Alexis de Tocqueville' (Bryce, 1910, vol. 1, p. 3). But the concerns had changed, outlooks had altered and democratic government seemed to Bryce, with deference to the Frenchman,

> a cause not so potent in the moral and social sphere as he deemed it; and my object has been less to discuss its merits than to paint

199

the institutions and people of America as they are, tracing what is peculiar in them not merely to the sovereignty of the masses, but also to the history and traditions of the race, to its fundamental ideas, to its material environment. (ibid., p. 4)

So the scope of democratic inquiry had changed; people had learned to live with the idea.

Where de Tocqueville had seen the 'tyranny of the majority', Bryce mused upon the 'fatalism of the multitude', an altogether more docile threat. *The American Commonwealth* was an example of meticulous, judicious empiricism. It reassured. Earlier fears of democracy's impact had been misplaced. Bryce's work was anodyne. What is more it set the tone for much of the subsequent discussion. The nature of democracy was debated in a climate of diminishing expectations. It was a variety of government, a process: as such its stability and efficiency as a form of social organization, rather than the quality of life associated with it, might be appropriate topics for the new discipline of political science to consider.

Nevertheless, Bryce's discussion of the problem of majority rule shows the consistency of this theme as a concern in nineteenth-century analysis of the idea of democracy. It was the outcome of a fear that democracy might prove just as tyrannical a threat to individual liberty as any other form of government. This was the counterpoint to a more idealistic interpretation of democracy which attempted a philosophical reconciliation of the values of equality and liberty.

EQUALITY AND LIBERTY

In America, Jefferson's Declaration had suggested a formula for a democratic society. It would be based upon an equal right to liberty. But what was the nature of that liberty? The tradition of philosophical thought which started with the idea of the individual – the basis of the liberal intellectual position – saw liberty in negative terms. In other words, liberty existed when the individual was left essentially free from the processes of society, to live without fear of the intrusion of others into a privatized lifestyle. Government could act as an umpire in such a society, but once it became partisan, representative of the interests of a group or an individual, then instead of preserving liberty it threatened tyranny.

This view of liberty anteceded the concept of democracy, and when that novel idea was expressed in terms of the equal right of each individual to claim this negative liberty, philosophical problems emerged. If the demand for communal equality affected individual liberty, then the task of the pro-democratic theorist was to find a synthesis of the two values. The practical outcome of a fear that equality and liberty might conflict was seen in America, where republican government – based on the notion of equality expressed in terms of popular sovereignty – was constrained by the Constitution. If this was not enough, then individual liberty was thought to be preserved further in the Bill of Rights. In Britain, the collision between values was also a concern, and a demand for political equality could be tolerated only if the social equality which it might imply was corralled away from severely damaging the fabric of a hierarchical society.

If democracy was an appealing idea to some, for others it became a potentially dangerous form of government when it appeared to attack the very individual liberty which its mission was to extend. The challenge was to achieve an acceptable accommodation of the values of equality and liberty, for the Jeffersonian premiss of an equal right to liberty posed an ethical dilemma only if they were regarded in a particular way. Negative liberty could indeed clash with the notion of equality if government acted against the individual in an effort to promote this democratic idea. But it might be possible to redefine the concept of liberty in a democratic context.

Such redefinition started with a more tolerant view of human nature. This was a function of a rationalist idealism which fuelled a conviction that improvement was possible, a belief in the latent capacity of individuals to develop the ability of self-government. If democracy was hence viewed as 'government of the self', rather than 'government of each by all the rest', some qualms could be assuaged. At core this view implied a confidence in people. Individualism did not mean selfishness; instead it could flourish as part of a commitment to society. This was the essence of the idea of 'republican virtue'. The democratic ethic was promoted, moreover, through the simple principle of participation in decisions of common concern, coupled with a realization of the constraints involved in living in an egalitarian society.

For Madison, commitment involved active citizenship. Individual liberty could be preserved and enhanced if each had a voice – however indirectly – in determining public policy, thereby solidifying an interest in the public good. True democracy should have this qualitative dimension: the superior society was a participatory society. In Britain too liberals like John Stuart Mill echoed the idea. Though anxious to preserve negative liberty – individualism – they could tolerate the suggestion that, if circumstances allowed, its benefits should be enjoyed by a greater proportion of the community.

In the *Principles of Political Economy* (1848), Mill argued that 'labouring people' should no longer be kept in a static state of dependence in a paternalistic society.

> The poor have come out of leading strings, and cannot any longer be governed or treated like children. To their own qualities must now be commended the care of their destiny. Modern nations will have to learn the lesson, that the well-being of a people must exist by means of the justice and self government . . . of the individual citizens . . . Whatever advice, exhortation, or guidance is held out to the labouring classes, must henceforth be tendered to them as equals, and accepted with their eyes open. The prospect of the future depends on the degree in which they can be made rational beings. (Mill, 1891, p. 501)

Education and participation became a civic responsibility, a form of democratic socialization, and was seen to be necessary in a variety of areas, not all of which were specifically political. Through such activity, moreover, liberty was encouraged: a positive liberty geared to the ideal of self-government. It was not a freedom from restraint but a freedom to create.

If each individual's rational capacity could be nurtured to its full potential, democracy became a viable form of self-government, in which equality as a value need not interfere with liberty as a right. This rationalism, though latent, could be encouraged. For Mill, possession of the right to vote become a powerful force helping the process. Political discussion developed rational faculties, yet what was the point of such debate if those encouraged to take part had no formal means of political self-expression?

> Political discussions fly over the heads of those who have no votes, and are not endeavouring to acquire them . . . No arrangement of the suffrage, therefore, can be permanently satisfactory, in which any person or class is peremptorily excluded; in which the electoral privilege is not open to all persons of full age who desire to obtain it. (Mill, 1886, pp. 67–8)

This is the most telling argument in favour of an extension of the right to vote. In similar fashion, de Tocqueville looked to jury service as a means of helping to develop the capacity to weigh decisions according to criteria of truth and justice. The free individual becomes an equal citizen of the democracy.

Education is linked to participation in the process of democratic socialization. If Mill and de Tocqueville realized this, then so too had

Jefferson. His 'vital interest in civic education was part of his hope for a republic that could develop moral faculties, identify natural leaders, and evoke an inward sense of equality' (McWilliams, 1977, p. 211). Self-government is a continuous self-sustaining process. Democratic liberty is rooted in the development of moral autonomy, the kind of rational self-awareness present too as an ideal in utilitarian thought. Such liberty, which is a consequence of self-determination, is not a passive concept. It relies upon the active commitment of citizens in society to aspire to the standards which democracy sets.

Democratic equality is based on an idea of mutual respect. Otherwise, why should an equal right to anything – life, liberty or the pursuit of happiness – be allowed? Mutual respect, the equality which for Jefferson was a self-evident truth derived from a divine ordinance, further implies a commitment to equality of worth rather than equality of treatment or even equality of opportunity, although they may stem from it. This ideal of equality neither involves a concession to conformity nor is a product of the 'depraved taste' of which de Tocqueville warned. It can instead be accommodated easily within a democratic ethos.

Defined in these ways, the ideas of equality and liberty are joined harmoniously in a definition of democracy which remains an idealistic prospect. De Tocqueville gave an example.

> Let us suppose that all the people take a part in government, and that each one of them has an equal right to take part in it. As no one is different from his fellows, none can exercise a tyrannical power; men will be perfectly free because they are all entirely equal; and they will all be perfectly equal because they are entirely free. (De Tocqueville, 1945b, p. 99)

In such a society liberty is a natural consequence of the existence of equality. The values are stitched together but form a seamless web of democracy. That was a nineteenth-century vision. The nineteenth-century concern was that a desire to promote equality regardless of the value of liberty could shatter the democratic identity which could be theoretically established between the two.

So democratic values can be held in their state of creative rather than destructive tension only if they are defined in an appropriate manner. Democracy is not merely about equality and liberty, nor is it sufficient to view it purely in terms of an equal right to liberty. It should involve instead the promotion of the twin concepts of rationalist liberty and humanitarian equality. When these values are expressed in this way they become compatible within the framework of a democratic society.

Humanitarian equality implies equality of worth, best recognized in the existence of the 'democratic citizen'. This view derives from a belief that everyone is of equal value, not that each should be treated the same. Equality of worth demands that the citizen should take on certain responsibilities within and to the community that justify that worth. The notion of democratic equality thus stands or falls with the confidence that there is a 'democratic citizen' who identifies with the communitarian spirit involved in a concept of civic altruism.

Rationalist liberty is associated naturally with the same idea. The 'democratic citizen' finds self-expression and self-fulfilment through participation. In turn this helps educate the individual in the ways of a democratic community. Education can do more than this. Through it the citizen can develop a capacity for self-government. Democratic liberty becomes the liberty to pursue and realize individual potential within the framework of an egalitarian society. Only if the humanitarian idea of equality is accepted, moreover, does the definition of democratic liberty come into play. Otherwise, as many realized in the nineteenth century, democratic values collide.

In focusing on the dangers of the unchecked advance of an equality which promoted conformity at the expense of individualistic liberty, writers such as de Tocqueville emphasized a growing nineteenth-century obsession with a perceived quantitative and qualitative 'tyranny of the majority'. The threat to an ethical ideal of democracy – resting on humanitarian equality and rationalist liberty – came from the unchecked sway of majority power. In America and in Britain, then, the democratic debate in the nineteenth century was marked by the twin concerns: the one involving an aspiration towards an ethical ideal, the other incorporating a design to control the abuse of that ideal.

THE PROBLEM OF THE MAJORITY

The doctrine of majority rule in America and in Britain was discussed in terms of its impact on the dominant faith in the benefits of individual liberty. This was because not everyone subscribed to the notion of democratic liberty perceived in positive terms, or to the belief in humanitarian equality. It was the individual that mattered, and the democratic experiment should be geared to the individual good, or at least the betterment of individual liberty. In contrast, the organizing principle of majority rule was a concept that aggregated individuals, and gave them political power *en masse*. It also conferred, as Cooper, de Tocqueville, John Stuart Mill and others pointed out, a moral authority which could structure ideas and outlooks within society. Flowing from the concern that equality and liberty could be antagonistic values in a democracy was a persistent nineteenth-century debate about the place of the individual within a society where public policy was determined by majority rule.

One way of looking at the problem of the majority was to see it in purely quantitative terms. In the context of a desire to preserve negative liberty, the fear that a majority would use the power of government to tyrannize was both real and earnest. It was the motive behind constitutional engineering in the United States. Madison and his contemporaries attempted to harness their republic, with its commitment to an abstract ethos of equality and liberty, to an institutional structure which divided and circumscribed powers, and which checked and balanced authority. In Britain a similar desire to preserve negative liberty in the face of a demand for political equality was achieved quite simply by restricting the right to vote.

It was the qualitative dimension of the idea of the 'tyranny of the majority', however, which was a more insidious threat to democratic society. If the majority influenced outlooks, attitudes and the liberty to be different, then a social conformity produced a society which was culturally mediocre. That view concerned liberal intellectuals on both sides of the Atlantic in the nineteenth century, and it was a problem which seemed to admit no real solution. But how valid a characterization was it? At the end of the century, Lord Bryce revisited the idea in *The American Commonwealth* to assess its contemporary relevance.

Bryce, too, identified a qualitative threat to intellectual and cultural life in America due to the dominance of the influence of the majority on public opinion. His analysis was reminiscent of the arguments of Cooper and to an extent de Tocqueville, but it was articulated in a slightly different way. The qualitative tyranny of the majority in America had been replaced by something else: the 'fatalism of the multitude'. It was the product of the power of public opinion, and attributable as well to one of the values upon which democracy was thought to rest. The passive, submissive attitude of the population – its 'fatalistic attitude of mind' – could be the outcome of the apparent condition of social equality in the United States.

Such equality had robbed the country of its opinion-making elite. Bryce suggested that in a society in which there was social egalitarianism 'the habit of intellectual command and individual self-confidence will have vanished from the leading class, which creates the type of national character, and will exist nowhere in the nation' (Bryce, 1910, vol. 2, p. 348). Walter Bagehot, in *Physics and Politics*, had made a similar point. It involved a belief that the elite, the group which was strongest physically or intellectually in a country, moulded its 'national character', created the model which defined the attitudes of the mass. In Matthew Arnold's terms, these people might be the cultured 'alien remnant'.

If the fact of social equality meant that no group undertook this function in America, there was nevertheless a substitute. Public opinion, which articulated the demands of the amorphous mass, created a mood, defined popular attitudes. Yet the dominance of such opinion had the consequence of inducing a sense of impotence among individuals. As Bryce put it:

> where complete political equality is strengthened and perfected by complete social equality, where the will of the majority is absolute, unquestioned, always invoked to decide every question, and where the numbers which decide are so vast that one comes to regard them as one regards the largely working forces of nature, we may expect to find certain feelings and beliefs dominant in the minds of men. (Bryce, 1910, vol. 2, p. 349)

What was the point of arguing? The weight of public opinion was a numbing force.

It was the majority which determined public attitudes – a point which would have been readily conceded by earlier critics of the majoritarian ethos of American democracy. Because the majority prevailed, the assumption was that its opinion was correct. 'The belief in the right of the majority lies very near to the belief that the majority must be right' (Bryce, 1910, vol. 2, p. 350). In America, deference to a majority of social equals was as important a trait in the character of democracy as deference to apparent social superiors was to the stability of British political life. It was easier to follow the dictates of public opinion than to argue against them. 'A citizen languidly interested in the question at issue finds it easier to comply with and adopt the view of the majority than to hold out against it' (ibid.).

The sheer geography of the country served to compound this sense of deference. Madison's 'extended sphere' had a large population from which the majority was formed. Confronting this, how could the individual be right, when a vast number had decided otherwise? America's size 'inspires a sort of awe, a sense of individual impotence, like that which man feels when he contemplates the majestic and eternal forces of the inanimate world' (Bryce, 1910, vol. 2, p. 351). And in such an atmosphere, the individual could not be blamed for experiencing a sense of 'self-distrust, a despondency, a disposition to fall into line, to acquiesce in the dominant opinion, to submit thought as well as action to the encompassing power of numbers' (ibid., pp. 351–2).

In pointing to the 'fatalism of the multitude', Bryce was presenting a variation on a critical theme which can be traced throughout the nineteenth century in commentaries on the American democratic experiment. But there was a sense in which, instead of being a weakness inherent in the republican society of the United States, that characteristic was its greatest strength. True, majority tyranny, as described by de Tocqueville, threatened a democratic ideal. But the fatalism which Bryce identified could be constructed as the foundation of the social consensus necessary for the experiment to work at all.

So Madison succeeded in spite of himself. In the end it is his analysis of American society that may have been flawed in a crucial respect. His view of the republic involved an idea of conflict between factions sparring for control of the instruments of government, which would then be used to promote one interest at the expense of others. Hence federalism and a separation of powers, and the arguments of 'Federalist 10'. But if there *had* been that antipathy within American society, could Madison's system have long survived? What the American Constitution managed to do was to resolve political conflict within the society so long as there was fundamental agreement on the broad outlines of the republican ideal. If that underlying consensus broke down, the result could be – and ultimately was – civil war. What Madison perceived as potential social conflict was in reality a political conflict over means rather than ends.

The 'fatalism of the multitude' thus becomes essential to the existence of harmony in American society. The weight of public opinion provides ballast in an atmosphere of social equality. Confidence in the republic was everything, and could be demonstrated when individuals were generally in broad agreement with popular sentiment. One benefit of this, as Bryce argued, was that it indicated a widespread support for institutions and an optimism in the future success of republicanism as a form of government. 'The foundation of the Republic is confidence in the multitude, in its honesty and good sense, in the certainty of its arriving at right conclusions' (Bryce, 1910, vol. 2, p. 354). The tendency of individuals to defer to those conclusions creates an atmosphere of political and social stability.

In describing a 'tyranny of the majority', de Tocqueville had been moved by a basic mistrust of the idea of social equality, and a pessimism about the capacity of the multitude to govern responsibly in the way he considered aristocracies had done in the past. Hence the concept he stressed as the dangerous consequence of the democratic idea was gleefully taken up in those countries where the notion of social equality was mistrusted even more than the possibility of political equality. This was particularly the case in Britain, where in practical terms the concern proved largely irrelevant. There the 'fatalism of the multitude' was induced not by a perception of the omnipotence of public opinion but by the historical weight of social deference. Stability was encouraged by the persistence of social hierarchy, even as the right to vote – political equality – was grudgingly conceded by the Reform Acts of the nineteenth century.

So the problem of the majority was a question of attitude. For those such as Cooper, de Tocqueville and Mill it was an issue of paramount concern. On the other hand, for Walt Whitman it was not really a concern at all. Fear of the majority could be assuaged by faith in the people. Tyranny threatened if the motives of a majority were mistrusted, but, if democracy was about faith in the capacities of ordinary individuals to live in a free and equal society, and to govern themselves instead of relying upon monarchs and aristocrats – or even the middle classes – to do that job for them, then the great nineteenth-century worry melted away. Reactions to the idea of democracy depended in turn upon the perspective from which it was judged. It became, in the context of the emerging industrial society in the United States and in Britain, a matter of ideology.

DEMOCRACY AND IDEOLOGY

In America democracy was so much part of the political fabric of the nation that it could be viewed as an ideology in itself. This all but stifled variations in its interpretation. The Declaration of Independence assumed a symbolic, emotional and mythical significance, and became a corner-stone of an all-encompassing liberal tradition. In Britain, where democracy was a challenge to be met, attitudes towards the idea, and interpretations of the ideal, were filtered through a greater diversity of ideological belief. The reason for this intellectual monism on one side of the Atlantic and pluralism on the other is, in a curious fashion, the outcome once again of the connection between social and political equality which was accepted in the United States and denied in Britain.

In European terms, to enter the ideological world in America is to enter a hall of mirrors. The new world, conceived as a liberal reaction to the persecutions encountered in the old, was from Puritan days onwards a place suffused by liberal ideas. But more than this, the non-conformists who had escaped from European oppression established liberalism as a conservative ideology – the ideology of the status quo – in America. Later, to be liberal in the United States was to be conservative – true to the nostalgic purpose of the Union defined by Jefferson and planned by Madison – and similarly to be conservative was to be liberal. This ideological somersaulting ignored alternatives. All other beliefs could be labelled 'un-American' and consigned to the ash-heap of history. If socialism was a reaction against a feudal past, then the lack of a feudal tradition in America doomed it to the fringes of ideological debate.

This lack of ideological variation in America which flows from the overwhelming dominance of the liberal–conservative, conservative–liberal belief is another aspect of the desire to find social cohesion within a society of social equals. What binds American society together is that common faith in a singular agreement on the democratic purpose of the nation. Dispute has been ever about means, never about ends. Interpretations of democracy in America involve a consideration of different strands of liberal thought. This allows the socialist critique of the late nineteenth century to be largely ignored.

The case is overstated. The republican tradition is too eclectic to be monolithic. The democratic argument in the United States can be better traced with an awareness of at least some ideological diversity. It was the development of industrial society which, in America as elsewhere, locked ideologies into conflict. After the Civil War, the advocates of the 'Gospel of Wealth' came to the conclusion that the ideals of *laissez-faire* capitalism and liberal democracy were compatible. Capitalism became the doctrine of democracy, but a democracy with only materialistic aspirations.

In this early age of affluence, however, there were others who looked at the democratic tradition through another ideological prism. The 'Social Gospel' was connected with a socialist analysis, whose proponents may have taken 'the model for their America' from 'the America that had been' (Rossiter, 1955, p. 129) but only to reinterpret once more that nostalgic ideal. The attempt to recreate the America they thought had been intended led these late-nineteenth-century socialists to construct a future from values established in the past. For them, such a socialist persuasion was not un-American; instead they argued that democracy in the United States should aspire to Jefferson's intent in the industrial age.

The predominant liberal-conservative ideology nevertheless continued to define the terms of the American political tradition, even though for a period after the Civil War that intellectual hegemony

209

splintered at the edges. Those who looked upon democracy as the political lieutenant of *laissez-faire* capitalism drew their inspiration from the ancient ideal of negative liberty. Their libertarian persuasion came into its American democratic inheritance. That conservative-liberal philosophy remained, and still remains, a powerful persuasion, even if in the late nineteenth century it was punched by populism and progressivism, as in the twentieth century it was to be temporarily out-pointed by the interventionist liberalism of the New Deal, or the social concern of the 'Great Society'.

Under these influences, the reinterpretation of the values of democracy became associated with a different ideological refrain. Minor key maybe but still audible, an ethical interpretation of democracy could be followed to its all-embracing conclusion: a democracy that included economic, social and religious as well as political values. Expressing the virtues of positive liberty and more significantly humanitarian equality, this democratic ideal found an ideological home among American socialists. As no ideology is nuclear, some of their ideas influenced liberal opinion, as populism and then progressivism were established as creeds of political reform. Yet the socialists of the late nineteenth century – among them powerful propagandists such as George, Bellamy and Lloyd – could not hope to redefine the 'spirit of the age'. Although industrialism precipitated ideological fracture, it brought with it new possibilities as well as new concerns. Materialism seduced support for the democratic ideal expressed in ethical terms once the quality of life became associated purely with economic well-being.

In Britain, political democracy was mistrusted by conservatives, feared by liberals and seen by socialists as a step towards social equality and emancipation. The argument was joined. The consensus was not ideological in the sense that democracy could, as in America, be identified within a particular strand of liberal thought. Instead democracy was absorbed within the framework of an established constitutional tradition. This meant that discussion about democracy, for the greater part of the century, was not about interpretations of an ideal. Britain had no real sense of democratic purpose. Political democracy was a cause to battle for or against: a new development ultimately to be tolerated and accommodated within the context of convention and precedent.

The social hierarchy which existed in Britain was taken to be the source of both political and social stability. The concept of deference implied acceptance of a status quo, with class division recognized as a fact of British life – indeed a national characteristic of which some were proud. Democracy conceived in terms of an equal right to vote could evolve within the theatre of politics, but democracy incorporating an ideal of social equality would be a more dramatic departure from tradition. The extension of the suffrage could be controlled by Parliament, but if the demand for equality spilled over to threaten the historic division between monarchy, aristocracy and the rest it was to be resisted at most costs. So Paine's *Rights of Man* might be suppressed, while Burke's reflections were lauded.

The egalitarian ideal which in America could be taken as the basis of a democratic society that demanded active citizenship and encouraged republican virtue fused the notions of social and political equality. Britain refused that egalitarian ideal. The implication is clear. Monarchy and aristocracy, and even the vestiges of monarchical and aristocratic rule, imply social hierarchy, even if within that structure an equal right to vote is admitted. A system of government which retains such a division cannot be called democratic in the egalitarian sense of the ideal. It is indeed the case that 'a society that is hierarchical . . . does not offer the possibility of more than a qualified form of democracy' (Sabine, 1952, p. 471). Britain remains an example of such a proposition.

Industrialization in Britain brought problems of social distress similar to those experienced in the United States. There too capitalism might produce economic misery for many, while others, far fewer, became rich: or at least, as wealth expanded, its distribution might be unevenly spread. The response was not, however, to look for a reinterpretation of nostalgic democratic values, since democracy itself was still to many an alien political force just as the consequences of industrial development were new and strange. Democracy might become part of the British political tradition, but it could never define it.

So the social conscience which emerged early in the nineteenth century – in the criticism of a Carlyle, or later on, a Ruskin – was not necessarily the product of an ethical vision of democracy. Indeed, those writers remained antagonistic to this novel concept. However, that social conscience became an influence in the evolution of British socialist ideology, in the sense that Carlyle's heirs also included William Morris. And the interpretation of society which can be found in this strand of social criticism was refined into a commitment to a sense of community and fellowship which ultimately incorporated an ethical ideal of democracy in all its dimensions.

The ethical strand in Anglo-American thought based upon a view of democracy which saw liberty in rationalist terms and equality as a humanitarian ideal thus converged in the two countries in the expression of a socialist ideology. If this ethical dimension of democracy is seen in such ideological terms, it is nevertheless a socialism rooted in liberal values. The ideal involves the sovereignty of the individual in the sense of self-government, and not the apotheosis of the state as government of each by all the rest. There is, then a 'sense in which socialism is itself a priori and parasitic on the norms of liberal theory . . . for its commitment to human equality' (Siedentop, 1979, p. 153). And even de Tocqueville would agree that it is philosophically possible to find liberty through equality.

When the ideal of democracy based upon a reconciliation of the values of equality and liberty acquires an ideological overcoat, it is one constructed from the material of a moralistic, libertarian socialist tradition. In America and in Britain in the nineteenth century, such socialist ideas were critical and analytical of contemporary society rather than inspirational of effective change. The subject of democracy was kept alive as a matter of debate throughout the nineteenth century, but the strand of democratic idealism which found its home in socialist thought and consequently socialism itself was mistrusted in both countries.

CONCLUSION

What in America was a concern to establish the true meaning of democracy as part of the republican tradition was in Britain an argument whether, and indeed how, to graft it on to an existing constitutional structure, without revolution, through controlled reform. Democracy in America began as a revolutionary idea. Britain was not be recreated there. The Founders envisaged something completely different, conceptually unique, although the British heritage remained strong. A system of government was designed which could not ignore Jefferson's original premisses: that the basis of society was equality and that each individual had a right to life, liberty and the pursuit of happiness. The republic should give expression to those values: confident that civic altruism – virtue – would ultimately pervade American society, but realistic enough to check, balance, diffuse and limit power just in case it did not.

Two problems in particular emerged as the union of the states became the United States. Between them the doctrine of majority rule and slavery defined the terms of the *ante-bellum* squabble over the nature of American democracy. Calhoun may have argued against the rule of numbers on general philosophical grounds in order to avoid a charge of sectional special pleading, but at least he confronted an important issue: minority rights versus majority rule. Critics such as Cooper and de Tocqueville explored another dimension of democracy, as they argued that it had to be seen in terms of the quality of life it might afford. That qualitative concern was an important consideration, since it lifted the idea of democracy from the purely political. If Cooper and de Tocqueville became deeply pessimistic about the capacity of American democracy to afford the opportunity of a better life, others were not so sure.

In drawing attention to what might be called the morality of democracy, the critics of America in the Jacksonian period expressed a concern that in another way underlined the controversy over slavery. That issue focused attention upon fundamental values in a direct and compelling way. Slavery united the abstract concerns of equality and liberty by being inimical to both. Slaves were by status unequal and by definition unfree. Lincoln understood that. On the other hand, if democracy was interpreted in a narrower sense as a form of government which just gave certain people the right to self-determination, values, as Stephen Douglas suggested, could be ignored.

If democracy was not concerned with morality then neither was slavery. The two sides of that debate could not be reconciled: the monologues co-existed uneasily as dialogue was avoided. It was fighting talk. From this perspective the Civil War was a battle of different ideas and interpretations of what democracy – and the Constitution – was all about. It was left to Lincoln from the victorious north to re-emphasize the ethical nature of American democracy, and its enduring values, by re-dedicating the republic to the pursuit of that aspiration at Gettysburg.

The new industrial age brought with it fresh challenges. Underlying the commitment to liberty and equality was an appreciation that democracy might be the defining term for all aspects of life. Whitman argued the need for a democratic culture, and others were quick to observe that a democratic political economy was also essential. It was a demand which involved a reinterpretation of Jefferson's original Declaration of Independence in the context of the growth of an industrial society. That meant that a political republic resting on democratic values was no longer enough. The logic of the argument led inexorably to the desire for a democratic commonwealth. It might be impractical, but this discussion was not about practicalities, even though it sponsored political movements connected to these new ideas. Once more the animating forces were values, aspirations, ideals. And the ethical strand of the American democratic tradition found a resting place among native socialists, even if the images of equality and liberty found a rhetorical home elsewhere.

213

In Britain the intellectual mould was cast within a different political tradition. There the nineteenth-century debate about democracy can be seen initially in the light of a reaction to two eighteenth-century revolutions, the American and the French. Both these events were based on the axiom that governments could be designed according to principles, among them equality and liberty. That idea proved politically unacceptable to many in Britain, where democracy, if it came at all, was to come on Burke's terms despite Paine's critique, and within the framework of a Whig interpretation of the constitutional past.

Bentham might devise a plan of government based upon utilitarian logic, and James Mill could provide an encyclopedic entry for the idea, but the supporters of the status quo, such as Lord Macaulay, rallied to a constitutional and institutional system which had the major merit of the supposed continuity of its historical tradition. Time had made the British system stable and good – or at least good enough to accommodate new demands. But that kind of complacency masked some very real fears. What de Tocqueville exported from America as the 'tyranny of the majority' was connected in Britain with the potential consequences of giving the working class the vote. Those who thought that that matter had been disposed of in 1832 read *Democracy in America*, saw Chartism, and prepared to meet the further demand for change.

Within the liberal intellectual establishment it was those such as John Stuart Mill who came closest to an appreciation of the ethical claims of democracy. However, he was concerned to protect minority rights from majority rule – in a way, echoing Calhoun – even as he appreciated that education and participation could create a democracy that the few might find less frightening. Bagehot knew it was a matter of control: control built upon ignorance and apathy; control which relied on deference; control which recognized democracy as a threat, ignored quality as an issue and instead was concerned to protect what had served the minority so well. Liberty and equality had little to do with an institutional system that looked to the party system to deflect the supposed tyranny of a working-class majority.

British commentators thus placed barriers in the way of political democracy, not so much to prevent its arrival as to mitigate its apparent effects. Arnold used culture. At mid-century, with the consequences of the second Reform Act threatening, he looked to a particular genius of British society, the cultured individuals who might capture the state and set the standards for others to achieve. It was an argument which was the counter-point to Whitman's ideas.

Whereas the American's cultural ideal was inclusive, based upon a democratic confidence in the capacity of his fellows, Arnold's description of culture as an alternative to anarchy betrayed the common British liberal's fear of being swamped by the mass. And Arnold's observation of America merely confirmed his prejudice.

The concern in Britain, then, was not so much with the morality of democracy, although again the younger Mill did try to contribute to that debate. Rather, there was some agonizing about the morality of the society upon which political democracy, that partial vision, was to be imposed. It was industrialization which caused that outcry. Carlyle questioned the moral basis of capitalism, but looked to the hero rather than the people for salvation. Ruskin discussed the concept of work as the basis of society's moral impoverishment without connecting that to ideas of either political or economic democracy. It was almost as if those concerned with the morality of the emerging industrial society in Britain missed the point that had been plain to their American counterparts. It was a theory of democracy conceived in ethical terms which could provide an interpretation of society in which values were important, and in which the quality of life might thereby be improved. Even William Morris connected his moral vision with the ideology of socialism rather than the ideal of democracy, although in his thought they amounted to the same thing.

This leads on to another aspect of the democratic debate in America and in Britain during the nineteenth century. In neither country was it self-contained. Events may have taken place and ideas been formed in the context of distinct traditions, but initially at least America looked to Britain for some inspiration and guidance, and throughout the century the latter was extracting warnings and lessons from the example of the former. Self-evidently the American War of Independence locked the two countries in conflict, but the subsequent severing of constitutional ties did not result in intellectual isolation or an embargo on the export and import of ideas between the old world and the new.

Thomas Paine proclaimed the republican ideal in America, and agitated for it in France and in Britain. Where Madison borrowed from abroad, Bentham looked to the United States. Cooper's experiences in Europe coloured his perceptions of home. Emerson first published Carlyle in the United States, and Carlyle used the American Civil War as an allegorical example to warn of the dangers of franchise reform. Whitman and Arnold talked about culture. Arnold indeed presumed to tell Americans what it was, and Whitman, while he could respect the thrust of Carlyle's critique, was dismissive of Arnold's analysis.

And of course there was de Tocqueville. In many ways he defined the terms of the entire debate. He observed the American experiment, reinforcing its philosophical credibility while serving Europe – and particularly Britain – with a warning. For any of his contemporaries who wished to come to terms with the nature of the emerging American democratic tradition it proved impossible to avoid *Democracy in America*. So de Tocqueville's lessons from abroad underlined John Stuart Mill's understanding of democracy and contributed to British perceptions of the idea.

The parallels are also striking in the discussions of the social critics. George lectured in Britain and found some converts to his socialism. That should be no surprise: at least they could talk a common language. Bellamy influenced and was influenced by British Fabians, so too was Lloyd. And again, Morris replied to Bellamy's utopia with one of his own. There was, then, a level of debate which transcended the national perspective. America may have pursued a unique goal, if that was seen in terms of a wish to interpret Jefferson's Declaration to practical effect. But it did so with eclectic intent, absorbing and adapting ideas from elsewhere as it invented its unique tradition. On the other hand, in Britain many continued to view America as a laboratory, an experiment to prove the validity of theories, a place which could provide proof of their concerns about democracy or else might be a vindication of their beliefs.

In terms of the link which was finally forged between democratic values and socialist ideology these intellectual cross-currents have another significance. The identification of democracy with rationalist ideas of liberty, and humanitarian notions of equality, placed the ideal in a particular corner of the socialist camp. That kind of moralistic and Christian social and socialist ethic ran counter to some European 'scientific' lines of analysis. The extent to which ideas from America informed this British strand of socialist thought cannot be measured, but there can be no doubt of the transatlantic contribution to the ideological debate. Now America is not seen usually as an influential source of socialist ideas. And it would be too much to try to construct a uniquely Anglo-American version of socialism, but the cross-cutting appeal between the two countries of such theories at the end of the nineteenth century is apparent, and the connection of them with the ideal of democracy can be made. It is worth at least a thought.

The attempt to define democracy in terms of values was in itself part of a recurrent nineteenth-century concern to find the meaning of the idea. Democracy should have a purpose: it should be judged as a superior form of political and social organization. But in order to warrant such consideration the ideal had to be appreciated in all its dimensions. In particular, it proved necessary to connect political and economic life. It was no use having principles in the one and not in the other. Nor could it be that economic ideas and organization were seen as somehow extrinsic to political and social consequences. If they were, then economic theories could be developed which largely ignored social costs. But that was not what democracy was all about. Political and economic and social concerns could be linked if it was appreciated that democracy should incorporate moral and humanitarian values. Democracy without those values denied the importance of such connections.

If there is an overriding theme which arises from this discussion of aspects of the nineteenth-century democratic traditions in America and in Britain, however, it is that the ethical ideal of democracy has been consistently challenged by critics who prefer to see democracy as a purely political process of government, a way of doing things. The experience of democratic government lends weight to this view to the extent that democracy in practice is held to fall short of its ideals. Contemporary events define the terms of the argument. In the late eighteenth century in Britain it made sense for Burke and Paine to talk of reform or revolution as viable options for constitutional change. But, as violent political and social upheaval appeared less likely, the concern to discuss such a possibility evaporated, and instead the debate revolved around the form and probable outcome of alterations in the right to vote.

In similar fashion in America the nature of the democratic ideal after the Civil War was conceived in terms of the competing claims of the 'Gospel of Wealth' on the one hand and the 'Social Gospel' on the other. But as the democratic tradition has emerged in the twentieth century the issue of its meaning has come to be seen progressively, as in Britain, in terms of 'what is' rather than 'what ought to be'. Underpinned by the philosophical justifications of pragmatism, and using the conceptual apparatus of pluralist analysis, democratic literature often invites comment upon the reality and not the prospect. There is a danger in that line of inquiry in both countries. It amounts to an ethical fall from grace – from the theoretical to the merely rhetorical.

Understanding of democracy is undermined, therefore, to the extent that the concept is ill-defined. So today the world is 'kept safe for democracy'. But what does this appeal mean? Is quality or stability to be preserved? Does democracy imply the institutional arrangements of a republic? Or can it be thought to exist in a country where a monarchical system masquerading as populist helps to preserve a hierarchical social structure enshrined in a constitution which is hide-bound by history and convention? If these questions emerge from a consideration of the traditions of democratic thought in America and in Britain in the nineteenth century – an analysis of democracy and its critics – it still remains for the twentieth century to answer them.

Bibliography

Abse, L. (1980), *John Ruskin, The Passionate Moralist* (London: Quartet).

Alexander, E. (1965), *Matthew Arnold and John Stuart Mill* (London: Routledge & Kegan Paul).

Angle, P. M. (ed.) (1958), *Created Equal? The Complete Lincoln–Douglas Debates of 1858* (Chicago: Chicago University Press).

Anthony, P. D. (1983), *John Ruskin's Labour* (Cambridge: Cambridge University Press).

Arnold, M. (1879), *Mixed Essays* (London: Smith, Elder).

Arnold, M. (1913) [1867], *The Poems of Matthew Arnold* (Oxford: Oxford University Press)

Arnold, M. (1965) [1869], *Culture and Anarchy* (Ann Arbor, Mich.: University of Michigan Press).

Arnold, M. (1974a) [1882], 'A Word About America', in R. Super (ed.) *Philistinism in England and America*, pp. 1–23 (Ann Arbor, Mich.: University of Michigan Press).

Arnold, M. (1974b) [1883], 'Numbers: or the Majority and the Remnant', ibid., pp. 143–64.

Arnold, M. (1974c) [1884], 'Interview to the *Boston Herald*', ibid., 'Reports of Public Lectures and Brief Notes to the Press', pp. 242–58.

Arnold, M. (1974d) [1885], 'Preface to Discourses in America', ibid., pp. 239–41.

Arnold, M. (1977) [1888], 'Civilisation in the United States', in R. Super (ed.) *The Last Word*, pp. 350–69 (Ann Arbor, Mich.: University of Michigan Press).

Bagehot, W. (1859), *Parliamentary Reform – an Essay Reprinted, with Considerable Additions, from the National Review* (London).

Bagehot, W. (1900) [1872], *Physics and Politics* (London: Kegan Paul).

Bagehot, W. (1963) [1865], *The English Constitution* (London: Fontana).

Bellamy, E. (1936) [1897], *Equality* (New York: D. Appleton-Century).

Bellamy, E. (1960) [1888], *Looking Backward, 2000–1887* (New York: New American Library).

Bewley, M. (1970), *Masks and Mirrors* (London: Chatto & Windus).

Billington, R. (ed.) (1950), *The Making of American Democracy*, 2 vols (New York: Rinehart).

Blaas, P. (1978), *Continuity and Anachronism* (The Hague: Martinus Nijhoff).

Blake, R. (1970), *The Conservative Party from Peel to Churchill* (London: Eyre & Spottiswoode).

Boorstin, R. (1953), *The Genius of American Politics* (Chicago: Chicago University Press).

219

Bowring, J. (ed.) (1962), *The Works of Jeremy Bentham*, 11 vols (New York: Russell & Russell).

Bradley, J. L. (ed.) (1984), *Ruskin: The Critical Heritage* (London: Routledge & Kegan Paul).

Brock, M. (1973), *The Great Reform Act* (London: Hutchinson).

Bryce, J. (1910) [1888], *The American Commonwealth*, 2 vols (London: Macmillan).

Bryce, J. (1921), *Modern Democracies*, 2 vols (London: Macmillan).

Burke, E. (1850) [1791], 'Appeal from the New to the Old Whigs', in H. Rogers (ed.), (1850), *The Works of the Hon. Edmund Burke* (London: H. G. Bohn) 2 vols, vol. 1, pp. 492–542.

Burke, E. (1910) [1790], *Reflections on the Revolution in France* (London: Dent).

Burke, E. (1912) [1775], *Speech on Conciliation with America* (London: Macmillan).

Calhoun, J. C. (1968a) [1853], 'A Disquisition on Government', in R. Crallé (ed.) *The Works of J. C. Calhoun*, 6 vols, pp. 1–107 (New York: Russell & Russell).

Calhoun, J. C. (1968b) [1853], 'A Discourse on the Constitution and Government of the United States', ibid., pp. 109–406.

Carlyle, T. (1897) [1843], 'Past and Present', in *Works*, 30 vols (London: Chapman & Hall), vol. 10.

Carlyle, T. (1904) [1841], 'Heroes, Hero-Worship and the Heroic in History', ibid., vol. 5.

Carlyle, T. (1905a) [1839], 'Chartism', ibid., vol. 29, pp. 118–204.

Carlyle, T. (1905b) [1867], 'Shooting Niagara and After?', ibid., vol. 30, pp. 1–48.

Carlyle, T. (1907) [1850], 'Latter-Day Pamphlets', ibid., vol. 20.

Carnegie, A. (1886), *Triumphant Democracy* (London: Sampson Low).

Cassirer, E. (1946), *The Myth of the State* (New Haven, Conn.: Yale University Press).

Chambers, W. N. (1963), *Political Parties in a New Nation* (New York: Oxford University Press).

Commager, H. S. (1950), *The American Mind* (New Haven, Conn.: Yale University Press).

Commager, H. S. (ed.) (1951), *Living Ideas in America* (New York: Harper & Brothers).

Cooper, J. F. (1931) [1838], *The American Democrat* (New York: Knopf).

Cooper, J. F. (1961) [1838], *Home as Found* (New York: Capricorn Books).

Cooper, J. F. (1982) [1837], *Gleanings in Europe: England* (Albany, NY: SUNY Press).

Cooper, T. V. (1885), *American Politics* (Boston: Russell & Henderson).

Courtney, W. (1879), 'Carlyle's Political Doctrines', *Fortnightly Review*, vol. 26, pp. 817–28.

Craven, A. (1959), *Civil War in the Making* (Baton Rouge, La.: LSU Press).

Current, R. N. (1963), *John C. Calhoun* (New York: Twayne).

Dekker, G., and Johnson, L. (1969), 'Introduction', in J. F. Cooper, *The American Democrat* (Harmondsworth: Penguin).

Delolme, J. (1789), *The Constitution of England* (London: Robinson & Murray).

Del Veccio, T. (1956), *Tom Paine: American* (New York: Whittier).

Destler, C. M. (1946), *American Radicalism, 1865–1901: Essays and Documents* (New London, Conn.: Connecticut College).

de Tocqueville, A. (1945a) [1835], *Democracy in America*, vol. 1 (New York: Knopf).

de Tocqueville, A. (1945b) [1840], *Democracy in America*, vol. 2 (New York: Knopf).

de Tocqueville, A. (1971) [1856], *The Ancien Regime and the French Revolution* (London: Fontana).

Dodson, J. (1867), 'The Private Business of Parliament', *Edinburgh Review*, vol. 125, pp. 85–107.

Dombrowski, J. (1936), *The Early Days of Christian Socialism in America* (Philadelphia, Penn.: Lippincott).

Elliot, C. H. (1791), *The Republican Refuted* (London).

Elwin, W., (1859), 'Reform', *Quarterly Review*, vol. 105, pp. 255–74.

Faulkner, P. (ed.) (1973), *William Morris – the Critical Heritage* (London: Routledge & Kegan Paul).

The Federalist (1937) [1787–8], (Everyman, edited by E. Rhys) (London: Dent).

Fennessy, R. (1963), *Burke, Paine and the Rights of Man* (The Hague: Martinus Nijhoff).
    Press).

Feuer, L. S. (1959), 'John Dewey and the Back to the People Movement in American Thought', *Journal of the History of Ideas*, vol. 20, pp. 545–68.

Fielding, K., and Tarr, R. (1976), *Carlyle Past and Present* (London: Vision Press).

Fitzhugh, G. (1960) [1856], *Cannibals All!* (Cambridge, Mass.: Harvard University Press).

Furness, C. (ed.) (1964), *Walt Whitman's Workshop* (New York: Russell & Russell).

Gabriel, R. (1956), *The Course of American Democratic Thought* (New York: Ronald Press).

George, H. (1937) [1879], *Progress and Poverty* (London: Vacher).

George, H. (1966) [1879], *Progress and Poverty*, condensed edn (London: Hogarth Press).

Godkin, E. L. (1966) [1896], *Problems of Modern Democracy* (Cambridge, Mass.: Harvard University Press).

Goldberg, M. (1976), 'A Universal "Howl of Excoration": Carlyle's Latter Day Pamphlets and their Critical Reception', in J. Clubbe (ed.), *Carlyle and His Contemporaries* (Durham, NC: Duke University Press), pp. 129–47.

Greg, W. R. (1852), 'Representative Reform', *Edinburgh Review*, vol. 96, pp. 452–508.

Grimes, A. (1955), *American Political Thought* (New York: Holt, Rinehart & Wilson).

Grimké, F. (1848), *Considerations upon the Nature and Tendency of Free Institutions* (Cincinnati, Ohio: H. H. Derby).

Hanham, H. (1964), *Elections and Party Management* (London: Longman).

Harris, D. (1966), *Socialist Origins in the United States* (Assen: Van Gorcum).

Harrison, F. (1876), 'Past and Present', *Fortnightly Review*, vol. 20, pp. 93–105.

Harrison, F. (1902), *John Ruskin* (London: Macmillan).

Harrison, F. (1975) [1875], *Order and Progress* (Brighton: Harvester Press).

Hart, H. L. A. (1982), *Essays on Bentham* (Oxford: Clarendon Press).

Hastings, G. W. (ed.) (1867), *Transactions of the National Association for the Promotion of Social Science* (London).

Hearnshaw, F. (1918), *Democracy at the Crossways* (London: Macmillan).

Heckscher, G. (1939), 'Calhoun's Idea of the "Concurrent Majority" and the Constitutional Theory of Hegel', *American Political Science Review*. vol. 33, pp. 585–90.

Heinberg, J. G. (1932), 'Theories of Majority Rule', *American Political Science Review*, vol. 26, pp. 452–69.

Herr, R. (1962), *Tocqueville and the Old Regime* (Princeton, NJ: Princeton University Press).

Himmelfarb, G. (ed.) (1963), *Essays on Politics and Culture* (New York: Anchor Books).

Hindus, M. (ed.) (1955), *Leaves of Grass – 100 Years After* (Stanford, Calif.: Stanford University Press).

Hobson, J. (1899), *John Ruskin, Social Reformer* (London: Nisbet).

Hofstadter, R. (1948), *The American Political Tradition* (New York: Knopf).

Hofstadter, R. (1969), *The Idea of a Party System* (Berkeley, Calif.: University of California Press).

Horwitz, M. (1966), 'Tocqueville and the Tyranny of the Majority', *Review of Politics*, vol. 28, pp. 293–307.

Horwitz, R. (ed.) (1977), *The Moral Foundations of the American Republic* (Charlottesville, Va: University of Virginia Press).

Hovell, M. (1918), *The Chartist Movement* (Manchester: Manchester University Press).

Hunt, J. (1982), *The Wider Sea: A Life of John Ruskin* (London: Dent).

Jefferson, T. (1943a) [1801], 'First Inaugural Address', in S. Padover (ed.), *The Complete Jefferson* (New York: Books for Libraries Press), pp. 384–7.

Jefferson, T. (1943b) [1805], 'Second Inaugural Address', ibid., pp. 410–15.

Johnson, A., and Woodburn, J. (eds) (1927), *American Orations* (New York: G. P. Putnam's Sons).

Jones, H. M. (1944), 'Arnold, Aristocracy and America', *American Historical Review*, vol. 49, pp. 393–409.

Krause, R. (1983), 'Classical Images of Democracy in America: Madison and Tocqueville', in G. Duncan (ed.), *Democratic Theory and Practice* (Cambridge: Cambridge University Press).

Laski, H. (1931), 'Alexis de Tocqueville and Democracy', in F. Hearnshaw (ed.), *The Social and Political Ideas of Some Representative Thinkers of the Victorian Age* (New York: Barnes & Noble).

Le Quesne, A. (1982), *Carlyle* (Oxford: Oxford University Press).

Lerner, R. (1963), 'Calhoun's New Science of Politics', *American Political Science Review*, vol. 57, pp. 918–52.

Lippincott, B. (1938), *Victorian Critics of Democracy* (Minneapolis, Minn.: Minneapolis University Press).

Lively, J., and Rees, J. (eds) (1978), *Utilitarian Logic and Politics* (Oxford: Clarendon Press).

Lloyd, H. D. (1936) [1894], *Wealth Against Commonwealth* (Washington, DC: National Home Library).

Locke, J. (1978) [1690], *Two Treatises of Government* (London: Dent).

Lockhart, J. G. (1835), 'M. Beaumont on the Americans', *Quarterly Review*, vol. 53, pp. 289–312.

Lunde, E. (1981), *Horace Greeley* (Boston, Mass.: Twayne).

Lynd, S. (1973), *Intellectual Origins of American Radicalism* (London: Wildwood House).

Macaulay, T. B. (1967) [1848], *The History of England*, 4 vols (London: Dent).

McDonald, E. (ed.) (1936), *Phoenix*, 2 vols (London: Heinemann).

McGee, J. (1931), *A Crusade for Humanity* (London: Watts).

McHenry, J. (1927) [1787], 'Papers on the Federal Convention of 1787', in Tansill (1927), pp. 923–52.

McWilliams, W. (1977), 'On Equality as the Moral Foundation for Community', in Horwitz (1977), pp. 183–213.

Madison, J. (1884) [1787], *Letters and Other Writings of James Madison*, 4 vols (New York).

Madison, J. (1927) [1787], 'Debates in the Federal Convention of 1787', in Tansill (1927), pp. 109–745.

Maine, H. (1976) [1885], *Popular Government* (Indianapolis, Ind.: Liberty Classics).

Medley, D. J. (1894), *A Students' Manual of English Constitutional History* (Oxford: Blackwell).

Meier, P. (1978), *William Morris: The Marxist Dreamer*, 2 vols (Brighton: Harvester).

Mill, J. S. (1886) [1861], *Considerations on Representative Government* (London: Longmans Green).

Mill, J. S. (1873) *Autobiography* (London: Longmans Green).

Mill, J. S. (1891) [1848], *Principles of Political Economy* (London: Routledge).

Mineka, F. and Lindley, D. (eds) (1972), *The Later Letters of John Stuart Mill, 1849–1873* (Toronto: University of Toronto Press).

Montesquieu, Baron de (1748), *De L'Esprit des Lois* (Genève: Barrillot & Fils).

Moore, D. C. (1976), *The Politics of Deference* (New York: Barnes & Noble).

Morgan, A. E. (1974) [1944], *Edward Bellamy* (Philadelphia, Penn.: Porcupine Press).

Morison, S., and Commager, H. S. (1930), *The Growth of the American Republic*, 2 vols (New York: Oxford University Press).

Morris, W. (1912) [1890], 'News from Nowhere', in *Collected Works*, 24 vols (London: Longmans Green), Vol. 16, pp. 3–211.

Morris, W. (1915a) [1877], 'The Lesser Arts', in *Collected Works*, Vol. 22, pp. 3–27.

Morris, W. (1915b) [1883], 'Art under Plutocracy', ibid., Vol. 23, pp. 164–91.

Morris, W. (1915c) [1885], 'The Hopes of Civilization', ibid., Vol. 23, pp. 59–80.

Morris, W. (1915d) [1886], 'Whigs, Democrats and Socialists', ibid., Vol. 23, pp. 27–38.

Morris, W. (1915e) [1886], 'Dawn of a New Epoch', ibid., Vol. 23, pp. 121–40.

Morris, W. (1915f) [1888], 'Art and its Producers', ibid., Vol. 23, pp. 342–55.

Morris, W. (1915g) [1894], 'How I became a Socialist', ibid., Vol. 23, pp. 277–81.

Noble, J. (1884), *The Parliamentary Reformer's Manual* (London).

Ostrogorski, M. (1902), *Democracy and the Organization of Political Parties*, 2 vols (London: Macmillan).

Padover, S. (ed.) (1960), *The World of the Founding Fathers* (New York: Thomas Yoseloff).

Paine, G. (1939), 'The Literary Relations of Whitman and Carlyle with Especial Reference to their Contrasting Views on Democracy', *Studies in Philology*, vol. 36, pp. 550–63.

Paine, T. (1953a) [1776], 'Common Sense', in N. Adkins (ed.) *Common Sense and Other Political Writings* (New York: Bobbs-Merrill), pp. 3–52.

Paine, T. (1953b) [1783], 'The American Crisis', ibid., pp. 55–70.

Paine, T. (1969) [1791, 1792], *The Rights of Man*, Parts 1 and 2 (Harmondsworth: Penguin).

Parrington, V. L. (1930), *Main Currents in American Thought*, 3 vols (New York: Harcourt, Brace).

Pelling, H. (1965), *The Origins of the Labour Party, 1800–1900* (Oxford: Clarendon Press).

Phillips, W. F. (1898), 'Edward Bellamy: Prophet of Nationalism', *Westminster Review*, vol. 150, pp. 498–504.

Railton, S. (1978), *Fenimore Cooper* (Princeton, NJ: Princeton University Press).

Raleigh, J. (1957), *Matthew Arnold and American Culture* (Los Angeles: University of California Press).

Reeve, H. (1866), 'The Reform Debate', *Edinburgh Review*, vol. 123, pp. 586–90.

Rogers, H. (1848), 'Revolution and Reform', *Edinburgh Review*, vol. 88, pp. 360–403.

Rosenblatt, F. (1916), *The Chartist Movement* (London: Frank Cass).

Rossiter, C. (1955), *Conservatism in America* (New York: Vintage Books).

Rozwenc, E. (ed.) (1963), *The Meaning of Jacksonian Democracy* (Boston, Mass.: D. C. Heath).

Ruskin, J. (1904) [1853], 'The Nature of Gothic', in *The Stones of Venice*, in E. Cook and A. Wedderburn (eds) *Complete Works*, 40 vols (London: George Allen), vol. 10, pp. 180–269.

Ruskin, J. (1905a) [1860], 'Unto this Last', ibid., vol. 17, pp. 59–80.

Ruskin, J. (1905b) [1863], 'Munera Pulveris', ibid., vol. 17, pp. 119–293.

Ruskin, J. (1905c) [1867], 'Time and Tide', ibid., vol. 17, pp. 299–482.

Ruskin, J. (1905d) [1872], 'Fors Clavigera', ibid., vol. 27, pp. 243–56.

Sabine, G. (1952), 'The Two Democratic Traditions', *Philosophical Review*, vol. 61, pp. 451–74.

Schleifer, J. (1980), *The Making of Tocqueville's Democracy in America* (Chapel Hill, NC: University of North Carolina Press).

Schlesinger, A. (1946), *The Age of Jackson* (Boston, Mass.: Little Brown).

Seigel, J. (ed.) (1971), *Thomas Carlyle: The Critical Heritage* (London: Routledge & Kegan Paul).

Siedentop, L. (1979), 'The Two Liberal Traditions', in A. Ryan (ed.), *The Idea of Freedom* (Oxford: Oxford University Press), pp. 153–74.

Stansky, P. (1983), *William Morris* (Oxford: Oxford University Press).

Stanwood, E. (1903), *A History of the Presidency* (Boston, Mass.: Houghton, Mifflin).

Stepanchev, S. (1976), 'Walt Whitman in Russia', in G. Allen (ed.), *Walt Whitman Abroad* (Oradell, NJ: Norwood).

Stephen, L. (1950), *The English Utilitarians*, 3 vols (London: London University Press).

Stephens, F. (1909), 'The Transitional Period, 1788–1789 in the Government of the United States', *University of Missouri Studies*, vol. 2, no. 6.

Stevas, N. St. J. (1959), *Walter Bagehot* (London: Eyre & Spottiswoode).

Storing, H. J. (1978), 'Slavery and the Moral Foundation of the American Republic', in Horwitz (1977), pp. 214–34.

Tansill, C. (ed.) (1927), *Documents Illustrative of the Formation of the Union of the American States* (Washington, DC: Govt. Printing Office).

Tawney, R. (1931), *Equality* (London: Allen & Unwin).

Thomas, D. O. (1977), *The Honest Mind* (Oxford: Clarendon Press).

Thomas, J. L. (1983), *Alternative America* (Cambridge, Mass.: Harvard University Press).

Thompson, E. P. (1955), *William Morris: Romantic to Revolutionary* (London: Lawrence & Wishart).

Thoreau, H. D. (1981) [1854], 'Walden', in C. Bode (ed.) *The Portable Thoreau* (Harmondsworth: Penguin), pp. 258–572.

Traubel, H. (1961), *With Walt Whitman in Camden*, 3 vols (New York: Rowman & Littlefield).

Trilling, L. (1965), *Matthew Arnold* (London: Allen & Unwin).

Van Doren Stern, P. (ed.) (1940), *The Life and Writings of Abraham Lincoln* (New York: Modern Library).

Vile, M. (1967), *Constitutionalism and the Separation of Powers* (Oxford: Clarendon Press).

Vile, M. (1976), *Politics in the USA* (London: Hutchinson).

Voltaire (1734), *Lettres Philosophiques* (Rouen).

Whitman, W. (1909) [1881], 'Calhoun's Real Monument', in *Complete Prose Works* (New York: Appleton), p. 69.

Whitman, W. (1965) [1871], 'Memories of President Lincoln', in H. Blodgett and S. Bradley (eds), *Leaves of Grass* (London: London University Press), pp. 328–56.

Whitman, W. (1982) [1871], 'Democratic Vistas', in M. Van Doren (ed.) *The Portable Walt Whitman* (Harmondsworth: Penguin), pp. 313–82.

Wills, G. (1978), *Inventing America* (New York: Doubleday).

Wills, G. (1981), *Explaining America* (New York: Doubleday).

Williams, G. (ed.) (1976), *John Stuart Mill on Politics and Society* (London: Fontana).

Williams, R. (1958), *Culture and Society* (Harmondsworth: Penguin).

Wood, G. S. (1969), *The Creation of the American Republic* (Chapel Hill, NC: University of North Carolina Press).

Wood, G. S. (1978), 'The Democratization of Mind in the American Revolution' in Horwitz (1977), pp. 102–28.

Yates, R. (1927) [1787], 'Secret Proceedings and Debates of the Convention Assembled in Philadelphia in the Year 1787', in Tansill (1927), pp. 746–843.

Zetterbaum, M. (1967), *Tocqueville and the Problem of Democracy* (Stanford, Calif.: Stanford University Press).

Index